PEACE AND CONFLICT 2014

David A. Backer
Jonathan Wilkenfeld
Paul K. Huth

Center for International Development and Conflict Management
University of Maryland

Paradigm Publishers
Boulder • London

All rights reserved. No part of this publication may be transmitted or reproduced in any media or form, including electronic, mechanical, photocopy, recording, or informational storage and retrieval systems, without the express written consent of the copyright holder.

Copyright © 2014 University of Maryland

Published in the United States by Paradigm Publishers, 5589 Arapahoe Avenue, Boulder, CO 80303 USA.
Paradigm Publishers is the trade name of Birkenkamp & Company, LLC,
Dean Birkenkamp, President and Publisher.

Library of Congress Cataloging-in-Publication Data for this title is available from the Library of Congress.

   ISBN 978-1-61205-435-3 hardcover
   ISBN 978-1-61205-436-0 paperback

Printed and bound in the United States of America on acid-free paper that meets the standards of the American National Standard for Permanence of Paper for Printed Library Materials.

18 17 16 15 14 1 2 3 4 5

CONTENTS

1 Introduction to Peace and Conflict 2014 — 1
David A. Backer, Jonathan Wilkenfeld, and Paul K. Huth

Regular Features

2 The Peace and Conflict Instability Ledger: Ranking States on Future Risks — 4
David A. Backer and Paul K. Huth

3 Global Trends in Armed Conflict, 1946–2012 — 18
David A. Backer and Paul K. Huth

4 Global Trends in Democratization: Leadership Transitions and Systemic Change — 23
Erica Frantz

5 Global Trends in Terrorism, 1970–2011 — 29
Gary LaFree and Laura Dugan

Special Theme—Disaggregation and the Microdynamics of Conflict and Peacebuilding

Introduction — 43
David A. Backer

6 Disaggregating Conflict by Actors, Time, and Location — 44
Karsten Donnay, Elena Gadjanova, and Ravi Bhavnani

7 The Political Geography of Climate Vulnerability, Conflict, and Aid in Africa — 57
Joshua W. Busby, Clionadh Raleigh, and Idean Salehyan

8 Exploring Inequality and Ethnic Conflict: EPR-ETH and GROW^{up} — 74
Lars-Erik Cederman, Luc Girardin, and Julian Wucherpfennig

9 Describing and Understanding Sexual Violence in Armed Conflict: The Role of Disaggregation — 88
Amelia Hoover Green

10 Localizing Peace, Reconstruction, and the Effects of Mass Violence — 105
Patrick Vinck and Phuong N. Pham

11 Crowdsourcing to Map Conflict, Crises, and Humanitarian Responses — 122
Patrick Meier

Additional Resources

12 Profiles of Active Armed Conflicts — 142
Jonathan Wilkenfeld

References — 169
Peace and Conflict Editorial Advisory Board — 185
Acknowledgments — 185
About the Authors — 186
About the Contributors — 186
About the Center for International Development and Conflict Management — 188

A Note on the 2014 Publication

Peace and Conflict is the flagship publication of the Center for International Development and Conflict Management at the University of Maryland. Its purpose is to make current academic research on conflict, democratization, terrorism, and international development more accessible and interpretable for people in the policy community and especially for an academic audience that wants to better understand how such research informs policy discussions.

This publication continues coverage of several topics that appeared in earlier volumes: the Peace and Conflict Instability Ledger and global trends in armed conflict, the spread of democracy, and terrorism. In addition, six chapters are included on a special theme: "Disaggregation and the Microdynamics of Conflict and Peacebuilding." This section, organized by David Backer, highlights the recent emergence of a new frontier in research, the novel datasets on which it is based, and important insights and applications. Also, a final chapter provides an overview of the armed conflicts that were active in 2012.

The publication is committed to the principle that research should be fully transparent and the findings replicable by other interested researchers. To that end, the analyses generally use data sources that have been released to the public.

The partnership between CIDCM and Paradigm Publishers facilitates wider dissemination of *Peace and Conflict* to the academic and policy communities, providing the opportunity for researchers, policy makers, and students to understand and extend our analyses. In addition, an executive summary can be obtained from the CIDCM website (www.cidcm.umd.edu) and is available from the Center upon request (cidcm@cidcm.umd.edu).

We continue to benefit from the advice and guidance offered by our Editorial Board, chaired by Ted Robert Gurr, the founding author of the *Peace and Conflict* publications. Board members played an important role in shaping the contents of *Peace and Conflict 2014*. As the various chapters came together, they provided careful reviews of each one, making the final collection a sharper and more cohesive product. We are very grateful for their valuable support. The members are identified at the end of this volume.

1. INTRODUCTION TO PEACE AND CONFLICT 2014

Since the publication of *Peace and Conflict 2012*, developments in many regions and countries attest to the continuing problems of armed conflict, as well as the complexities of crisis management and post-conflict peacebuilding. For instance, the Egyptian military's forcible removal of former president Mohamed Morsi in July 2013, and subsequent violent repression of the Muslim Brotherhood, highlights the deep challenges to democratization. While Egypt now teeters on the precipice of full-scale civil war, Syria has been engulfed in massive internal violence since mid-2011, exhibiting large-scale victimization of civilian populations, deep divisions among the rebel forces opposing the Assad regime, and growing internationalization of the conflict, with many regional actors supporting the opposing sides. In January 2013, the Malian government teetered on the edge of collapse under the threat of Islamist-led fighters moving from territory they controlled in northern Mali, but a French intervention turned back the rebels. The political crisis has stabilized, at least for the short term, as a peace agreement was reached with Tuareg rebel forces, new elections were held, and a UN peacekeeping operation was authorized. In Kenya, national elections held in April 2013 did not result in the widespread violence associated with the previous round of national elections in December 2007, which is a positive sign for the stability of the country.

These events in the several countries exemplify the types of topics taken up by the authors in various chapters of *Peace and Conflict 2014*. For example, the political crisis in Egypt raises larger questions about the prospects of democratization during periods of leadership transition, which Erica Frantz addresses in Chapter 4. The Syrian civil war has resulted in widespread attacks on civilians, but no reports of high levels of sexual violence. In Chapter 10, Amelia Hoover Green tackles the matter of why civil wars vary in the extent to which sexual violence is committed by opposing armed forces. The long-standing ethnic conflict in Mali, contrasted with episodic variation in Kenya, raises questions about ethnic grievances as a cause of armed violence, which are central to the analysis by Lars-Erik Cederman, Luc Girardin, and Julian Wucherpfennig in Chapter 8. The involvement of forces linked to al-Qaeda in the Malian conflict connects to the analysis by Gary LaFree and Laura Dugan of global and regional trends in terrorism in Chapter 5.

As with previous editions, *Peace and Conflict 2014* is organized into two main sections. The first section, comprised of Chapters 2–5, presents the standard, recurring features of *Peace and Conflict*. In this section, the authors offer analyses of global trends in political instability, armed conflict, democracy, and terrorism. The second section, comprised of Chapters 6–11, is devoted to the special theme of "Disaggregation and the Microdynamics of Conflict and Peacebuilding." In this section, the authors discuss an important recent shift in research, describing new sources of data that are being collected and used, detailing the distinctive insights that associated analysis provides, and explaining the implications for policy and practice. In addition, Chapter 12 presents another regular feature of *Peace and Conflict*: a review of active armed conflicts around the world.

In Chapter 2, David Backer and Paul Huth report the latest results from the Peace and Conflict Instability Ledger, a worldwide ranking of countries' risk of facing significant political instability and armed conflict during the period of 2012–2014. Particular attention is paid to those 25 countries at the greatest risk of instability, as well as those countries that have experienced the largest changes in risk scores—both positive and negative—over the previous five years. Not surprisingly, the Ledger categorizes countries such as Afghanistan, Pakistan, and Iraq among the most at risk. Interestingly, Egypt is in the "some risk" category, while Syria is in the "low risk" category, whereas both have recently suffered considerable turmoil and violence. The chapter acknowledges the inherent imperfections of forecasting and offers suggestions about how the Ledger and related analysis could be improved to yield a better fit to observed outcomes.

In Chapter 3, Backer and Huth report on global trends in armed conflict from 1946–2012, including both interstate and intrastate confrontations. They provide information on the onset, recurrence, and termination of conflicts. In particular, conflict recurrence remains a persistent problem for countries emerging from civil wars.

In Chapter 4, Frantz examines global trends in democratization from 1947–2004, with a focus on the relationship of leadership transitions to successful or failed democratization efforts. She finds that leadership changes typically do not correspond with fundamental changes in political systems. Yet when leaders are forced out of power by coups coupled with mass protests and demonstrations, there is a substantial spike in the likelihood of systemic change. These general patterns provide a larger context for assessing the prospects for democratization following the ongoing unrest in Egypt.

In Chapter 5, LaFree and Dugan present a careful analysis of trends in terrorism from 1970–2011, using information on more than 104,000 terrorist attacks recorded in the Global Terrorism Database. A striking pattern is the pronounced U-shape pattern in the number and severity of terrorist attacks from 1992–2011, where a sharp decrease in terrorism during the 1990s was followed by a steep increase in terrorism since the early 2000s. One new feature of their analysis—connecting to the special theme of *Peace and Conflict 2014*—is a disaggregation at the county level of over 3,000 terrorist attacks in the United States from 1970–2011. A central finding is that attacks in the United States are heavily concentrated in a small number of counties around major cities. The recent Boston Marathon terrorist attacks seem to fit well with this general pattern.

In Chapter 6, Karsten Donnay, Elena Gadjanova, and Ravi Bhavnani provide an overview of recent research that disaggregates conflicts by actors, timing, and location. They highlight various topics, including the targeting of civilian populations, in-fighting and side-switching among rebel groups, and the relationship between subnational inequality among groups and the onset of violent conflicts. They make a strong case that researchers using disaggregated data on both conflict behavior and the attributes of combatant actors has generated insights on policy-relevant issues such as the effectiveness of counterinsurgency strategies, the causes of civilian migration during armed conflicts, and the probability that rebel groups will target civilian populations with violence.

In Chapter 7, Joshua Busby, Clionadh Raleigh, and Idean Salehyan encapsulate groundbreaking work being done as part of the Climate Change and African Political Stability (CCAPS) program over the past five years. In the process, they provide an overview of the design and applications of two newly created disaggregated datasets on conflict behavior in Africa: the Armed Conflict Location and Event Dataset (ACLED) and the Social Conflict in Africa Database (SCAD). They also discuss the Climate Security Vulnerability Model (CSVM), which has been developed to study the political and security consequences of climate change at the subnational level in Africa. Of note, the CSVM has been used to address questions such as whether foreign assistance is being targeted to those areas most vulnerable to climate change and whether areas of strategic interest to the United States are also areas of high climate vulnerability.

In Chapter 8, Cederman, Girardin, and Wucherpfennig review the noteworthy advances made in the study of ethnic conflict via the Ethnic Power Relations (EPR) research program. Among the major products of this vibrant program is a family of new datasets with comprehensive information on access to political power at the national level by over 800 ethnic groups around the world and their conflict behavior from 1946–2009. A number of associated studies provide strong evidence that patterns of political exclusion and discrimination suffered by ethnic groups, as well as high levels of economic inequality between groups, are related to the onset of civil-war violence.

In Chapter 9, Hoover Green discusses recent efforts to collect more disaggregated and reliable data on sexual violence during armed conflicts. She convincingly argues that problems in collecting data warrant caution. Nonetheless, researchers have made considerable progress, with notable findings emerging across studies. One is that the occurrence of sexual violence during armed conflicts varies considerably. Another is that patterns of sexual violence do not seem to closely follow patterns of lethal violence. Instead, the causes of sexual violence can be quite distinct, roughly divided between those that emphasize strategic use of sexual violence as an element of military strategy and organizational explanations centered on the command-and-control systems of armed forces.

In Chapter 10, Patrick Vinck and Phuong Pham shift the attention to studying challenges to successful post-conflict peacebuilding and reconstruction at the local level. Their central argument is that peacebuilding too often involves top-down strategies, which fail to appreciate local dynamics of how civilian populations react to post-war reconstruction policies set by national governments and intergovernmental institutions. They distill results from general population surveys conducted during and after civil wars in six countries between 2005 and 2010. This unique body of research reveals that individuals' experiences of conflict are diverse, as are their views and preferences about peacebuilding efforts, which often differ from priorities established by political authorities.

In Chapter 11, the final contribution to the special theme section, Patrick Meier highlights the very recent use of information crowdsourced from social media to monitor and address humanitarian crises. He reviews the impressive initiatives to track the onset and escalation of violence in Libya in 2011 and on an ongoing basis in Syria since 2011, as well as the application of similar approaches in the wake of two natural disasters in 2012: Typhoon Pablo in the Philippines and the Oklahoma tornado. He also reflects on the challenges of using social media as a source, including the volume, veracity, and representativeness of the information. Despite these potential complications, Meier argues that crowdsourcing from social media is a valuable new tool for improving crisis monitoring and humanitarian responses by national governments and intergovernmental institutions.

Finally, in Chapter 12 Jonathan Wilkenfeld provides descriptive histories of the 26 intermediate and major armed conflicts in 22 countries that were active as of December 31, 2012. Each case is illuminated with details about the origins and evolution of the conflict and any change in status since the publication of *Peace and Conflict 2012*.

David A. Backer
Jonathan Wilkenfeld
Paul K. Huth

2. THE PEACE AND CONFLICT INSTABILITY LEDGER: RANKING STATES ON FUTURE RISKS

David A. Backer and Paul K. Huth

This chapter presents the latest results of the Peace and Conflict Instability Ledger. The focus of the analysis is the ranking of countries around the world according to their estimated risk of experiencing significant bouts of political instability or armed conflict during the three-year period of 2012–2014. Those risk estimates are obtained using a statistical forecasting model, developed based on historical data, that confirms strong correlations between the onset of instability or conflict and several factors. The most current data available for these factors, from the individual countries, are plugged into the forecasting model, yielding projections of the risk that they face in the future. Once again, the findings illuminate a concentration of serious vulnerabilities in Sub-Saharan Africa and South Asia. Awareness of these risks, as well as where they worsened and improved, is an important resource in conflict preparedness and management.

Methodology

The Ledger represents a synthesis of leading research on conceptualizing, explaining, and forecasting political instability. The definition established by the Political Instability Task Force (PITF) is employed.[1] This definition guided the PITF's compilation of state failure events during 1955–2006, which encompass a wide variety of types, including revolutionary wars, ethnic wars, adverse regime changes, and genocides or politicides. While the set of events is heterogeneous, they share a fundamental similarity: their onset signals the arrival of a period in which government's capacity to deliver core services and to exercise meaningful authority has been disrupted, threatening its overall stability.

The specification of the Ledger's forecasting model involved identifying factors for which agreement about their relative importance was consistent among researchers. Empirical studies demonstrate historical associations between instability and five factors in four domains of government and society.[2] Table 2.1 provides a brief overview of the theoretical relationship between each of these factors and the risk of instability. A fuller discussion is given in *Peace and Conflict 2008* (Hewitt 2008).

> *The specification of the Ledger's forecasting model involved identifying factors for which agreement about their relative importance was consistent among researchers. Empirical studies demonstrate historical associations between instability and five factors in four domains of government and society.*

---

[1] The initial compilation of state failure events was done in 1994–1995 at the University of Maryland's Center for International Development and Conflict Management, under the direction of Ted Robert Gurr. The roster of genocides and politicides was provided by Barbara Harff. The PITF presents full definitions for revolutionary wars, ethnic wars, adverse regime changes, genocide, and politicide in Esty et al. (1999).

[2] Significant contributions to this literature include Collier et al. (2003); Collier and Hoeffler (2004); Esty et al. (1999); Fearon and Laitin (2003); Goldstone et al. (2005); Hegre and Sambanis (2006); Hegre et al. (2001); King and Zeng (2001); Sambanis (2002, 2004); and the United States Agency for International Development (2005).

Table 2.1 Factors Influencing the Risk of Instability

Factor	Domain	Description
Institutional Consistency	Political	The Ledger accounts for the impact of institutional consistency. This refers to the extent to which the institutions comprising a country's political system are uniformly and consistently autocratic or democratic. Political institutions with a mix of democratic and autocratic features are inconsistent, a common attribute of polities in the midst of a democratic transition. Based on a series of findings reported in the academic literature, we expect regimes with inconsistent institutions to be more likely to experience political instability (Gurr 1974; Gates et al. 2006; Hegre et al. 2001).
Economic Openness	Economic	The Ledger accounts for the impact of economic openness, which is the extent to which a country's economy is integrated with the global economy. Countries that are more tightly connected to global markets have been found to experience less instability (Hegre et al. 2003; Goldstone et al. 2000).
Infant Mortality Rates	Economic and Social	The Ledger examines the impact of infant mortality rates, an indicator that serves as a proxy for a country's overall economic development, its level of advancement in social welfare policy, and its capacity to deliver core services to the population. In this respect, this indicator taps into both the economic and social domains of a country. Research findings reported by the PITF have been especially notable for the strong relationship found between high infant mortality rates and the likelihood of future instability (Esty et al. 1999; Goldstone et al. 2005).
Militarization	Security	To account for the security domain, the Ledger focuses on a country's level of militarization. Instability is most likely in countries where the opportunities for armed conflict are greatest. In societies where the infrastructure and capital for organized armed conflict are more plentiful and accessible, the likelihood for civil conflict increases (Collier and Hoeffler 2004). Extensive militarization in a country typically implies that a large portion of the society's population has military skill and training, weapons stocks are more widely available, and other pieces of military equipment are more diffused throughout the country. The likelihood of instability is greater in this setting because increased access to and availability of these resources multiplies the opportunities for organizing and mobilizing.
Neighborhood Security	Security	The likelihood of political instability in a state increases substantially when a neighboring state is currently experiencing armed conflict. This risk is especially acute when ethnic or other communal groups span across borders. A number of studies have shown that neighborhood conflict is a significant predictor of political instability (Sambanis 2001; Hegre and Sambanis 2006; Goldstone et al. 2005).

Leveraging these relationships, the Ledger uses a statistical model to obtain risk scores for all 164 countries with a population of at least 500,000 in 2011. This analysis employs annual observations for each country for every year that data exist for all five factors. Each observation records whether the country experienced an onset of a new instability event in any of the subsequent three years. The data can thereby be analyzed to assess the empirical relationship between the five factors and the risk of future instability. To maintain comparability with the results presented in past volumes of *Peace and Conflict*, we continue to estimate the model using "training data" from 1950–2003. The logistic regression procedure produces weights for the five factors that reflect the relative influence each has on explaining future instability. For the updated Ledger, we then apply the weights to 2011 data—the last year for which complete data are available for all five factors—to produce a forecast indicating the risk of instability at any time during the period 2012–2014. In the absence of significant change to any of the five factors, risks change only gradually from year to year. Therefore, a high-risk country that experiences no major structural change to its regime, socioeconomic status, or security situation in the period 2012–2014 will likely remain at high risk during and beyond this forecast period.

The full listing of all 164 countries is presented at the end of the chapter. The tabulation includes an indication of how each country is performing on each of the risk factors, which enables a quick assessment of how these indicators relate to the ultimate risk estimates. In this fashion, the full Ledger table serves as a diagnostic tool, offering comprehensive information about all countries so that comparisons can be drawn about how the levels of each factor influence risk.

To ease interpretation of the results, the Ledger presents each country's likelihood of future instability as a risk ratio. The risk ratio gives the relative risk of instability in a country compared to the average estimated likelihood of instability for the 28 members of the Organization for Economic Cooperation and Development (OECD). The OECD supplies a worthwhile baseline because its membership is widely viewed to contain the most stable countries in the world. The estimated probability of the average OECD country's experiencing an instability event in the period 2012–2014 is 0.007. To illustrate, Timor-Leste's estimated probability of experiencing instability in the next three years is 0.072, which yields a risk ratio of approximately 10.1. Presented in this way, the analysis indicates that Timor-Leste's risk of instability is about 10 times that of the OECD—a more useful characterization of its risk than the raw probability 0.072 by itself.

The risk ratios are estimated with varying levels of confidence, depending on the particular attributes of a given country. This is a standard, but underappreciated, aspect of statistical inferences. For example, in the historical analysis underlying the Ledger, infant mortality rates were found to be positively related to the onset of instability. The level of uncertainty for that estimate was sufficiently small to rule out the possibility that the model was pointing erroneously to a positive relationship when the "true" relationship was actually negative (or nonexistent). Yet uncertainty around the estimate remains. The uncertainty exists because certain countries with high infant mortality rates have not experienced instability (e.g., Malawi, Saudi Arabia, or Bolivia), whereas certain countries with a low rate of infant mortality have experienced instability (e.g., Israel). These cases that deviate from the normal pattern introduce "noise" in the estimated relationship between instability and infant mortality rates. This kind of uncertainty accompanies each of the estimates for the variables in the model. Information extracted from the model can be used to compute the total amount of uncertainty surrounding the estimate of instability risk for an individual country. The Ledger reports a single best estimate of the overall risk of instability for each country. In addition, the Ledger reports the level of uncertainty, in terms of a confidence range of values within which the best estimate lies. Statistically speaking, the "true" risk of instability lies within this range with a 95 percent probability.

Countries are assigned to different risk categories, according to the procedure described in Box 2.1. This procedure establishes meaningful risk categories. Within a given category, a solid empirical basis exists to indicate that the identified states are comparable in terms of risk. Meanwhile, states assigned to different categories are distinct. In particular, states in lower risk categories are unlikely to have a true risk in excess of that of countries assigned to higher risk categories. The graphical display of the confidence range shows how it extends across risk categories. For some countries, the range is confined largely within one category. For others, large segments extend across multiple categories, which suggests that assessments of their risk of instability should be more cautious.

> **Box 2.1 Classification of Countries into Risk Categories**
>
> Information from the confidence intervals for the risk scores is leveraged to inform the classification of countries into separate risk categories, using the following approach:
>
> - The list of 164 countries is sorted from highest to lowest risk scores.
> - The country with the highest risk score (Afghanistan) anchors the first group of countries.
> - Moving down the list, any country for which the upper bound on its confidence range is higher than Afghanistan's risk score is assigned to the same group as Afghanistan. Such an overlap indicates that there is little difference in their respective risk scores.
> - The initial country on the list with an upper bound on its confidence range that is less than Afghanistan's score begins a new group. In this instance of the Ledger, the country is Niger.
> - Moving further down the list, any country with an upper bound greater than Niger's risk score of 18.5 would be grouped with Niger.
> - The first two groups are combined to form the "highest risk" category.
> - Moving down the list in a similar manner, the third group of states (beginning with Bangladesh) will be assigned to the "high risk" category, the fourth group (beginning with Armenia) makes up the "moderate risk" category, the fifth group (beginning with Jordan) makes up the "some risk" category, and all remaining countries are assigned to the "low risk" category.
> - The risk score for the last country in a category serves as a threshold for characterizing the portion of a confidence range that falls into that category. For example, the last country in the highest risk category, Haiti, has a risk score of 12.3, while the last country in the high risk category, Angola, has a risk score of 6.7. Therefore, a confidence range that spans 6.7 and/or 12.3 would fall into multiple categories.
>
> This approach allows for clearer delineation of categories, bases on the statistical estimates.

Like any statistical model, the Ledger is not a perfect prediction tool. Yet empirical evidence demonstrates that it is relatively reliable: for every several cases the analysis forecasts correctly, one is forecast incorrectly. Only a share of these will be false negatives: instances of instability in places not anticipated by the model. Events that are unusual—unprecedented, some might argue—will be among these anomalies.

For instance, the previous edition of *Peace and Conflict* discussed the events that came to be known as the Arab Spring—a wave of mass protests, beginning in early 2011, that affected multiple countries in both North Africa (Egypt, Libya, Tunisia) and the Middle East (Bahrain, Jordan, Syria, Yemen). The fact that these events occurred at all, especially on such a scale within and across countries, and advanced as far as they did, even resulting in political transitions in several cases, came as a surprise to many, not least those used to long-standing, entrenched autocratic regimes across the region. In other words, the countries were not generally forecast to be places of significant upheaval, including by the Peace and Conflict Instability Ledger (Hewitt 2012). Part of the explanation is that this analysis of risk focuses on the prospects of instability at a level beyond what has been observed in most of the aforementioned countries. The projections of the Ledger were admittedly inaccurate in the cases of Libya and Syria, both of which descended into full-scale civil war. Neither of these countries conformed to the historic tendencies exhibited by most consolidated autocracies, where such devastating conflict is actually outside the norm. Elsewhere in the region, circumstances have been consistent with expectations. There has been serious turmoil, without bringing about the wholesale collapse of governments and the complete disruption of the provision of basic services, the risk of which is what the Ledger was specifically designed to gauge.

Thus, we continue to maintain confidence in the Ledger. At the same time, we acknowledge the need for and continue to explore ways of improving the reliability of forecasting of instability and conflict.

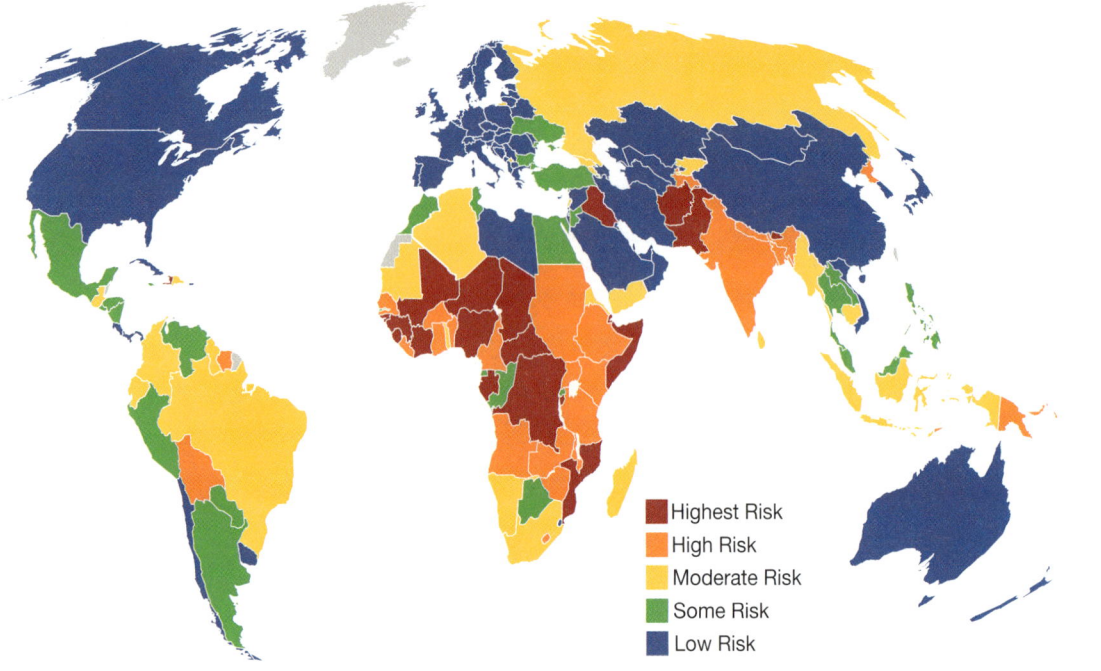

Figure 2.1 Risk of Instability, 2012–2014

- Highest Risk
- High Risk
- Moderate Risk
- Some Risk
- Low Risk

Results

Figure 2.1 shows how the countries in the analysis were classified according to their estimated risk scores. A quick glance at the map offers an overview of the geographic landscape of the risk of instability. Undoubtedly, Africa remains the most serious concern. Of the 47 African countries covered in the Ledger, 33 (70 percent) qualify for either the high or highest risk category. Of all the countries worldwide in those categories, African countries comprise 72 percent (33 of 46). A similar concentration of states qualifying at high or highest risk exists in South Asia, a grouping that contains crucial states like Afghanistan and Pakistan, which are pivotal because their fates have direct repercussions for global trends in terrorism.

> *Africa remains the most serious concern. Of the 47 African countries covered in the Ledger, 33 (70 percent) qualify for either the high or highest risk category.*

Table 2.2 lists the 25 countries with the highest risk scores. Since the publication of *Peace and Conflict 2012*, this group has undergone some changes. Six states (Cameroon, Ethiopia, Kenya, Malawi, Zambia, Zimbabwe) have dropped out of the top 25. Six other states have taken their place (Côte d'Ivoire, Guinea, Nepal, Niger, South Sudan, and Timor-Leste). All six of the states that dropped out of the top 25 listing were from Africa, offset by four African states that joined. The net effect leaves 17 African countries in the top 25 listing, which is the fewest since the methodology for calculating the Ledger was adjusted in 2008. As recently as 2010, 22 African countries were in the top 25. The trend is favorable, but should be treated cautiously because some of the underlying factors are subject to fluctuation.

Once again, the risk scores generally declined among countries that were previously in the highest, high, or moderate risk categories. According to *Peace and Conflict 2012*, 44 countries were classified in one of those three categories, and these countries had an average risk score of 13.7. In the latest estimates, the average for the same set of countries is 11.7, a modest but statistically significant difference.

The reduction cannot be traced to just one or two factors. Rather, the net effect of changes in several factors contributes to the overall decline. Some countries experienced shifting political situations that greatly amplified the risk of instability. Of note, Guinea and Guinea-Bissau faced new neighborhood conflicts, while Côte d'Ivoire and Guinea gained partial democratic status to accompany irregular institutions. Elsewhere, evolving circumstances substantially lowered the risk of instability. In particular, the neighborhood conflicts that confronted Bolivia, Cameroon, and Nigeria dropped below threshold levels in 2011, while the Kyrgyz Republic and Pakistan experienced shifts toward more autocratic institutions. As a broader backdrop, improving conditions were prevalent and often coincided in the set of at-risk countries. In 43 of the 44 countries, infant mortality rates fell by appreciable amounts, demonstrating developmental progress. In addition, 37 of the 44 countries exhibited increases in economic openness, often by large amounts. Also, 39 of the 44 countries reduced their levels of militarization.

In sum, looking back at the set of states that qualified in any of the three top risk categories from *Peace and Conflict 2012*, the reduction in average levels of risk is a reason for encouragement. Despite the worsening of security conditions in a couple of instances, conflicts abated elsewhere, and there was a general trend toward less militarization. A number of countries slipped toward more autocratic practices, but fortunately these were isolated cases, rather than a widespread pattern. Another positive sign is that gains in the social and economic domains were pervasive.

Table 2.2 Highest Estimated Risk for Instability, 2012–2014

Rank	Country	Risk Score
1	Afghanistan	27.5
2	Guinea-Bissau	26.3
3	Djibouti	25.5
4	Guinea*	23.1
5	Burundi	22.7
6	Congo, Dem. Rep.	20.8
7	Somalia	20.0
8	Niger*	18.5
9	Mali	17.9
10	Pakistan	17.6
11	Sierra Leone	16.5
12	Cote d'Ivoire*	16.4
13	Central African Republic	15.1
14	South Sudan*	14.5
15	Nigeria	14.1
16	Bhutan	14.0
17	Mozambique	14.0
18	Iraq	13.4
19	Haiti	12.3
20	Bangladesh	11.7
21	Chad	11.6
22	Benin	11.6
23	Nepal*	11.1
24	Gabon	10.3
25	Timor-Leste*	10.1

* New to the top 25 in the most recent rankings.

Table 2.3 Largest Increases in Risk of Instability

Forecast Period	Country	Risk Ratio	Net Change	Regime Consistency	Partial Democracy	Infant Mortality	Economic Openness	Militarization	Neighborhood War
2007–09	Pakistan	4.7		25	○	66	49%	571	○
2012–14		17.6	12.9	36	●	59	59%	535	●
2007–09	Guinea	10.4		1	○	90	66%	174	○
2012–14		23.1	12.7	1	●	29	99%	120	●
2007–09	Bhutan	2.8		36	○	51	149%	889	●
2012–14		14.0	11.2	9	●	42	150%	813	●
2007–09	Cote d'Ivoire	8.3		0	○	87	157%	104	○
2012–14		16.4	8.1	0	●	81	184%	88	○
2007–09	Gabon	2.3		16	○	55	160%	501	○
2012–14		10.3	7.1	9	●	49	257%	437	○
2007–09	Sudan	3.9		16	○	61	90%	398	●
2012–14		9.7	5.8	4	○	57	89%	770	●
2007–09	Guinea-Bissau	21.6		36	●	104	62%	645	○
2012–14		26.3	4.7	36	●	98	49%	417	●
2007–09	Zimbabwe	5.7		16	○	54	102%	407	○
2012–14		9.3	3.6	1	●	43	299%	398	○
2007–09	Thailand	0.9		25	○	13	180%	624	○
2012–14		2.8	1.9	49	●	11	275%	683	●
2007–09	Myanmar	4.8		64	○	54	10%	1101	○
2012–14		5.8	1.0	9	○	48	19%	1062	●

NOTE: Infant mortality represents deaths per 1,000 live births. Economic openness column refers to the percentage of a country's GDP accounted for by the value of its imports plus exports. Militarization refers to the number of active military personnel per 100,000 people. The symbol ● means "yes" and the symbol ○ means "no."

To appreciate how changing circumstances can influence risk estimates, consider the countries that experienced significant change over the last five years. Table 2.3 lists the 10 countries with the largest increase in risk scores over the past five years. The top row for each country presents the estimated risk score for the forecast period of 2007–2009, generated based on 2006 data. The second row for each country presents the new risk score for the 2012–2014 forecast period. In many of these cases, the increase in risk can be traced to a single factor: a transition to more democratic governance that led to classification as a partial democracy. Among the 10 countries that experienced the greatest increase in risk over the past five years, eight were classified as partial democracies according to 2011 data, including seven that were not in this position five years prior.

Undoubtedly, the process of democratization is a welcome development because it brings desirable qualities to governance (e.g., greater citizen participation, broader competition for leadership positions, and more expansive civil liberties). For many observers, though, the heightened dangers of instability during this period are often underappreciated. Partial democracies are at greater risk for instability than autocracies or full democracies. Repressive tactics adopted by autocratic governments often smother the potential for significant political instability. Coherent and mature democracies possess the capacity to address group grievances and manage the competition between groups that vie for political power and other resources, thereby reducing the risks of instability. Partial democracies typically possess neither the qualities of full autocracies nor those of democracies, leaving them more vulnerable to the drivers of instability and conflict (Hegre et al. 2001; Fearon and Laitin 2003; Pate 2008). Indeed, the historical data over the past half-century show a strong empirical relationship between partial democracy and the future onset of instability or conflict.

Table 2.4 Largest Reduction in Risk of Instability									
Forecast Period	Country	Risk Ratio	Net Change	Regime Consistency	Partial Democracy	Infant Mortality	Economic Openness	Militarization	Neighborhood War
2007–09	Zambia	16.5		25	●	72	168%	136	●
2012–14		7.4	–9.1	49	●	53	267%	122	●
2007–09	Nigeria	21.7		16	●	92	156%	113	●
2012–14		14.1	–7.6	16	●	78	200%	100	○
2007–09	Sierra Leone	23.7		25	●	131	84%	206	●
2012–14		16.5	–8.1	49	●	119	171%	175	○
2007–09	Congo, Dem. Rep.	25.7		25	●	116	118%	176	●
2012–14		20.8	–4.9	25	●	111	308%	198	●
2007–09	Madagascar	9.3		49	●	52	91%	119	○
2012–14		4.7	–4.6	0	○	43	123%	101	○

NOTE: Infant mortality represents deaths per 1,000 live births. Economic openness column refers to the percentage of a country's GDP accounted for by the value of its imports plus exports. Militarization refers to the number of active military personnel per 100,000 people. The symbol ● means "yes" and the symbol ○ means "no."

Table 2.4 presents a list of five countries that showed the largest improvement in risk scores. Most of these were partial democracies before. Only Madagascar experienced a lessening of autocratic politics. The rest remained at the status quo, or else became more autocratic—an undesirable outcome, but one that substantially reduces the risk of instability. All made gains on the social and economic fronts. Moreover, all but the DRC exhibited improvements in security conditions.

Conclusion

The latest risk estimates from the Peace and Conflict Instability Ledger offer some positive news for the set of countries most vulnerable to conflict or instability. Average levels of risk have declined across the set of countries qualifying at the highest, high, or moderate risk. The changes in factors that heighten risks—emergence of neighborhood conflict, shifts toward autocracy, partial democratic transitions, significant worsening of socioeconomic conditions—were largely absent in the world's most vulnerable states. In fact, improvements in socioeconomic and security conditions were commonplace, in some cases helping to offset increased vulnerabilities in other areas.

These findings have important implications for the notable hotspots of instability around the world, including the countries experiencing turmoil, violence, and in certain instances political change as a result of the Arab Spring, as well as many others in Africa and South Asia. In these settings, the hope that accompanies the removal of long-standing autocratic regimes should be tempered by a recognition of the challenges ahead. The early stages of any democratic reforms should be monitored closely because the dangers for observing significant instability events will be especially high—Egypt is a clear example. The historical evidence indicates that two types of political change can lower this risk. One is a return to strong autocratic rule. The ability to maintain stability is often advanced as a justification for intrusions on democracy, as with the Egyptian military deposing President Morsi. Of course, this has been accompanied by considerable violence, which might only die down as the result of the military tightening its grip. The other political change that reduces risk of instability is continuing a trajectory towards full-fledged democracy. Reaching that point is hard, however, if key actors prove unwilling to countenance electoral competition with the legitimate prospect for alternation of power, as well as protections of rights, tolerance, inclusiveness, participation, accountability, and the other hallmarks of democracy.

The analysis also emphasizes that other ways exist of mitigating the risks of instability, which may help to offset negative circumstances or sluggish performance on the political front. In particular, it is vital to enhance the delivery of core social services (health, education, etc.), economic benefits (jobs, trade, infrastructure development, etc.), and security (demilitarization, reduction in crime). Doing so will enhance the likelihood that a government is viewed as legitimate, reducing the chances of popular upheaval, intergroup antagonism, and armed rebellion.

The analysis also emphasizes that other ways exist of mitigating the risks of instability, which may help to offset negative circumstances or sluggish performance on the political front. In particular, it is vital to enhance the delivery of core social services (health, education, etc.), economic benefits (jobs, trade, infrastructure development, etc.), and security (demilitarization, reduction in crime).

Ultimately, the key to effective policy responses to heightened risks of instability depends heavily on an ability to trace back from the estimate to the particular factors that exert the most influence on it. The Peace and Conflict Instability Ledger places an emphasis on making information about the risk estimates as accessible and interpretable as possible, so that diagnosing the foundations of these risks can be more effective. Moreover, by explicitly reporting confidence ranges associated with each country estimate, the Ledger offers policymakers enhanced leverage for making more confident assertions about the substantive importance of any year-to-year change observed in a particular country, which is crucial for making precise assessments about progress in at-risk countries. This chapter suggests how information from the Ledger can be used to help clarify risk trends in a particular country. Employed alongside the detailed information available to country experts, the Ledger can be a powerful diagnostic tool in any policy maker's toolkit for assessing risk levels across countries.

The Peace and Conflict Instability Ledger

The Peace and Conflict Instability Ledger ranks states according to the forecasted risk of future instability. See pp. 16–17 for a description of the information in the table, including the color codes, and a detailed explanation of the confidence range (note 12).

Regional Rank (2014)	Regional Rank (2012)	Country	Regime Consistency	Partial Democracy	Infant Mortality	Economic Openness	Militarization	Neighborhood War	Risk Category	Risk Score	Confidence Range	Active Armed Conflict in 2012
											Africa	
1	3	Guinea-Bissau	●	●	●	●	●	●	●	26.3	17.0–37.4	
2	4	Djibouti	●	●	●	●	●	●	●	25.5	13.5–40.4	
3	27	Guinea	●	●	●	●	●	●	●	23.1	13.6–36.4	
4	2	Burundi	●	●	●	●	●	●	●	22.7	13.6–34.9	
5	1	Congo, Dem. Rep.	●	●	●	●	●	●	●	20.8	9.7–38.4	■
6	9	Somalia	●		●	●	●	●	●	20.0	12.8–29.4	■
7	36	Niger	●	●	●	●	●	●	●	18.5	12.5–26.2	
8	7	Mali	●	●	●	●	●	●	●	17.9	9.4–31.9	
9	8	Sierra Leone	●	●	●	●	●	●	●	16.5	7.6–29.7	
10	28	Cote d'Ivoire	●	●	●	●	●	●	●	16.4	8.6–28.6	
11	10	Central African Rep.	●		●	●	●	●	●	15.1	8.1–25.0	
12	NR	South Sudan			●	●	●	●	●	14.5	7.1–25.3	
13	6	Nigeria	●	●	●	●	●	●	●	14.1	7.5–24.0	■
14	11	Mozambique	●	●	●	●	●	●	●	14.0	8.3–22.2	
15	12	Chad	●		●	●	●	●	●	11.6	5.6–21.7	
16	14	Benin	●	●	●	●	●	●	●	11.6	6.8–17.7	
17	17	Gabon	●		●	●	●	●	●	10.3	5.4–18.9	
18	38	Sudan	●		●	●	●	●	●	9.7	5.4–15.8	■
19	22	Liberia	●	●	●	●	●	●	●	9.7	5.4–15.8	
20	16	Kenya	●	●	●	●	●	●	●	9.4	5.2–15.6	
21	20	Uganda	●		●	●	●	●	●	9.3	5.0–15.0	
22	15	Zimbabwe	●	●	●	●	●	●	●	9.3	4.5–16.3	
23	19	Malawi	●	●	●	●	●	●	●	9.2	5.1–15.2	
24	21	Burkina Faso	●		●	●	●	●	●	8.4	4.7–13.8	
25	5	Ethiopia	●		●	●	●	●	●	7.8	4.4–13.0	■
26	26	Senegal	●	●	●	●	●	●	●	7.6	4.3–12.6	
27	13	Zambia	●	●	●	●	●	●	●	7.4	3.6–13.0	
28	29	Lesotho	●	●	●	●	●	●	●	7.3	3.3–13.6	
29	18	Cameroon	●		●	●	●	●	●	7.2	3.9–12.0	
30	25	Comoros	●		●	●	●	●	●	7.1	3.4–13.3	
31	23	Tanzania	●		●	●	●	●	●	7.0	3.5–12.0	
32	24	Angola	●		●	●	●	●	●	6.7	2.1–14.9	
33	35	Togo	●		●	●	●	●	●	6.5	3.3–10.8	
34	30	Ghana	●	●	●	●	●	●	●	6.2	2.7–11.9	
35	31	Namibia	●	●	●	●	●	●	●	6.0	3.1–10.1	
36	34	Eritrea	●		●	●	●	●	●	5.5	2.8–9.8	
37	33	South Africa	●	●	●	●	●	●	●	4.8	2.6–8.7	
38	40	Madagascar	●		●	●	●	●	●	4.7	2.6–7.4	
39	39	Mauritania	●		●	●	●	●	●	4.3	2.0–7.6	
40	32	Botswana	●	●	●	●	●	●	●	3.5	1.9–6.0	
41	43	Gambia, The	●		●	●	●	●	●	3.5	1.9–6.2	
42	37	Rwanda	●		●	●	●	●	●	2.7	1.2–5.1	■
43	42	Equatorial Guinea	●		●	●	●	●	●	2.3	1.1–4.3	
44	41	Congo, Rep.	●		●	●	●	●	●	2.2	1.1–4.1	
45	45	Swaziland	●		●	●	●	●	●	1.4	0.7–2.7	
46	44	Cape Verde	●		●	●	●	●	●	0.9	0.4–1.8	
47	46	Mauritius	●		●	●	●	●	●	0.7	0.3–1.3	

Regional Rank (2014)	Regional Rank (2012)	Country	Regime Consistency	Partial Democracy	Infant Mortality	Economic Openness	Militarization	Neighborhood War	Risk Category	Risk Score	Confidence Range	Active Armed Conflict in 2012
											Asia	
1	1	Afghanistan	●	●	●	●	●	●	●	27.5	17.1–41.9	■
2	2	Pakistan	●	●	●	●	●	●	●	17.6	11.6–25.7	■
3	3	Bhutan	●	●	●	●	●	●	●	14.0	7.8–22.6	
4	4	Bangladesh	●	●	●	●	●	●	●	11.7	7.4–17.5	
5	5	Nepal	●	●	●	●	●	●	●	11.1	6.8–16.7	
6	8	Timor-Leste	●	●	●	●	●	●	●	10.1	6.8–14.2	
7	6	India	●	●	●	●	●	●	●	8.8	4.9–15.2	■
8	7	Papua New Guinea	●	●	●	●	●	●	●	8.3	4.4–14.0	
9	10	Cambodia	●	●	●	●	●	●	●	6.6	3.4–11.3	
10	11	Tajikistan	●	●	●	●	●	●	●	6.3	3.1–12.3	
11	18	Myanmar	●	●	●	●	●	●	●	5.8	2.7–10.0	■
12	16	Korea, Dem. Rep.	●	●	●	●	●	●	●	5.6	2.1–11.9	
13	12	Sri Lanka	●	●	●	●	●	●	●	4.8	2.2–9.4	
14	13	Indonesia	●	●	●	●	●	●	●	4.1	2.3–6.7	
15	9	Kyrgyz Republic	●	●	●	●	●	●	●	4.0	1.9–7.3	
16	15	Philippines	●	●	●	●	●	●	●	3.5	2.0–5.8	■
17	14	Solomon Islands	●	●	●	●	●	●	●	3.3	1.8–5.7	
18	17	Thailand	●	●	●	●	●	●	●	2.8	1.3–5.3	■
19	19	Laos	●	●	●	●	●	●	●	2.2	1.1–3.7	
20	20	Malaysia	●	●	●	●	●	●	●	1.7	0.6–4.1	
21	24	Uzbekistan	●	●	●	●	●	●	●	1.6	0.8–2.7	
22	21	Mongolia	●	●	●	●	●	●	●	1.5	0.6–3.3	
23	22	Turkmenistan	●	●	●	●	●	●	●	1.2	0.5–2.5	
24	23	Korea, Rep.	●	●	●	●	●	●	●	1.1	0.4–2.5	
25	25	Kazakhstan	●	●	●	●	●	●	●	1.1	0.5–2.3	
26	26	China	●	●	●	●	●	●	●	0.7	0.2–1.5	
27	27	Fiji	●	●	●	●	●	●	●	0.7	0.3–1.6	
28	28	Vietnam	●	●	●	●	●	●	●	0.6	0.2–1.1	
29	29	Singapore	●	●	●	●	●	●	●	0.5	0.1–1.3	
30	32	Japan	●	●	●	●	●	●	●	0.4	0.1–0.9	
31	30	New Zealand	●	●	●	●	●	●	●	0.3	0.1–0.7	
32	31	Australia	●	●	●	●	●	●	●	0.3	0.1–0.7	
											Eastern Europe	
1	1	Armenia	●	●	●	●	●	●	●	6.6	3.4–11.3	
2	NR	Kosovo	●	●	●	●	●	●	●	5.6	2.6–10.6	
3	2	Georgia	●	●	●	●	●	●	●	5.3	2.7–9.4	
4	3	Russia	●	●	●	●	●	●	●	3.8	1.6–7.8	■
5	4	Ukraine	●	●	●	●	●	●	●	2.3	1.0–4.5	
6	6	Albania	●	●	●	●	●	●	●	2.0	1.0–3.6	
7	7	Bulgaria	●	●	●	●	●	●	●	2.0	0.9–3.8	
8	5	Moldova	●	●	●	●	●	●	●	1.9	0.9–3.4	
9	11	Azerbaijan	●	●	●	●	●	●	●	1.7	0.8–3.1	■
10	9	Romania	●	●	●	●	●	●	●	1.7	0.8–3.2	
11	13	Latvia	●	●	●	●	●	●	●	1.6	0.6–3.2	
12	8	Montenegro	●	●	●	●	●	●	●	1.3	0.6–2.8	
13	NR	Macedonia	●	●	●	●	●	●	●	1.3	0.5–2.5	
14	12	Serbia	●	●	●	●	●	●	●	1.0	0.4–2.2	
15	10	Bosnia	●	●	●	●	●	●	●	0.9	0.3–2.0	
16	14	Croatia	●	●	●	●	●	●	●	0.8	0.3–1.7	
17	15	Estonia	●	●	●	●	●	●	●	0.6	0.2–1.4	
18	16	Czech Republic	●	●	●	●	●	●	●	0.6	0.2–1.4	
19	18	Poland	●	●	●	●	●	●	●	0.4	0.2–0.9	

Regional Rank (2014)	Regional Rank (2012)	Country	Regime Consistency	Partial Democracy	Infant Mortality	Economic Openness	Militarization	Neighborhood War	Risk Category	Risk Score	Confidence Range	Active Armed Conflict in 2012
	**Eastern Europe (continued)**											
20	19	Lithuania	●		●	●	●	●	●	0.4	0.1–0.8	
21	20	Slovak Republic	●		●	●	●	●	●	0.3	0.1–0.7	
22	17	Belarus	●		●	●	●	●	●	0.3	0.1–0.7	
23	21	Hungary	●		●	●	●	●	●	0.3	0.1–0.6	
24	22	Slovenia	●		●	●	●	●	●	0.2	0.0–0.4	
	**Latin America and the Caribbean**											
1	1	Haiti	●	●	●	●	●	●	●	12.3	6.7–20.3	
2	2	Bolivia	●	●	●	●	●	●	●	7.6	4.2–12.7	
3	18	Suriname	●	●	●	●	●	●	●	6.6	3.6–10.8	
4	3	Ecuador	●	●	●	●	●	●	●	6.0	2.9–10.5	
5	6	Guyana	●	●	●	●	●	●	●	5.4	2.9–8.9	
6	7	Guatemala	●	●	●	●	●	●	●	4.3	2.5–7.2	
7	8	Dominican Republic	●	●	●	●	●	●	●	4.2	2.3–6.8	
8	5	Brazil	●	●	●	●	●	●	●	4.1	2.1–6.8	
9	4	Colombia	●	●	●	●	●	●	●	4.0	2.2–6.9	■
10	9	Peru	●	●	●	●	●	●	●	3.5	1.9–5.9	
11	11	Mexico	●	●	●	●	●	●	●	3.5	1.9–5.9	
12	10	Honduras	●	●	●	●	●	●	●	3.3	1.6–5.8	
13	15	Nicaragua	●	●	●	●	●	●	●	3.2	1.7–5.5	
14	14	Paraguay	●	●	●	●	●	●	●	3.0	1.5–5.1	
15	16	Argentina	●	●	●	●	●	●	●	2.9	1.5–5.1	
16	17	El Salvador	●	●	●	●	●	●	●	2.7	1.4–4.6	
17	13	Venezuela	●		●	●	●	●	●	2.4	1.1–4.7	
18	12	Jamaica	●	●	●	●	●	●	●	2.4	1.2–4.3	
19	20	Panama	●		●	●	●	●	●	1.4	0.7–2.6	
20	19	Trinidad and Tobago			●	●	●	●	●	1.3	0.6–2.5	
21	21	Uruguay	●		●	●	●	●	●	0.7	0.3–1.3	
22	23	Costa Rica	●		●	●	●	●	●	0.5	0.3–1.0	
23	22	Chile	●		●	●	●	●	●	0.5	0.2–1.0	
24	24	Cuba	●		●	●	●	●	●	0.3	0.2–0.9	
	**Middle East and North Africa**											
1	1	Iraq	●	●	●	●	●	●	●	13.4	6.2–24.7	■
2	2	Yemen			●	●	●	●	●	6.1	3.4–10.1	■
3	7	Algeria	●		●	●	●	●	●	4.8	2.5–8.2	■
4	4	Lebanon	●	●	●	●	●	●	●	3.8	1.7–7.0	
5	5	Jordan	●		●	●	●	●	●	3.7	1.8–6.5	
6	3	Turkey	●	●	●	●	●	●	●	3.1	1.6–5.3	■
7	8	Tunisia	●		●	●	●	●	●	2.2	1.0–4.1	
8	9	Morocco	●		●	●	●	●	●	1.9	0.8–3.8	
9	6	Egypt	●		●	●	●	●	●	1.8	0.7–3.9	
10	10	Iran.	●		●	●	●	●	●	1.3	0.6–2.3	
11	12	Libya	●		●	●	●	●	●	1.3	0.4–3.2	
12	11	Syria	●		●	●	●	●	●	0.8	0.3–1.6	■
13	15	Oman	●		●	●	●	●	●	0.7	0.2–1.5	
14	17	Israel	●		●	●	●	●	●	0.6	0.2–1.2	■
15	16	Bahrain	●		●	●	●	●	●	0.5	0.2–1.2	
16	14	Kuwait	●		●	●	●	●	●	0.5	0.2–1.2	
17	13	Saudi Arabia	●		●	●	●	●	●	0.3	0.1–0.7	
18	18	Qatar	●		●	●	●	●	●	0.2	0.1–0.6	
19	19	United Arab Emirates	●		●	●	●	●	●	0.2	0.1–0.5	

Regional Rank (2014)	Regional Rank (2012)	Country	Regime Consistency	Partial Democracy	Infant Mortality	Economic Openness	Militarization	Neighborhood War	Risk Category	Risk Score	Confidence Range	Active Armed Conflict in 2012
									North Atlantic			
1	2	United States	●		●	●	○	●	●	0.8	0.3–1.6	■
2	1	Belgium	●	●	●	●	○	●	●	0.6	0.2–1.4	
3	4	Greece	●		●	○	●	●	●	0.5	0.2–1.0	
4	3	Canada	●		●	●	○	●	●	0.5	0.2–1.0	
5	6	France	●		●	●	○	●	●	0.3	0.1–0.8	
6	7	United Kingdom	●		●	●	○	●	●	0.3	0.1–0.7	
7	5	Cyprus	●		●	○	●	●	●	0.3	0.1–0.7	
8	9	Spain	●		●	●	○	●	●	0.3	0.1–0.6	
9	11	Switzerland	●		●	●	○	●	●	0.3	0.1–0.6	
10	8	Italy	●		●	●	○	●	●	0.3	0.1–0.6	
11	14	Norway	●		●	○	●	●	●	0.3	0.1–0.6	
12	18	Finland	●		●	●	●	●	●	0.2	0.1–0.6	
13	15	Austria	●		●	●	○	●	●	0.2	0.1–0.5	
14	12	Portugal	●		●	●	○	●	●	0.2	0.1–0.5	
15	10	Germany	●		●	●	○	●	●	0.2	0.1–0.5	
16	16	Netherlands	●		●	●	○	●	●	0.2	0.1–0.5	
17	13	Denmark	●		●	●	○	●	●	0.2	0.1–0.5	
18	17	Ireland	●		●	●	○	●	●	0.2	0.1–0.4	
19	19	Sweden	●		●	●	○	●	●	0.2	0.0–0.4	
20	NR	Luxembourg	●		●	●	○	●	●	0.1	0.0–0.3	

Notes and Explanations for the Peace and Conflict Instability Ledger

The Ledger reflects a theoretical model that relates the future likelihood of instability events in a given country to five explanatory factors. A statistical analysis, using "training data" for more than 160 countries during the period of 1950–2003, found that all of these factors are strongly associated with the future risk of instability. Based on the estimates from the model for the causal weight assigned to each factor, data from 2011—the last year for which complete data are available for all of the factors—are used to produce a forecast indicating the risk of instability in the period 2012–2014. The notes below describe the information presented in the table, including the factors and the color codings they are assigned, which reflect a country's standing based on 2011 values.

(1) Regional Rank (2014): Rank of the country's risk score within the region, according to the analysis reported in *Peace and Conflict 2014*.

(2) Regional Rank (2012): Rank of the country's risk score within the region, according to the analysis reported in *Peace and Conflict 2012*.

(3) Country: The Ledger examines only those countries with populations greater than 500,000 in 2011.

(4-5) Regime Consistency and Partial Democracy: The risk of future instability is related to the extent to which the institutions comprising a country's political system are uniformly and consistently autocratic or democratic. Political institutions with a mix of democratic and autocratic features are deemed inconsistent, a common attribute of polities in the midst of a democratic transition (or a reversal from democratic rule to more autocratic governance). Regimes with inconsistent institutions are expected to be more likely to experience political instability. In the Ledger, highly consistent democracies (Polity score greater than or equal to 6) and autocracies (Polity score less than or equal to –6) receive a green marker. A red marker is assigned to regimes with inconsistent characteristics that also qualify as partial democracies according to PITF. Regimes with these characteristics have been found to have the highest risk for instability. A yellow marker is assigned to partial autocracies because the propensity for instability in these regimes is somewhat less than in partial democracies.

(6) Infant Mortality: This indicator serves as a proxy for overall governmental effectiveness in executing policies and delivering services that improve social welfare in a country. High rates are associated with an increased likelihood of future instability. Countries with the best records (scoring in the bottom 25th percentile of global infant mortality rates) are indicated with a green marker. Countries with the worst record (scoring in the highest 25th percentile) are indicated with a red marker. Countries in the middle 50th percentile are indicated with a yellow marker.

(7) Economic Openness: Integration with global markets reduces the likelihood of political instability and armed conflict. Policies that integrate global and domestic markets can produce higher growth rates and sometimes reduce inequality, thereby lessening common drivers for civil unrest related

16   Chapter 2

to economic grievances. The measure for economic openness employed here is the proportion of a country's GDP accounted for by the value of all trade (exports plus imports). Countries with economic openness in the lowest 25th percentile are considered to be at the highest risk and designated with a red marker. The highest 25th percentile of countries are at low risk and assigned a green marker. The middle 50th percentile is assigned a yellow marker.

(8) Militarization: Instability is most likely in countries where the opportunities and means for conflict are greatest. In societies where the infrastructure and capital for organized armed action are more plentiful and accessible, the likelihood of civil conflict is higher. The Ledger measures militarization as the number of individuals in a country's active armed forces as a percentage of the country's total population. Countries with militarization scores in the bottom 25th percentile are indicated with a green marker. Countries in the top 25th percentile are indicated with a red marker. The middle 50th percentile is indicated with a yellow marker.

(9) Neighborhood War: Countries with neighbors that are engaged in armed conflict (internal or interstate) face a higher risk of instability. Regional armed conflict can have contagion effects, especially when ethnic or other communal groups span across borders. The most recent data released from the Uppsala Conflict Data Program is used to determine the conflict status of states in 2011 (see Gleditsch et al. 2002). For a neighbor to be considered involved in armed conflict, the conflict must produce 25 or more battle-related fatalities per year. A red marker indicates when at least one neighbor is involved in armed conflict. A green marker indicates the absence of armed conflict in all neighboring states.

(10) Risk Category: Based on their risk score (see Box 2.1), countries are placed in one of five categories: highest risk (red), high risk (orange), moderate risk (yellow), some risk category (green), or low risk (blue).

(11) Risk Score: Based on the results from estimating a statistical model using global data from the period 1950–2003, data from 2011 were used to obtain a three-year forecast for each country of the relative risk (compared to an average member of the OECD) of experiencing instability during for the period 2012–2014.

(12) Confidence Range: The confidence range provides information about the degree of uncertainty corresponding to a country's estimated risk score. Statistically speaking, the "true" risk of instability lies within this range with a 95 percent probability. The width of the confidence range is drawn to scale. The widest confidence range observed in the data has been set to the width of the full column, with all other confidence ranges drawn accordingly. When the bar is one color, the confidence range is confined to a single risk category. In cases where the confidence range spans multiple risk categories, the different colors of the bar reflect the extent of the overlap with those categories. The color blue indicates the low risk range, green the some risk range, yellow the moderate risk range, orange the high risk range, and red the highest risk range. Figure 2.2 illustrates how to read the information contained in the graphic for each country's confidence range, using a sample country (Iraq).

(13) Active Armed Conflict in 2012: A red marker indicates that a country was involved in intermediate or major armed conflict as of December 31, 2012, according to information compiled by the Uppsala Conflict Data Program (see Chapter 12). This designation means that there was an ongoing contested incompatibility between the government and at least one other armed group, resulting in at least 25 battle-related deaths in 2012 and a cumulative total of at least 1,000 battle-related deaths since the start of the conflict.

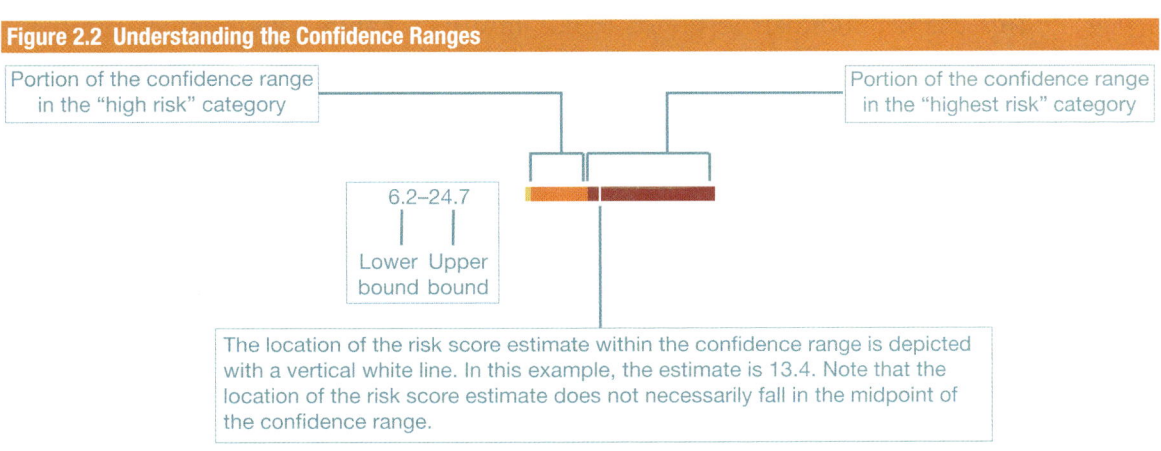

Figure 2.2 Understanding the Confidence Ranges

3. GLOBAL TRENDS IN ARMED CONFLICT, 1946–2012

David A. Backer and Paul K. Huth

According to the latest information available from the Uppsala Conflict Data Program (UCDP) and Peace Research Institute Oslo (PRIO), 26 intermediate and major armed conflicts were active worldwide in 2012 (Gleditsch et al. 2002).[1] This number matches what was reported in the past two editions of *Peace and Conflict* (Hewitt 2010, 2012).[2] In fact, the number is the same as in 1995, though some fluctuation was observed in the interim. When the Cold War era ended in 1990, 38 conflicts were active, the peak in the post-World War II period. By 1995, the number had declined sharply, representing the largest five-year decrease over the period. After a slight resurgence, the number dropped to just 20 conflicts in 2004, a level not observed since the mid-1970s. In 2005, however, the number of conflicts increased by seven, equaling 1960 as the largest annual jump after World War II. The number has since remained relatively stable.

Yet individual conflicts hardly remain static. Subsequent to the publication of *Peace and Conflict 2012*, several conflicts changed status. One existing conflict reached the threshold of 1,000 cumulative battle-related deaths in 2012: Nigeria with Boko Haram. Two dormant conflicts re-emerged in 2012: Azerbaijan with Nagorno-Karabakh and the Democratic Republic of the Congo with M23. The civil war involving the government of Libya, forces loyal to Muammar Gaddafi, and the National Transitional Council commenced and became a major armed conflict in 2011, but was no longer active in 2012. Four conflicts re-emerged in 2011: Myanmar with KIO, Pakistan with BLA and BRA, Senegal with MFDC, and Syria with FSA and Jabhat al-Nusra li al-Sham. The conflict in Pakistan had been inactive in 2010, while the conflict in Senegal was no longer active in 2012. Seven other recent conflicts were terminated: Chad with UFR (2011), Iran with PJAK (2012), Myanmar with both KNU (2012) and RCSS (2012), Peru with Sendero Luminoso (2011), Sri Lanka with LTTE (2010), and Uganda with LRA (2012).

This chapter summarizes global trends in armed conflict, examining patterns in different types of conflict, new onsets of conflict, recurrences of past conflicts, and terminations of existing conflicts. A major finding is that after the Cold War era concluded, countries cycling in and out of recurring conflict has been a more common occurrence.

Definitions

The UCDP/PRIO Armed Conflict Dataset defines conflict as "a contested incompatibility that concerns government and/or territory where the use of armed force between two parties, of which at least one is the government of a state, results in at least 25 battle-related deaths" (UCDP/PRIO Armed Conflict Dataset Codebook: 4). Our analyses focus on conflicts that have produced at least 25 battle-related fatalities in any given year, as well as accumulated at least 1,000 such fatalities over the entire course of the conflict (1,000 fatalities in a single year is characterized as a *major conflict*, while 1,000 fatalities distributed over multiple years is an *intermediate conflict*).

---

[1] Chapter 12 provides an overview of the intermediate and major armed conflicts that were active in 2012.
[2] Subsequent to the original release of the 2009 data, which were the basis of Hewitt (2012), UCDP reclassified two ongoing cases (Russia with the Forces of the Caucasus Emirates, Thailand with Patani insurgents) as intermediate conflicts, bringing the total number of active conflicts for that year to 28.

The UCDP/PRIO dataset identifies four types. *Internal armed conflict* involves a state and one or more domestic non-state actors such as opposition groups or guerilla forces (e.g., India and insurgents in Kashmir). *Internationalized internal armed conflict* adds the feature of outside intervention by at least one other state in support of any of the protagonists (e.g., the civil war in the Democratic Republic of the Congo from 1996–2001). *Interstate armed conflict* involves two or more states (e.g., Iran and Iraq from 1980–1988). Finally, *extrasystemic armed conflict* involves a state and a non-state actor and occurs outside the territory of the state (e.g., France and the Viet Minh from 1946–1954). No extrasystemic armed conflicts have been recorded since the mid-1970s.

A conflict is considered as a *new onset* in the year that the 1,000-fatality threshold is reached for the first time. A conflict is considered as a *recurrence* in a given year when returning to active status (i.e., reaching the 25-fatality threshold again) following one or more years of inactivity (i.e., below the 25-fatality threshold in each), after having previously reached the 1,000-fatality threshold. A *termination* occurs when an existing conflict becomes inactive in a given year (i.e., fewer than 25 fatalities). The reduction in visible hostilities may present an opportunity for the antagonists to implement a more durable peace, though the definition does not explicitly capture whether a formal cease-fire or any other agreement is in place. In fact, terminations are frequently temporary.

Trends in Active Armed Conflicts

Figure 3.1 presents the numbers of active internal conflicts and interstate conflicts each year from 1946–2012. The total has largely been confined to a narrow range since 1990, aside from the dip in the early 2000s, which was quickly reversed. Another conspicuous pattern is that interstate conflict has become essentially a non-factor since 2003.

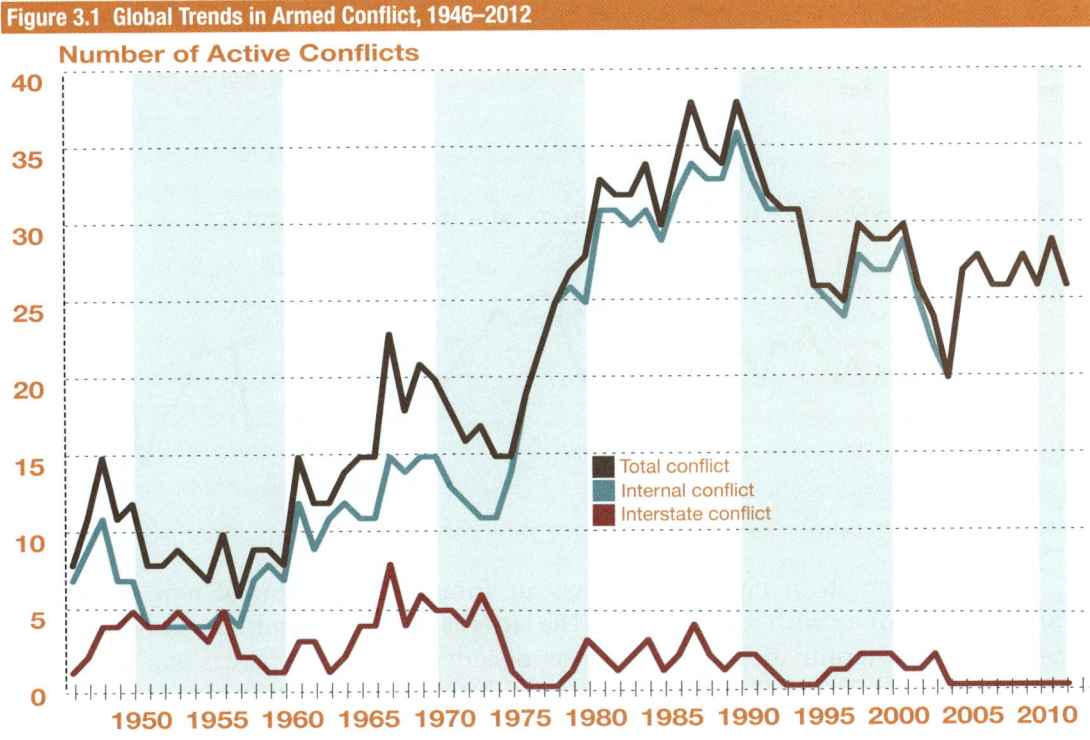

Figure 3.1 Global Trends in Armed Conflict, 1946–2012

A better understanding of the trends can be achieved by disaggregating the data into new onsets, recurrences, and terminations. As reported by Hewitt (2012), recurrences have been prevalent and far more common than new onsets of conflict over the last 25 years. These patterns lead to a stubborn persistence of conflicts at around the same level. Although certain conflicts subside year to year, and new onsets have been rare over the past decade, other conflicts reignite on a regular basis.

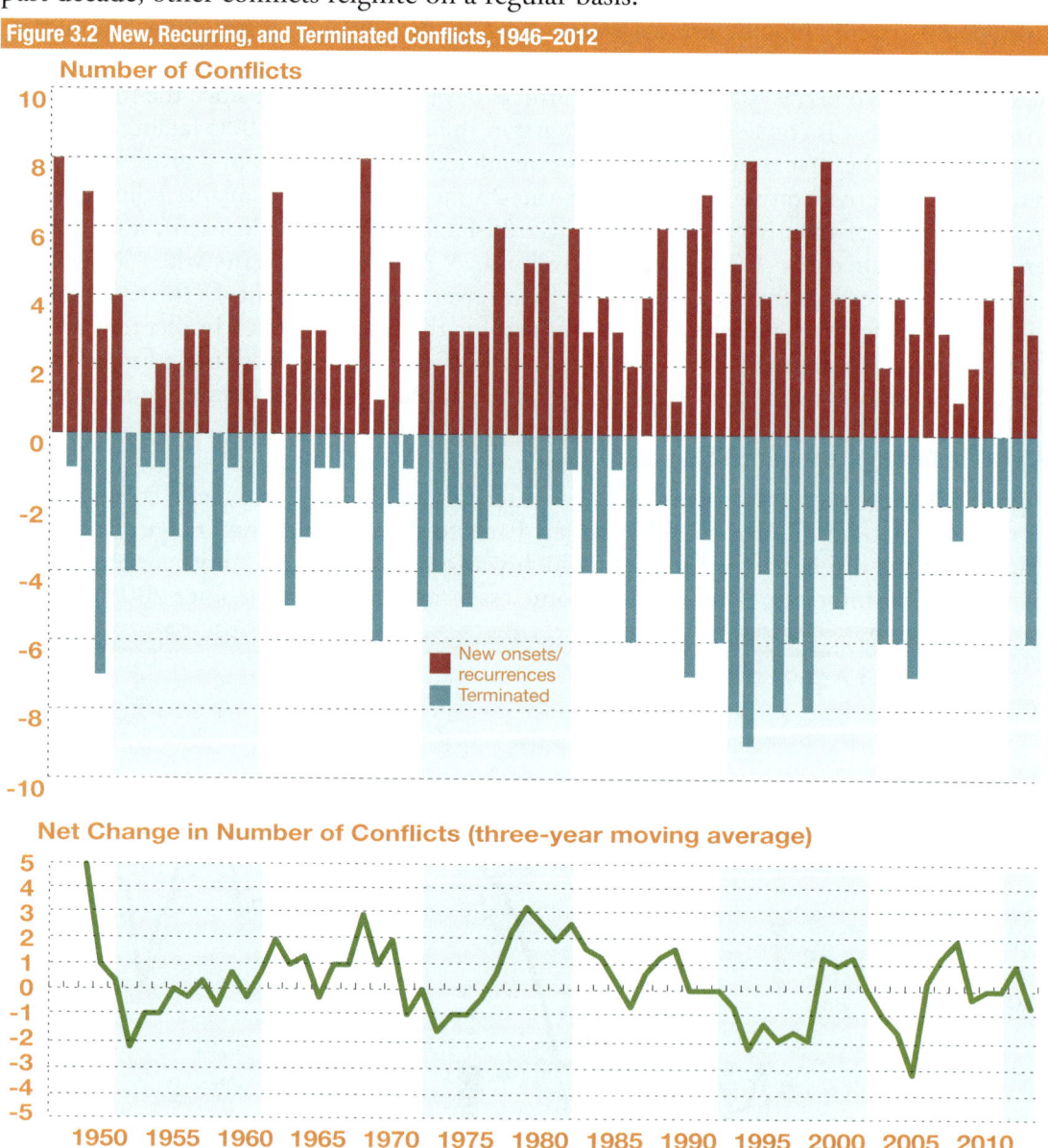

Figure 3.2 New, Recurring, and Terminated Conflicts, 1946–2012

The top graph in Figure 3.2 shows an annual comparison of new onsets and recurrences of conflict with terminations. The latter is represented with negative numbers to emphasize that terminations reduce the set of active conflicts, whereas new onsets and recurrences increase the set. During the post-Cold War period, when active conflicts have declined worldwide, the total of new onsets and recurrences is actually higher than before:

the average annual incidence during 1990–2012 was 4.2 cases, compared to 3.4 cases from 1946–1989. The frequency of terminations has risen by an even greater amount: from an average of 2.6 cases per year during 1946–1989 to 4.5 cases during 1990–2012. Thus, there is increased flux, with the annual incidence of basic changes in conflict status up by 45 percent.

The bottom graph in Figure 3.2 considers the net effects of these changes. It depicts the three-year moving average—smoothing annual fluctuations, which can be erratic, into short-term trends—of the number of new onsets and recurrences minus the number of terminations. During the Cold War era, the trends were typically in the direction of more conflict. This was especially true during much of the 1960s and from the mid-1970s through the early 1980s, which were characterized by waves of independence movements and post-colonial struggles, especially in Africa and Asia, as well as revolutionary wars—often with proxy dimensions—in these regions and other parts of the world. The pattern has been inverted since the end of the Cold War. Most of the trends are toward less conflict, and often strongly so. This was evident during the early 1990s, tied to post-conflict and post-authoritarian transitions as part of the ongoing third wave of democratization, especially in Latin America and Sub-Saharan Africa. It was again evident during the late-1990s and early 2000s, following a brief resurgence of conflict—often of the ethnic and separatist variety—in the mid-1990s. As the top graph in Figure 3.2 shows, conflict terminations surged and outnumbered onsets and recurrences by 13 from 1991–1997 and by 10 from 2002–2004. Each of these intervals was followed by a sharp spike in active conflicts: net additions of five cases in 1998 and seven cases in 2005. In both instances, terminations were unusually low in number: just three in 1998 and none in 2005. A modest favorable trend also emerged over the recent years, capped by six terminations of conflicts in 2012—by far the most since 2004.

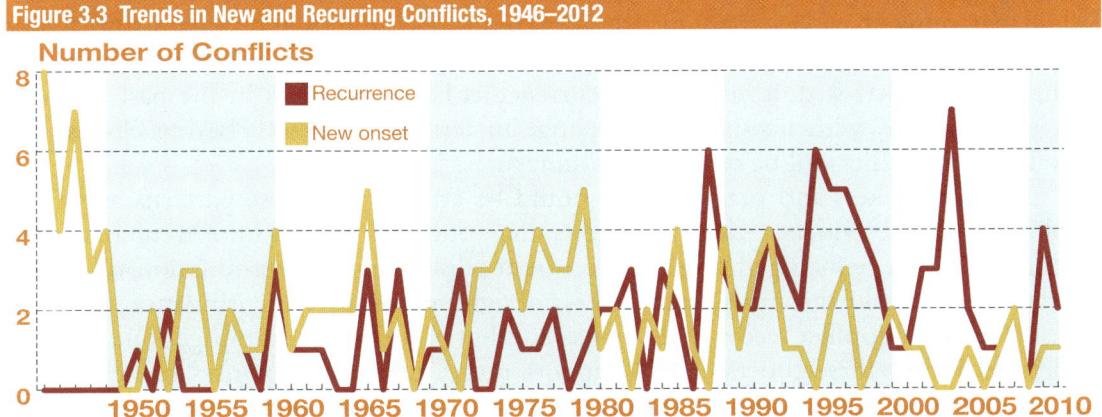

Figure 3.3 Trends in New and Recurring Conflicts, 1946–2012

Figure 3.3 displays separate trend lines for new onsets and recurrences. The positive news is that new onsets have been uncommon, never exceeding three in any year over the past two decades. In the past decade alone, four years have exhibited zero new onsets. No previous stretch since the end of World War II has been so lacking in new conflicts. At the same time, recurrences have become far more frequent, rising from an annual average of just 1.1 cases from 1946–1989 to 2.9 cases per year from 1990–2012, whereas new onsets dropped from 2.3 cases to 1.3 cases in the same periods.

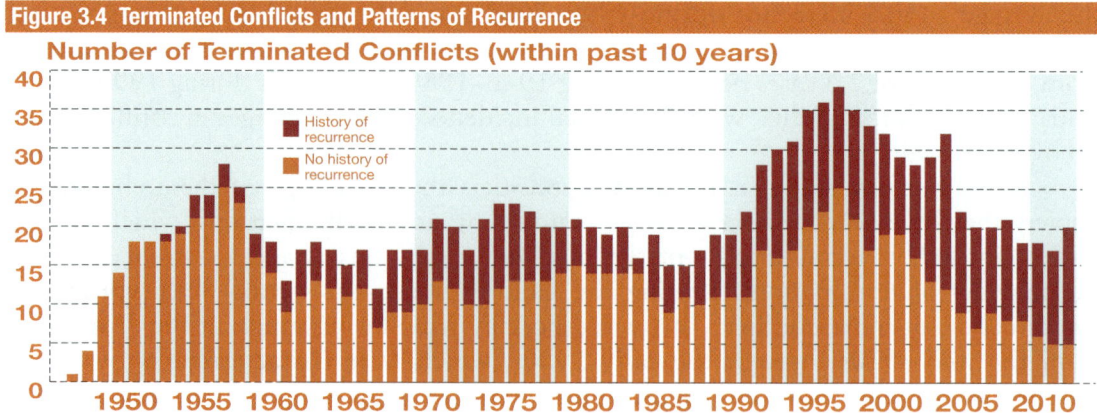

Figure 3.4 depicts the number of recently terminated conflicts. For each year, the bar reflects conflicts that terminated during the previous 10 years and remained inactive. This set of recently terminated conflicts has a latent risk of recurring. Terminated conflicts are removed from the set after 10 years on the assumption that a decade without recurrence is sufficient for a durable peace. The set expands substantially with the increase in conflict terminations during the early 1990s. The red portion of each bar indicates the terminated conflicts with a history of recurrence—i.e., terminating, subsequently restarting, and then terminating again. The share of terminated conflicts with such a history grew from 32 percent during 1955–1990 to 49 percent during 1990–2012.

Conclusion

The number of armed conflicts worldwide has leveled off. Surges of terminations during the early 1990s and early 2000s lowered the number of active conflicts considerably. While new onsets have declined, recurrences are more common and remain sufficiently frequent, preventing a sustained downward trend. Moreover, the share of recently terminated conflicts with a history of recurrence is far higher than in the past. If these patterns continue, with no significant change in terminations with lasting effects, the prevalence of conflict will be relatively stationary.

Policy makers and practitioners should be attentive to these patterns and their implications. The evidence clearly suggests that one area where improvements must be achieved is in reducing the risk of recurrence following the termination of armed conflict. In principle, this can be achieved via designing and implementing more effective measures of post-conflict recovery, as well as conflict prevention and mitigation. A better understanding of these processes will support more informed responses to help usher conflict-affected societies through the challenging steps of reconciliation, reconstruction, and stabilization, equipping them with the resilient capacity to avoid renewed violence. Otherwise, the troubling cycle, whereby armed violence reignites after a promising stage in which it subsided to minimal levels, will persist in all too many countries.

4. GLOBAL TRENDS IN DEMOCRATIZATION: LEADERSHIP TRANSITIONS AND SYSTEMIC CHANGE

Erica Frantz

In March 2013, Venezuelan president Hugo Chavez passed away after a bout with cancer. Venezuela had a long history of democracy prior to his election in 1998, but Chavez eroded many of the country's democratic institutions while in office.[1] During his time in power, Chavez expanded the powers of the president considerably and extended the president's term in office, all while holding semi-competitive elections on a regular basis. His actions effectively transformed the Venezuelan political system into an anocracy: though the country was no longer democratic, it was not fully autocratic either. Largely due to the centrality of Chavez to Venezuelan politics, his passing sparked a flurry of media commentary surrounding the country's future. Chavez's named successor, former vice president Nicolas Maduro, was elected president in April 2013, amid heavy criticism by members of the opposition. The consensus among observers, however, is that the likelihood of democratization in Venezuela is higher than it has been for many years.

Similar discussions emerged after the death of North Korean leader Kim Jong-il in December 2011. Observers debated how the country would be governed under Kim's handpicked successor, Kim Jong-un. Nearly everyone saw the elder Kim's passing as an opportunity that did not exist previously for larger political change in North Korea. Other recent deaths of leaders in office likewise sparked speculations about whether political change loomed on the horizon. Additions to the list include Malam Bacai Sanha of Guinea Bissau in January 2012, Bingu wa Mutharika of Malawi in April 2012, John Atta Mills of Ghana in July 2012, and Meles Zenawi of Ethiopia in August 2012.

> *The major finding is that a leadership transfer increases the likelihood that a country's political system will experience a transition, yet such systemic change is still rare.*

A leader's death in office is often assumed to raise the potential of political transformation. Whether that assumption matches reality is poorly understood. In line with the special theme of *Peace and Conflict 2014*, this chapter looks under the hood of the state at the impact of transfers in leadership: how frequently are they associated with systemic changes and under what conditions? The analysis examines the 885 leadership transitions around the world from 1947–2004, the years for which these data are available in the post-World War II era. Though more recent leadership transfers, like the aforementioned cases, are not included in this sample, prior patterns are illuminating. The major finding is that a leadership transfer increases the likelihood of a country's political system experiencing a transition, yet such systemic change is still rare. In the vast majority of cases, leaders come and go, and the political system persists, at least in the year of the leader's departure. Yet not all leadership transfers are the same. The probability of systemic change is noticeably higher when leaders are forced out of power—via coups d'état, for example—than when they are voted out or die while in office.

---

1 Chavez also was re-elected in 2000, under the new constitution Venezuelans approved the previous year.

The next section provides definitions and describes the data used in the analysis. Subsequent sections summarize trends in the distribution of political systems and patterns of systemic change and assess their relationship to the nature of leadership transfers.

Definitions & Data

The analysis follows a conventional approach by characterizing political systems using Polity scores (Polity 2011), which are differentiated into three categories: autocracy, anocracy, and democracy (see Box 4.1).[2] Transitions between any two of the categories represent instances of systemic change, involving significant movement in a country's "patterns of authority" (Polity 2010).[3] Meanwhile, the information on leadership transfers is obtained from the Archigos dataset (Goemans, Gleditsch, and Chiozza 2009a). The Archigos and Polity datasets are merged to conduct the analysis. Because the Polity data are recorded in a country-year format, the handful of cases in which the leader entered and exited power the same calendar year are excluded from the analysis. Both the political system and the leader are coded as of January 1 for each year.

Box 4.1 Categories of Political Systems

The Polity Project scores all independent countries of the world with a population of at least 500,000 in terms of the autocratic and democratic features in the nature of political competition, executive constraints, and openness in the executive recruitment process (Polity 2011). To characterize a country's political system, its autocratic and democratic scores are combined into an overall score, measured on a 21-point scale ranging from –10 to 10. Based on this overall score, a country can be categorized as an autocracy, anocracy, or democracy.

Autocracies are countries with scores from –10 and –6 on the Polity scale. Autocracies are typified by closed political recruitment, lack of restraints on executive political power, and limitations on political competition. Autocracies observed in 2011 include hereditary monarchies, such as Saudi Arabia; one-party states, such as China; and countries ruled by strongmen, such as Belarus.

Anocracies are countries with scores from –5 to 5 on the Polity scale. Anocracies are hybrid political systems, with both authoritarian and democratic features. Some anocracies hold elections that are contested, but not freely nor fairly, such as Chad. Other anocracies are weakly institutionalized electoral democracies, such as Cambodia.

Democracies are countries with scores from 6 to 10 on the Polity scale. Democracies exhibit open political recruitment, restraints on executive power, and political competition. Democracies include both parliamentary systems, such as the United Kingdom and India; and presidential systems, such as the United States, South Africa, and Argentina.

Political Systems Worldwide

As of 2011, 95 democracies existed around in the world, which represents an all-time high in the post-World War II era (see Figure 4.1). The number of autocracies, by contrast, has plummeted to 20, the lowest since 1945. Democracies now comprise 58 percent of

---

[2] These categories define different types of political systems, rather than different types of political regimes. Regimes refer to "the set of formal and informal rules and procedures for selecting national leaders and policies" (Geddes 1999, 116). Polity scores, by contrast, measure the "qualities of democratic and autocratic authority in governing institutions" (Polity 2010). Regimes can come and go within the same political system, just as political systems can change during the same regime. For example, most observers view the 1971 transfer of power in Uganda from Milton Obote to Idi Amin as a case of regime change, despite the fact that the underlying patterns of authority remained the same (in fact, the Polity scores for Uganda remained fairly consistent across both leaders' tenures). At the same time, few observers view Joseph Mobutu's 1992 decision to legalize opposition parties in the former Zaire as regime change, though the country's Polity score increased by three points in response, moving it from an autocracy to an anocracy. Therefore, the term "political system" is used—rather than "regime"—when referring to Polity classifications.

[3] The absence of systemic change does not necessarily mean the absence of major political upheaval. For example, in Libya, when Muammar Qaddafi ousted King Idris in 1969 in a coup, the identity of the leadership group changed dramatically from individuals associated with the monarch to military officers affiliated with the coup. Despite this disruption, Libya's political system remained autocratic, and consequently the Polity score did not change at that time.

the world's states, whereas the share of autocracies is just 12 percent. Another 49 states are anocracies, amounting to a 30 percent share that has more or less persisted since the end of the Cold War. Indeed, the collapse of the Soviet Union was a pivotal moment for the distribution of political systems worldwide, ushering in an era in which democracies are increasingly more common, autocracies less so as a result, and anocracies—which had been unusual during the prior era—remain a steady presence.

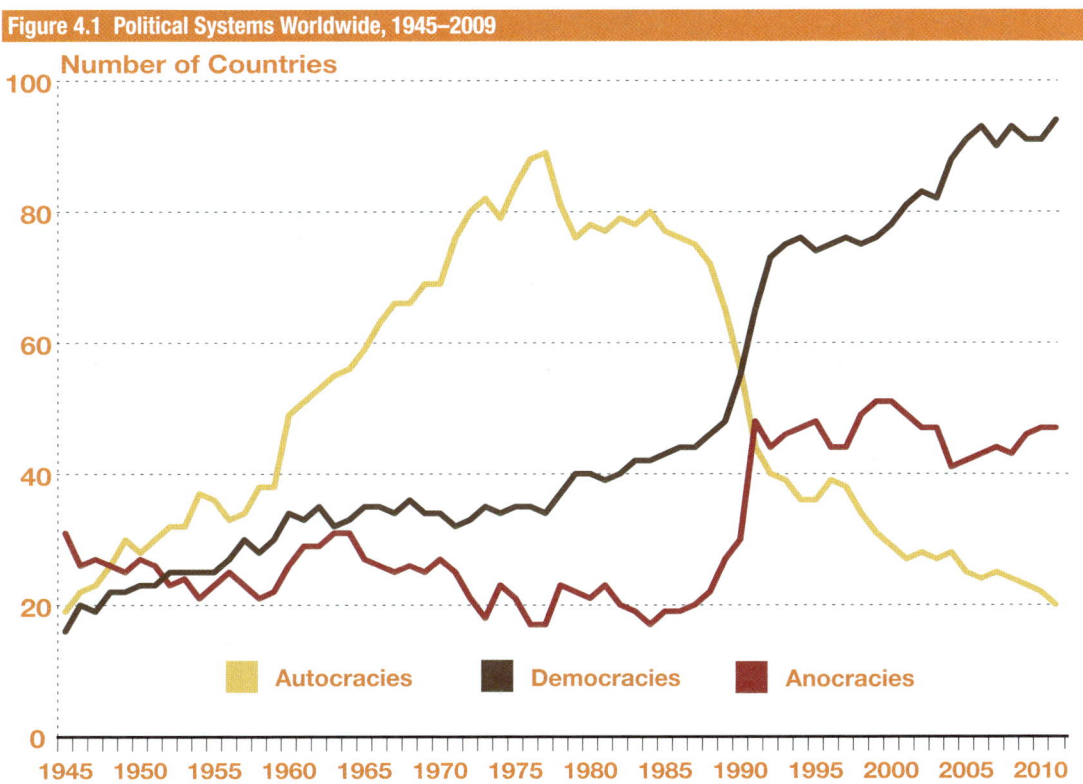

Systemic Change

In 2011, the number of systemic changes nearly doubled relative to recent years (see Figure 4.2). Between 2007 and 2010, no more than four states experienced systemic change in any given year, compared to seven in 2011. Kyrgyzstan, Niger, and Thailand transitioned from anocracies to democracies, while Libya, Morocco, and Myanmar transitioned from autocracies to anocracies. Bahrain was the lone country that moved in a more autocratic direction, transitioning from anocracy to autocracy.

> *Of note, 2011 constituted the first full year of the Arab Spring, but limited evidence of political transformation in North Africa and the Middle East is observed in the Polity data. Despite the momentous events that occurred across the region beginning in December 2010, systemic changes were recorded in only three countries by the end of 2011. Two of these countries exhibited greater levels of democracy.*

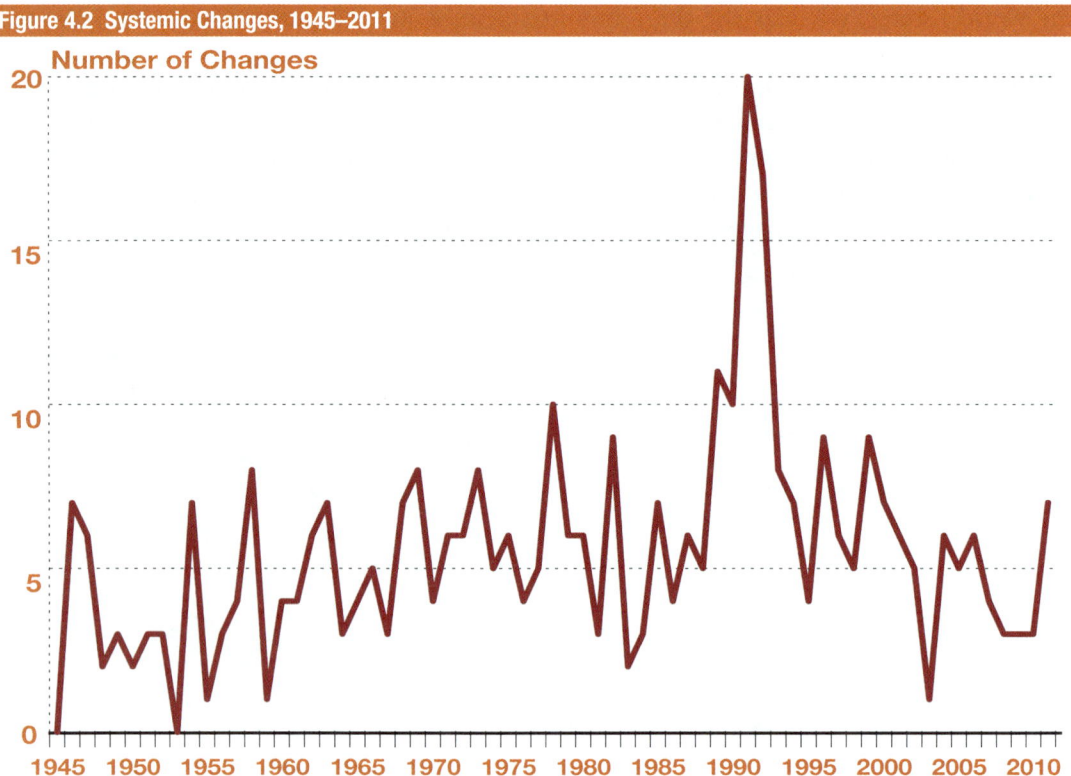

Figure 4.2 Systemic Changes, 1945–2011

Of note, 2011 constituted the first full year of the Arab Spring, but limited evidence of political transformation in North Africa and the Middle East is observed in the Polity data. Despite the momentous events that occurred across the region beginning in December 2010, systemic changes were recorded in only three countries by the end of 2011. Two of these countries exhibited greater levels of democracy. Tunisia, where everything started, is conspsicuously absent from the list. Thus, patterns of authority in many of the Arab Spring countries are fairly entrenched and resilient, at least in the face of mass-driven protests.

The Role of Leadership Transfers in Systemic Change

As the Arab Spring demonstrates, systemic change is difficult to engender. In fact, the likelihood of systemic change in any given year is only 4 percent on average (see Table 4.1). In 62 percent of these cases, the transition is from autocracy to anocracy or vice versa. Subtle changes can accumulate over time to produce systemic change, like with Venezuela under Chavez. Significant events such as foreign invasions, domestic rebellions, and leadership transfers can also serve as triggers.

Table 4.1 The Likelihood of a Systemic Change, 1947–2004						
			By Type of Leader Exit			
Any Year	With a Leader Exit	Without a Leader Exit	Regular	Irregular	Death in Office	Foreign Intervention
4%	2%	17%	10%	40%	8%	44%

In particular, a leadership transfer is a vulnerable moment for a political system. Decisions over who should succeed the incumbent can create tensions among elites and lead to destabilizing splits. Members of opposition groups, as well as foreign enemies, are attuned to this vulnerability and often view the period surrounding the transfer as an opportunity to seize power or pressure the leadership group for political transformation. These activities have the potential not only to propel the downfall of the existing leadership group, but also to induce dramatic changes in the structure of the political system.

When a leadership transfer occurs, the likelihood of systemic change is 17 percent. This number may seem low. Yet the likelihood of systemic change absent a transfer of leadership is only 2 percent. Systemic change, though infrequent under all conditions, is far more likely when leaders are replaced. Transitions to democracy—from either anocracy or autocracy—appear to be particularly dependent on leadership transfers. Only 34 percent of democratizations occur absent a transfer of leadership, compared to 47 percent of transitions to autocracy and 59 percent of transitions to anocracy. This indicates that a defining moment of democratization is the outgoing leader's departure from power.

> *Systemic change, though infrequent under all conditions, is far more likely when leaders fall from power. Transitions to democracy—from either anocracy or autocracy—appear to be particularly dependent on leadership transfers.*

Of course, not all leadership transfers are the same. Some are regular, meaning they comply with existing rules and norms, as with elections.[4] Others are irregular, meaning that they occur illicitly or by force, as with coups (Goemans, Gleditsch, and Chiozza 2009b). About two-thirds (65 percent) of leaders leave power through regular means, with the rest exiting through irregular means (23 percent), death in office (11 percent),[5] or foreign intervention (1 percent). The distribution of cases differs quite a bit when leadership transfers are differentiated by system type (see Table 4.2). Regular leadership transfers comprise the bulk of cases in democracies, a little more than half of cases in anocracies, and only about a quarter of cases in autocracies. These disparities are not surprising given that a central and standard element of democratic governance is the selection of leaders through free and fair elections. Elections—albeit not fully competitive ones—are common in non-democratic systems as well, but they are less likely to serve as a means by which leadership transfers occur. Absent institutional mechanisms to enable and enforce periodic leadership transfers, including limits on the number and length of terms in office, contenders often resort to force instead to get their turn. Such leadership transfers are far more destabilizing to political systems than those that occur through established norms and processes.[6] Whereas only 10 percent of regular leadership transfers are associated with systemic change, this rate quadruples with irregular leadership transfers.

---

[4] Transitions are considered regular when they occur through elections, even if the elections are not competitive. What matters is that the transition is dictated by an existing set of rules and norms.

[5] In the Archigos dataset, this category also includes leaders who committed suicide, as well as leaders who retired due to ill health (i.e., who were on the verge of death). Assassinations are considered irregular transfers.

[6] A natural assumption might be that illegal seizures of powers, such as coups, are transitions to autocracy, by definition. According to the Polity Codebook, however, "a sudden change in a polity's executive…through a violent or non-violent coup d'état does not necessarily constitute a change in authority patterns for the polity. Polity codes will be unaffected by a change in personal leadership if regime authority patterns and structures remain unchanged."

Table 4.2 How Leaders Exit Power, 1947–2004				
System Type	Regular	Irregular	Death in Office	Foreign Intervention
Democracies (n=448)	88%	5%	6%	1%
Anocracies (n=237)	54%	37%	7%	2%
Autocracies (n=200)	26%	45%	26%	3%

When mass actions accompany irregular leadership transfers, the likelihood of systemic change is even greater: riots increase the likelihood from 34 to 52 percent, while anti-government protests increase the likelihood from 37 to 49 percent.[7] Thus, irregular leadership transfers that coincide with mass actions (regardless of cause and effect) increase the likelihood of systemic change considerably, compared to transfers absent those activities. Regardless of the form of mass action, about half of the systemic changes that emerge in these contexts move countries towards greater levels of democracy, but the other half move them in the opposite direction.

Thus, when leaders die in office, more of the same can usually be expected—in terms of the nature of the political system.

What are the consequences of a leader's death in office for the political system—the question posed at the outset of this chapter? Death in office, while not the predominant mode of exit for leaders, occurs in about 10 percent of cases. Of the 100 leaders who died in office during the time period under analysis, 54 percent led autocracies, 30 percent led democracies, and 16 percent led anocracies. Autocratic leaders are about four times more likely to die of natural causes while in office (26 percent of cases) than their anocratic (7 percent) or democratic (6 percent) counterparts. Autocratic leaders, because they are sheltered from institutional mechanisms of leadership transfer that could make them step down, often manage to hold onto power until they are no longer physically able.[8] The death of an autocrat in office may trigger speculation that systemic change is on the way, but this outcome is uncommon (9 percent of cases).[9] Thus, when leaders die in office, more of the same can usually be expected—in terms of the nature of the political system.

Conclusion

This chapter shows that patterns of authority within countries over time tend to be fairly stable, as systemic changes happen infrequently. Certain events, however, increase the potential of transitions. Transfers of power between leaders boost the likelihood of systemic change more than eight times. Yet not all leadership transfers are identical. When transfers happen by force, such as ousting leaders via coups, systemic changes are somewhat common. By contrast, when transfers occur via routinized, institutional mechanisms like elections, systemic changes are rare. The same is true when leaders die in office. On balance, this evidence implies that democracy will not be observed in Venezuela post-Chavez, at least in the near term, despite the hopes of many that his death would precipitate systemic change. While some may view this assessment as disappointing, the silver lining is that autocracy will probably not materialize there, either.

---

7 Data on riots and anti-government demonstrations come from Banks (2001) and are available only through 1999.

8 One might assume that autocratic leaders are older upon leaving power than their democratic and anocratic peers, but on average the age at exit is actually about the same across all system types.

9 The likelihood of systemic change after a leader's death is 13 percent in anocracies and 3 percent in democracies.

5. GLOBAL TRENDS IN TERRORISM, 1970–2011

Gary LaFree and Laura Dugan

This chapter reports new results from the most recent version of the Global Terrorism Database (GTD), maintained by the National Consortium for the Study of Terrorism and Responses to Terrorism (START) at the University of Maryland. The GTD currently includes data on more than 104,000 terrorist attacks that occurred from 1970–2011.[1] The operational definition of terrorism is *the threatened or actual use of illegal force by non-state actors, in order to attain a political, economic, religious or social goal, through fear, coercion, or intimidation*. Thus, the GTD excludes state terrorism and genocide, topics that are important and complex enough to warrant their own separate reviews.

START relies entirely on unclassified sources, primarily print and electronic media articles, to identify terrorist attacks and systematically record details of the attacks. At present, this process begins with a universe of over one million articles published daily worldwide, in order to identify the relatively small subset of articles that describe terrorist attacks. We accomplish this using customized search strings to isolate an initial pool of potentially relevant articles, followed by more sophisticated machine learning techniques to further refine the search results. For this subset of articles, additional manual review is required to identify the unique events that satisfy the GTD inclusion criteria and are subsequently researched and coded according to the specifications of the GTD Codebook. Approximately 5,000 to 8,000 articles are manually reviewed, and approximately 600 to 900 attacks are identified and coded for each month of data collection.[2]

Using the GTD, this chapter provides an update on worldwide trends in terrorism, reporting baseline information concerning the distribution of terrorist attacks and fatalities, terrorist targets, tactics and weapons employed by terrorists, and the regional distribution of terrorist attacks since 1970. Unlike many of the most prominent databases on peace and conflict, the GTD can be disaggregated down to each specific event, reporting the day on which events occurred and for a subset of the data down to the latitude and longitude where each event happened. In keeping with the special theme of this volume, we also present a spatial analysis of terrorism at the county level for the United States and disaggregate global terrorist events by month and day.

---

1 GTD is comprehensive for this time period, with the exception of 1993 data, most of which were misplaced by the original collectors, prior to the transfer of the records to START, and have never been recovered (LaFree and Dugan 2007). Consequently, all findings exclude attacks from 1993. The GTD data are updated annually and made available publicly through START's website: http://www.start.umd.edu/gtd. Data collection for 2012 was underway as this chapter was being prepared. Under a contract with the US State Department, an abridged version of the GTD will support the statistical annex for the US State Department's *2012 Country Reports on Terrorism*.

2 Event databases can have limitations. The media may report inaccuracies and lies, and there may be conflicting information or false, multiple, or no claims of responsibility. Maintaining consistency is also challenging. The longer the lag between events and data collection, the greater the chances that some data will no longer be available. By the time we computerized the original GTD data, which ended in 1997, and secured funding for new data collection in 2005, we were eight years behind. In working to make the data current, we had to rely on historical sources; for more recent years, we approached real-time data collection. Availability of sources erodes over time, causing underreporting or missing data. This is most problematic when media—especially small, regional, and local newspapers—are not archived. In addition, compiling and maintaining databases is expensive. Amid budget crises and cost-cutting pressures, data collection can be an attractive target for elimination.

Global Trends in Terrorism

Given the amount of publicity that terrorism receives in the print and electronic media, many would likely assume that terrorist attacks and fatalities have been steadily rising since 1970, the starting point of the dataset. As Figure 5.1 shows, however, trends in terrorism over time have actually been more complex. Through the mid-1970s, worldwide terrorist attacks were relatively infrequent, with fewer than 1,000 incidents each year until 1977.[3] From 1978 to 1979, however, the number of attacks increased by 74 percent, from 1,527 to 2,663. The annual frequency generally continued to increase until the 1992 peak (5,081 attacks), with smaller peaks in 1984 (3,494 attacks) and 1989 (4,322 attacks). After 1992, the number of terrorist attacks dropped dramatically to a 20-year low in 1998 (but see footnote 2). In fact, total attacks in 2000 (1,815), the year prior to the 9/11 attacks, were just a few hundred more than the corresponding figure for 1978 (1,527). Attacks rose again sharply around the time that the United States and its allies invaded Iraq in 2003. By 2011, total attacks (5,066) were barely less than the record level experienced in 1992. This ebb and flow results in one of the most striking features of Figure 5.1: the pronounced U-shape pattern in total terrorist attacks from 1992 to 2011.

Figure 5.1 Total and Fatal Terrorist Attacks, 1970–2011

Fatal attacks exhibit a similar U-shaped pattern. The specific characteristics of the trends differ somewhat: total attacks rose more rapidly than total fatalities during the 1980s and again during the first decade of the twenty-first century. Despite these differences, the two series are highly correlated (r = 0.96), with fatal attacks, on average,

---

[3] Enders, Sandler, and Gaibulloev (2011) compared GTD and ITERATE data over time and found that from 1978 to 2005, the two databases provide very similar trends. From 1970 to mid-1977, however, the number of attacks in ITERATE, which is limited to international attacks, consistently exceeds the number of international attacks reported by GTD, leading us to suspect that GTD undercounts events during this earlier period.

accounting for just over half of all attacks (2,515 fatal attacks per year compared to 5,081 total attacks per year worldwide). Until 1979, the GTD recorded fewer than four hundred fatal terrorist attacks per year. Between 1978 and 1979, fatal attacks more than doubled (from 374 to 836). Throughout most of the 1980s, fatal attacks hovered close to 1,000 each year. The trend shifted again in 1988, rising to a peak of 2,175 fatal terrorist attacks in 1992. Like total attacks, fatal attacks declined after that year, bottoming out in 1998 with 451 fatal attacks and then rising again to surpass the 1992 peak in 2011 (2,515).

It is tempting to attribute the rise in total and fatal attacks before 1991 and their rapid fall-off thereafter to the collapse of the Soviet Union. Indeed, some evidence exists of a decline in attacks by Marxist-Leninist-inspired groups after 1991 (LaFree, Yang, and Crenshaw 2009). At present, however, we know of no rigorous tests of this claim.

Targets, Tactics, and Weapons of Terrorism

Next, we examine the distribution of targets, tactics, and weapons of terrorist attacks. Our last contribution to *Peace and Conflict* (LaFree and Dugan 2012) included data through 2008. Therefore, we opt to present information on total attacks for the entire available time frame, then differentiate attacks from 1970–2008 and from 2009–2011, as well as provide the percentage change between these two periods.

Targets

Table 5.1 Distribution in Targets of Terrorism

Category	Total (N=108,346)	1970–2008 (N=92,860)	2009–2011 (N=15,486)	Change from 1970–2008 to 2009–2011
Private Citizens and Property	21.7%	20.3%	30.3%	49.4%
Business	14.3%	14.9%	10.3%	–30.8%
General Government	13.5%	12.9%	17.3%	34.2%
Police	12.1%	12.0%	13.0%	9.0%
Military	11.6%	12.8%	4.6%	–64.2%
Transportation	5.1%	5.2%	4.8%	–6.6%
Utilities	4.3%	4.6%	2.6%	–43.2%
Diplomats	2.6%	2.9%	1.3%	–55.1%
Religious Figures/Institutions	2.4%	2.3%	3.0%	34.5%
Educational Institutions	3.4%	2.0%	4.3%	113.3%
Journalists and Media	1.9%	2.0%	0.9%	–56.7%
Airports and Airlines	1.1%	1.2%	0.4%	–69.4%
Other Terrorists	1.1%	1.0%	1.7%	77.1%
Other	6.0%	6.1%	5.5%	–9.4%

Table 5.1 presents the analysis of targets of global terrorist strikes.[4] Overall, there is considerable variation in target types. The top three targets for the entire series—and prior to 2009—are private citizens and property, businesses, and the general government, which together account for almost 50 percent of observations in both periods. While we excluded many attacks against police and the military as being noncivilian and

---

[4] The total number of targets exceeds the total number of terrorist attacks because each attack can have multiple targets.

therefore outside of our operational definition of terrorism, these two targets still jointly account for nearly 24 percent of total attacks. The "other" category encompasses a diverse range of targets, including telecommunication, maritime, and non-governmental organizations. While our definition of terrorism emphasizes civilian targets, these results suggest that purely civilian targets—"private citizens and property," without a specific institutional or organizational affiliation—account for just over one-fifth of all attacks.

> *The share of attacks on unaffiliated private citizens exhibited the largest increase, of 10 percentage points.... Significant decreases were observed in attacks targeting airports and airlines, the military, and journalists/media.*

As Table 5.1 also shows, there have been major changes in targeting by terrorists after 2008. The share of attacks on unaffiliated private citizens exhibited the largest increase, of 10 percentage points. General government and police ranked second and third as targets in the 2009–2011 period, with increased shares. Over this same period, businesses were attacked considerably less, dropping the rank to fourth. The target that exhibited the most dramatic increase was educational institutions, whose share more than doubled. The data also reveal a sharp increase in terrorists targeting other terrorists. Significant decreases were observed in attacks targeting airports and airlines, the military, and journalists/media. The first of these declines is consistent with the conclusion that airport security has improved in recent years. The decline in military targets is likely a reflection of scaled-back military engagements in Iraq and Afghanistan since 2008. The large drop in attacks on journalists and the media is interesting given recent concerns that journalists are frequently targeted by terrorists (Carr 2012). Yet attacks against airports/airlines and journalists/media are relatively infrequent, which means that small changes in numbers yield high percentage changes. Despite the differences noted, the six most commonly targeted entities (private citizens, business, government, police, military, transportation) remained the same during the two time frames and jointly accounted for more than three-quarters of all terrorist targets (78 percent from 1970–2008 and 80 percent from 2009–2011). Nevertheless, there were clearly major changes in terrorist targeting over time, which would be worthwhile to examine in more detail.

Tactics

The coding of the GTD also permits the examination of long-term trends in tactics used by terrorists. For purposes of this analysis, we divided terrorist tactics into eight categories: *bombings, armed assaults, assassinations, facility or infrastructure attacks, kidnappings, barricade/hostage taking, unarmed assaults,* and *hijackings.*

Bombings are attacks using explosive devices, including bombs detonated manually or by remote timer and suicide bombings. *Armed assaults* are in-person attacks whose primary objective is to cause physical harm or death directly on human targets by any means other than explosives. Hence, we classify the use of an explosive or an incendiary device as a bombing, but the use of a projectile grenade in the hands of an attacker as an armed assault. *Assassinations* are attacks that kill or attempt to kill specific high-profile individuals. Such attacks are considered assassinations even if accomplished with another tactic. A recent example occurred in October 2011, when suspected members of al-Qaeda in the Arabian Peninsula placed a bomb in the car of an Air Force colonel in Yemen, killing the colonel and two passengers. This attack was classified as an assassination, rather than a bombing, given the colonel's prominent position. *Facility or infrastructure attacks* are those whose primary objective is to cause damage to non-human targets, such as buildings or monuments. *Kidnappings* involve hostage taking of persons or groups of persons distinguished by the intention to move and hold the hostages in a clandestine location. *Barricade/hostage attacks* are those whose primary objective is to obtain political or other concessions in return for the release of the hostages. Such attacks are distinguished from kidnappings because the incident occurs and usually plays out at the target location without holding the hostages in a separate clandestine location. *Hijackings* are attacks that involve the forcible takeover of vehicles, including airplanes, buses, and ships, for the purpose of obtaining some concession, such as the payment of a ransom or the release of political prisoners. Hijackings differ from barricade/hostage attacks in that the target is the vehicle, regardless of whether there are people inside.

In both periods, bombings are the most common tactic, followed by armed attacks, with the shares of each increasing modestly from 1970–2008 to 2009–2011.

Table 5.2 shows the distribution of terrorist tactics.[5] In both periods, bombings are the most common tactic, followed by armed attacks, with the shares of each increasing modestly from 1970–2008 to 2009–2011. The largest increase in share was for kidnappings. Meanwhile, the share of assassinations dropped by more than half. Facilities attacks became somewhat less common. Hostage-taking, hijackings, and unarmed assaults were rarely used and became even more uncommon after 2008. A decline in aerial hijackings supports our tentative supposition that airport security may have improved.

Table 5.2 Distribution in Tactics of Terrorism				
Category	Total (N=105,190)	1970–2008 (N=89,419)	2009–2011 (N=15,771)	Change from 1970–2008 to 2009–2011
Bombing	45.2%	44.5%	49.4%	11.1%
Armed Assault	26.6%	26.0%	29.8%	14.4%
Assassination	13.9%	15.3%	6.8%	−55.9%
Facility Attack	7.1%	7.2%	6.0%	−17.0%
Kidnapping	5.6%	5.2%	7.6%	44.9%
Barricade/Hostage Taking	0.7%	0.8%	0.2%	−78.9%
Hijacking	0.4%	0.5%	0.3%	−24.4%
Unarmed Assault	0.4%	0.5%	0.0%	−94.9%

Weapons

A logical tendency is to think that most terrorist strikes are complex and carefully orchestrated and rely heavily on sophisticated weaponry. This inclination is heightened by high-profile cases like the coordinated 9/11 attacks in the United States and subsequent ones in London and Mumbai, as well as treatments of terrorism in the media and movies.

---

5 Terrorist attacks can rely on multiple tactics. Thus, the number of tactics may be larger than the number of attacks. Attacks where no tactic was determined are excluded from the analysis.

Table 5.3 Distribution in Weapons of Terrorism				
Category	Total (N=100,398)	1970–2008 (N=86,200)	2009–2011 (N=14,198)	Change from 1970–2008 to 2009–2011
Explosives	49.9%	48.5%	58.2%	19.9
Firearms	38.2%	39.3%	31.7%	−19.2
Incendiary	8.7%	9.0%	6.9%	−22.8
Melee	2.8%	2.8%	2.7%	−4.4
Chemical	0.2%	0.2%	0.1%	−43.6
Equipment Sabotage	0.2%	0.1%	0.3%	173.8
Biological	0.0%	0.0%	0.0%	−59.5
Radiological	0.0%	0.0%	0.0%	−100.0

Table 5.3 examines the types of weapons used by terrorists.[6] Contrary to the typical view of terrorism, the vast majority of terrorist attacks relied on ordinary, accessible weapons: explosives and firearms. These two types accounted for close to 90 percent of all attacks. For the most part, the explosives used were readily available, especially dynamite, grenades, and improvised devices placed inside vehicles ("car bombs"). Similarly, the most commonly used firearms were widely available, especially automatic weapons, shotguns, and pistols. Incendiaries accounted for a declining share of weapons. Given the dominance of explosives and firearms as weapons of choice, the most important shift in the use of weapons over recent years has been toward explosives and away from firearms. Equipment sabotage, where attackers attempt to disrupt the functioning of an existing system (e.g., removing bolts to dismantle vehicles or cutting cables from bridges), was uncommon in both periods, but the share of cases nearly tripled from 1970–2008 to 2009–2011. Melee attacks, where the perpetrator comes into direct contact with the target using low-technology weapons such as fists or knives, accounted for a consistent share. All other types of weapons declined in share. This includes the use of more sophisticated weapons that are highly regulated by the international community and subject to sanctions, such as those involving chemical, biological, and radiological agents, which are exceedingly rare. Among the attacks, 200 involved chemical agents (183 from 1970–2008 and 17 from 2009–2011),[7] 32 involved biological agents (30 versus 2),[8] and 13 involved radiological agents (all from 1970–2008).[9]

> *All other types of weapons declined in share. This includes the use of more sophisticated weapons that are highly regulated by the international community and subject to sanctions, such as those involving chemical, biological, and radiological agents, which is exceedingly rare.*

---

[6] Each attack can involve multiple weapons; this table lists all mentioned weapons for each attack.

[7] Chemical agents range from letters containing rat poison to tainted water supplies.

[8] Ten of the 32 biological weapons cases were the US anthrax attacks of 2001—in which seven people died. Other biological agents include salmonella and ricin.

[9] Ten of the thirteen radiological weapons were monazite, while plutonium and iodine were each used once. No detail was provided about the thirteenth chemical weapon.

Regional Differences in Terrorist Activity

Given the high profile of terrorist attacks originating in the Middle East/North Africa in recent years, it is easy to disregard the number of terrorist attacks originating in other parts of the world. To study this aspect, we divide countries into nine regions: East and Central Asia, Eastern Europe, Latin America, the Middle East and North Africa, North America, South Asia, Southeast Asia and Oceania, Sub-Saharan Africa, and Western Europe.[10] The countries and territories classified in each region are listed in Table 5.4.

Table 5.4 Classification of Countries by Region	
Region	Countries/Territories
East & Central Asia	China, Hong Kong, Japan, Kazakhstan, Kyrgyzstan, Macao, North Korea, South Korea, Taiwan, Tajikistan, Turkmenistan, and Uzbekistan
Eastern Europe	Albania, Armenia, Azerbaijan, Bosnia-Herzegovina, Bulgaria, Belarus, Croatia, Czechoslovakia, Czech Republic, Estonia, Georgia, Hungary, Latvia, Lithuania, Kashmir, Kosovo, Macedonia, Moldova, Montenegro, Poland, Romania, Russia, San Marino, Serbia, Serbia- Montenegro, Slovak Republic, Slovenia, Soviet Union, Ukraine, and Yugoslavia
Latin America & the Caribbean	Antigua and Barbuda, Argentina, Bahamas, Barbados, Belize, Bermuda, Bolivia, Brazil, Cayman Islands, Chile, Colombia, Costa Rica, Cuba, Dominica, Dominican Republic, Ecuador, El Salvador, Falkland Islands, French Guiana, Grenada, Guadeloupe, Guatemala, Guyana, Haiti, Honduras, Jamaica, Martinique, Nicaragua, Panama, Paraguay, Peru, Puerto Rico, St. Kitts and Nevis, Suriname, Trinidad and Tobago, Uruguay, Venezuela, and the Virgin Islands (US)
Middle East and North Africa	Algeria, Bahrain, Cyprus, Egypt, Iran, Iraq, Israel, Jordan, Kuwait, Lebanon, Libya, Morocco, North Yemen, Oman, Qatar, Saudi Arabia, South Yemen, Syria, Tunisia, Turkey, United Arab Emirates, West Bank and Gaza Strip, Western Sahara, and Yemen
North America	Canada, Mexico, and the United States
South Asia	Afghanistan, Bangladesh, Bhutan, India, Maldives, Mauritius, Nepal, Pakistan, Seychelles, Sri Lanka
Southeast Asia & Oceania	Australia, Brunei, Cambodia, Fiji, French Polynesia, Guam, Indonesia, Laos, Malaysia, Myanmar, New Caledonia, New Hebrides, New Zealand, Papua New Guinea, Philippines, Samoa (Western Samoa), Solomon Islands, Singapore, South Vietnam, Thailand, Timor-Leste, Tonga, Vanuatu, Vietnam, and Wallis and Futuna
Sub-Saharan Africa	Angola, Benin, Botswana, Burkina Faso, Burundi, Cameroon, Cape Verde, Central African Republic, Chad, Comoros, Congo (Brazzaville), Congo (Kinshasa), Djibouti, Equatorial Guinea, Eritrea, Ethiopia, Gabon, Gambia, Ghana, Guinea, Guinea-Bissau, Ivory Coast, Kenya, Lesotho, Liberia, Madagascar, Malawi, Mali, Mauritania, Mauritius, Mozambique, Namibia, Niger, Nigeria, Rwanda, Sao Tome and Principe, Senegal, Sierra Leone, Somalia, South Africa, Sudan, Swaziland, Tanzania, Togo, Uganda, Zaire, Zambia, and Zimbabwe
Western Europe	Andorra, Austria, Belgium, Corsica, Denmark, East Germany, Finland, France, Germany, Gibraltar, Great Britain, Greece, Iceland, Ireland, Italy, Luxembourg, Malta, Isle of Man, Netherlands, Northern Ireland, Norway, Portugal, Spain, Sweden, Switzerland, and West Germany

---

10 GTD identifies 13 regions. For purposes of this analysis, we combined some regions (e.g., Caribbean with Latin America, Southeast Asia with Australia and the rest of Oceania) in order to simplify the figures. Countries like Cyprus are listed according to their geography (Middle East), not their governance (Greece-Turkey).

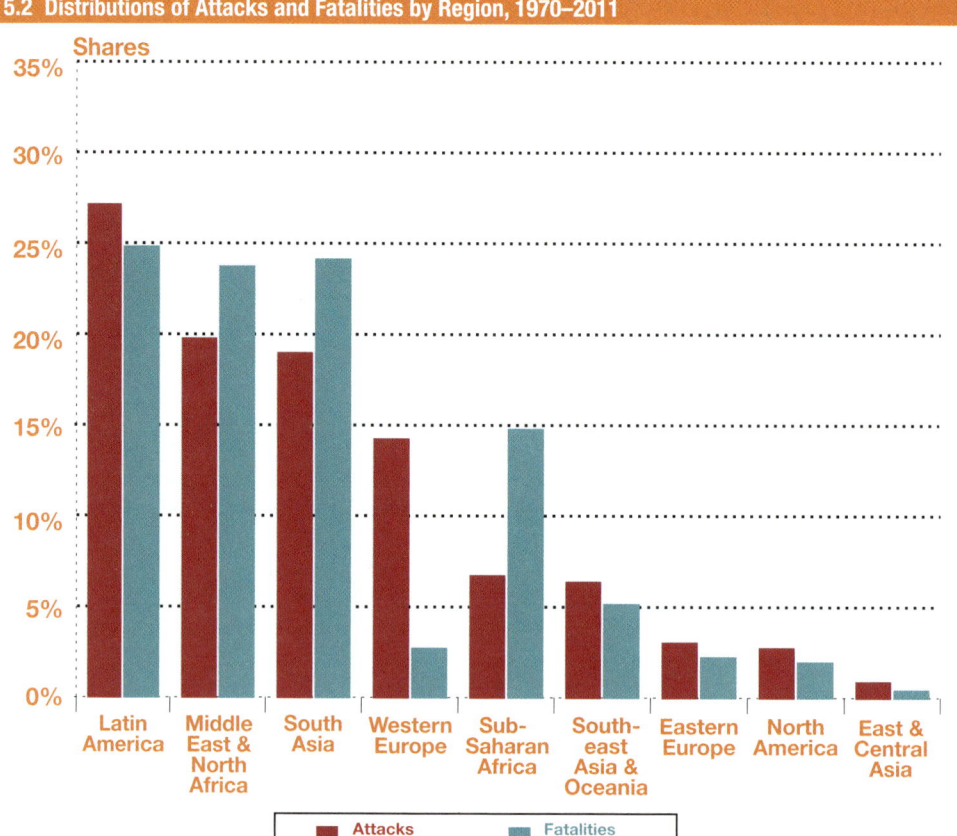

Figure 5.2 Distributions of Attacks and Fatalities by Region, 1970–2011

Figure 5.2 displays total attacks and fatalities from 1970–2011 by region.[11] The most striking result is that Latin America experienced the highest share of attacks (27 percent). In this region, highly active terrorist groups operated for prolonged stretches during the past four decades, including the Shining Path (Sendero Luminoso), the Farabundo Martí National Liberation Front (FMLN), and the Revolutionary Armed Forces of Colombia (FARC). Over the period spanned by the GTD, militant groups in the Middle East/North Africa region were next most active, accounting for nearly 20 percent of total attacks. South Asian countries rank third, with 19 percent of attacks. This is unsurprising given the persistent conflicts in Afghanistan, Pakistan, India, and Sri Lanka. The remaining regions account for 34 percent of attacks. While activity in Western European countries is now far less frequent than during the height of conflicts in Northern Ireland, the Basque area of Spain, and Italy, the region accounts for 14 percent of attacks. Both Sub-Saharan Africa and Southeast Asia/Oceania registered less than half the number of attacks observed in Western Europe. Eastern Europe, North America, and East and Central Asia each account for less than four percent of the total.

Regional patterns for fatalities are substantially different. Latin America remains the leader, but the number of fatalities from terrorist attacks in this region barely exceeded the corresponding figures for the Middle East/North Africa and South Asia. In addition, the ratio of fatalities to attacks varies widely across the regions. Sub-Saharan Africa averaged

---

11 We exclude two attacks that occurred in international territory and three attacks for which the country was missing.

nearly five deaths per terrorist attack, compared to one death for every 2.4 attacks in Western Europe. Part of the explanation may be limitations in the data, such as selective, inconsistent media coverage. Yet a good deal of the observed variation in lethality is likely due to the political context and the extent of the security presence and access to quality medical care. Consider that seven countries in Sub-Saharan Africa averaged more than 10 fatalities per attack: Rwanda (22.3), Djibouti (14.2), Mozambique (12.1), Chad (12.0), Burundi (10.9), Ethiopia (10.4), and Guinea (10.1). Also, the Lord's Resistance Army (LRA) in Uganda staged a series of brutal terrorist attacks resulting in large numbers of fatalities throughout the 1990s and 2000s. Since 2009, the LRA perpetrated two attacks with over 50 fatalities and three others with at least 20 fatalities. Some of these incidents took place in remote, rural settings, where police and doctors are limited in number. This contrasts with the attacks in Western Europe, which often target urban areas with an existing infrastructure of elite counter-terrorism units and first responders.

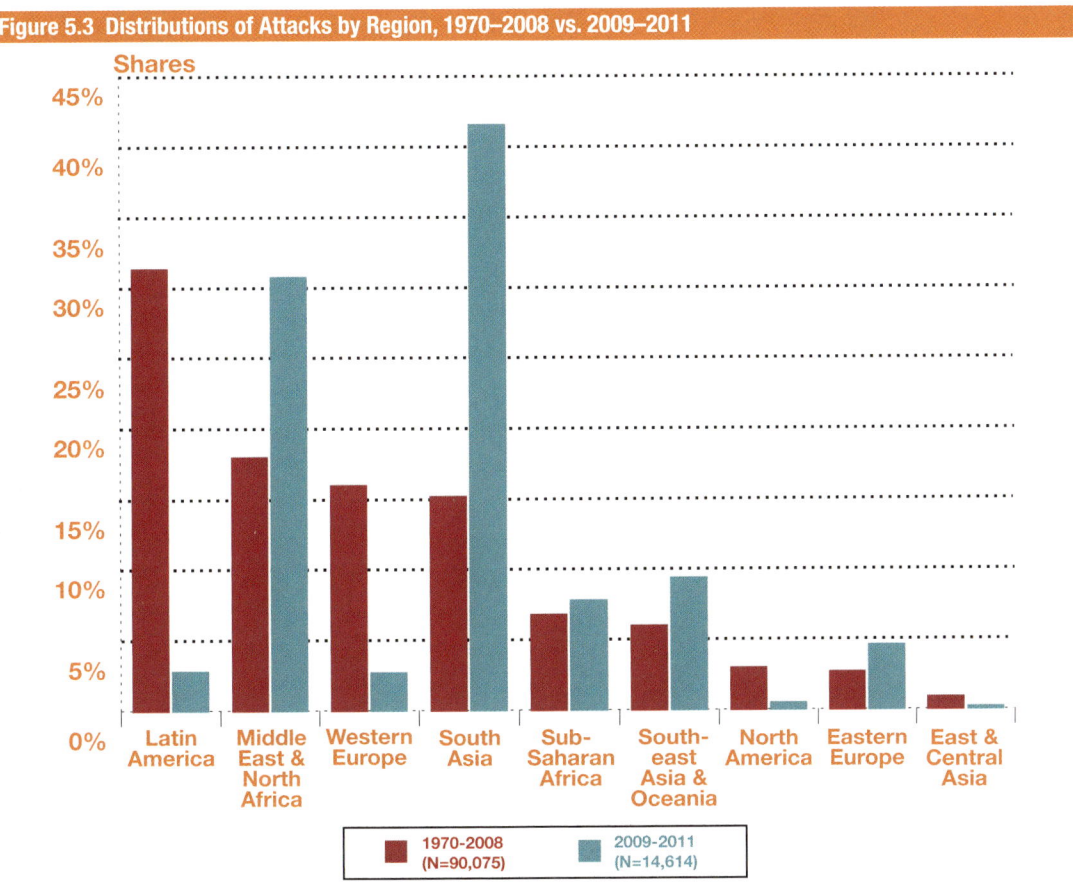

Figure 5.3 Distributions of Attacks by Region, 1970–2008 vs. 2009–2011

Figure 5.3 compares the shares of total attacks by region during 1970–2008 and 2009–2011. Two of the top three regions in the first period—Latin America and Western Europe—rank sixth and seventh in the second period. Only 3 percent of terrorist attacks recorded by the GTD from 2009–2011 took place in Latin America. Terrorism rates in this region during earlier years were driven up with attacks committed by leftist organizations (e.g., FARC in Colombia, Sendero Luminoso in Peru, FMLN in El Salvador), whose fortunes declined substantially after the collapse of the Soviet Union. North America and East and Central Asia also experienced declines in the shares of terrorist activity between the two periods. Meanwhile, South Asia and the Middle East/North Africa have been elevated in importance during the recent years. Likewise, Southeast Asia and Oceania and Eastern Europe exhibited significant increases in shares of attacks. Sub-Saharan Africa's proportion remained about the same.

Table 5.5 Top 25 Most Attacked Countries & Territories

Rank	1970–2008 (N=94,800)		2009–2011 (N=9,889)	
	Country	Share of Attacks	Country	Share of Attacks
1	Colombia	7.86%	Iraq	24.78%
2	Peru*	6.71%	Pakistan	16.36%
3	El Salvador*	5.91%	India	13.52%
4	India	5.47%	Afghanistan	10.01%
5	Iraq	4.65%	Thailand	5.01%
6	Northern Ireland	4.28%	Russia	4.04%
7	Spain*	3.56%	Philippines	4.00%
8	Pakistan	3.46%	Somalia**	2.98%
9	Sri Lanka*	3.21%	Colombia	2.54%
10	Philippines	3.09%	Nigeria**	1.90%
11	Turkey	3.04%	Yemen**	1.73%
12	Algeria	2.67%	Algeria	1.53%
13	United States*	2.58%	Greece**	1.21%
14	Chile*	2.55%	Nepal**	0.84%
15	Guatemala*	2.27%	Northern Ireland	0.82%
16	Lebanon*	2.23%	Israel	0.69%
17	Nicaragua*	2.18%	Sudan**	0.62%
18	South Africa*	2.15%	Congo (Kinshasa)**	0.60%
19	Afghanistan	1.75%	Turkey	0.57%
20	Israel	1.68%	Bangladesh**	0.44%
21	Italy*	1.66%	Kenya**	0.37%
22	West Bank and Gaza Strip	1.66%	Syria**	0.34%
23	Corsica*	1.49%	Iran	0.31%
24	Thailand	1.28%	Indonesia**	0.30%
25	Russia	1.28%	West Bank and Gaza Strip	0.28%

* This country was only in the top 25 from 1970–2008.
** This country was only in the top 25 from 2009–2011.

Given the substantial differences in attacks by region, it is unsurprising that they also vary greatly by country. Table 5.5 shows the 25 most frequently attacked countries/territories during 1970–2008 and 2009–2011. High-conflict territories, such as Corsica, Northern Ireland, and the West Bank and Gaza Strip, are listed separately. The importance of Latin America as a site of terrorism from 1970–2008 is underscored by the fact that Colombia, Peru, and El Salvador exhibited the highest number of attacks for this period. By contrast, Peru and El Salvador are not in the top 25 list for 2009–2011, while Colombia fell to number nine. In addition, three other Latin American countries made the top 25 for 1970–2008: Chile, Guatemala, and Nicaragua. None is among the top 25 for the 2009–2011 period.

Prior to 2009, the top 25 included four countries and territories in Western Europe, six in South and Southeast Asia, and six in the Middle East/Northern Africa. South Africa is the lone country from Sub-Saharan Africa in the top 25, while Russia is the only East European country. The United States finishes as 13th among the top 25 countries prior to 2009.

During the subsequent period, several Latin American and West European countries and territories, among others, dropped out of the top 25, a circumstance often associated with the end of long civil conflicts. They are replaced primarily by countries from Sub-Saharan Africa, the Middle East/North Africa, and South and Southeast Asia. In addition, Greece entered the list, which is an exception to the general trend of declining terrorism in Western Europe. Not surprisingly, Iraq ranks highest in total attacks in 2009–2011, accounting for nearly 25 percent of all attacks during this period. Of note, only 16 of these attacks targeted US nationals—this relatively small number is a likely consequence of the fact that most attacks on American military personnel are counted as warfare, rather than terrorism, and therefore excluded from the GTD. Only three other Middle Eastern/Northern African countries or territories entered the top 25 for 2009–2011. Nevertheless, Yemen, Israel, and the Palestinian Territories combined with Iraq to make the Middle East/North Africa the region that was the most frequent target of terrorism during this period, with just over 27 percent of all attacks.

The United States failed to rank among the top 25 for the last three years of the series. The GTD includes 38 terrorist attacks committed in the United States during 2009–2011. A closer examination of these attacks reveals that the majority of them were domestic, perpetrated most often by eco-terrorist groups (21 percent) or by groups or individuals without a clear organizational affiliation (39 percent).

Spatially Disaggregating the GTD—An Illustration with the United States

A substantial share of the academic research on political violence has involved studies with the country-year as the unit of analysis. A novel aspect of the GTD is the ability to disaggregate terrorism attacks around the world by both space and time. In keeping with the special theme of this issue of *Peace and Conflict*, we provide a closer look into these features of the GTD. At present, only about 40 percent of the GTD is geocoded to the county level. Nonetheless, we demonstrate the potential utility of such analysis, using the United States as an example.

Figure 5.4 shows attacks within the United States from 1970–2011. In all, the GTD includes 2,362 attacks during this period. We created a proportional symbol map to display the concentration of terrorist attacks across 3,140 US counties.[12] The size of the dots is proportional to the number of events that took place in an area, with larger dots representing a higher frequency.

---

12 The term "county" is also used for county-equivalent geographic subdivisions, including parishes and boroughs.

Figure 5.4 Terrorist Attacks in US Counties, 1970–2011

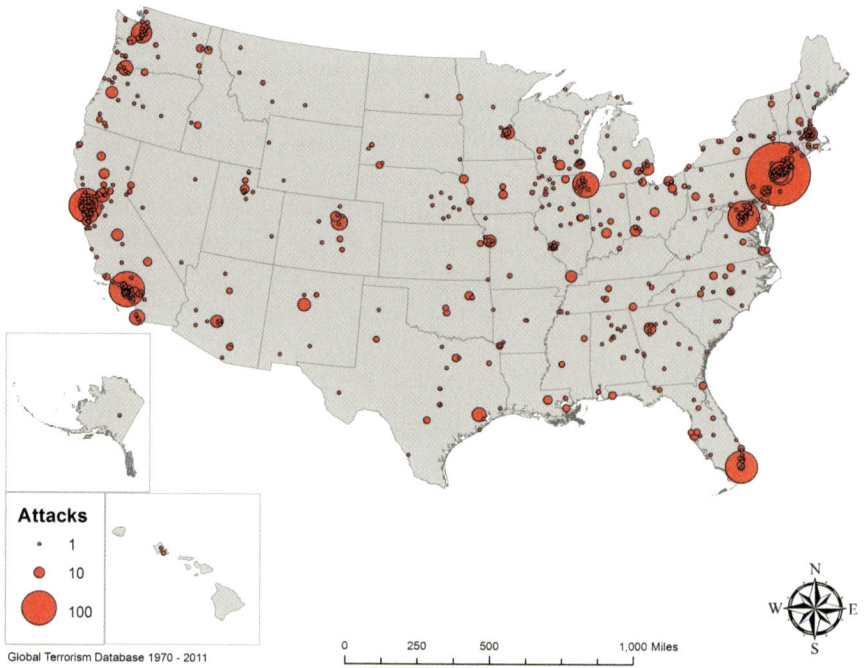

Of significant note, each of the 50 US states suffered at least one terrorist attack between 1970 and 2011. Not surprisingly, however, attacks were concentrated in major population centers. In fact, 33 percent occurred in just five counties: New York County, NY (Manhattan) (n=337); Los Angeles County, CA (n=158); San Francisco County, CA (n=98); Miami-Dade County, FL (n=96); and the District of Columbia (n=81). Meanwhile, 88 percent of counties had no recorded attacks.[13]

Disaggregating the GTD by Time

The GTD also allows us to place events down to the day that they occurred. The observed variation has implications for counter-terrorism policy and operational decisions.

Figure 5.5 shows the distribution of attacks by month. The increase in terrorist violence from February through May coincides with the onset of spring "fighting season" in Afghanistan, where attacks rose by 93 percent during 2003–2011. This compares to 19 percent for the rest of the world, which includes many climates that are less sensitive to the northern hemisphere's seasonal changes.

Figure 5.6 shows the distribution of attacks by day of the week. Attacks were most frequent on Mondays and least frequent on Saturdays—a difference of 19 percent. In fact, attacks are more common from Monday through Thursday than Friday through Sunday. This pattern may be driven by the desire of terrorists to optimize media coverage and to strike at times when people are likely to be present during the work day. All nine regions exhibit fewer attacks on Saturdays than on Mondays. The drop varies, however, from 3 percent in Western Europe to 34 percent in Latin America.

---

[13] Counties and county equivalents change somewhat over time. These estimates are based on the number of counties and county equivalents in 2010. Data for 1993 are excluded.

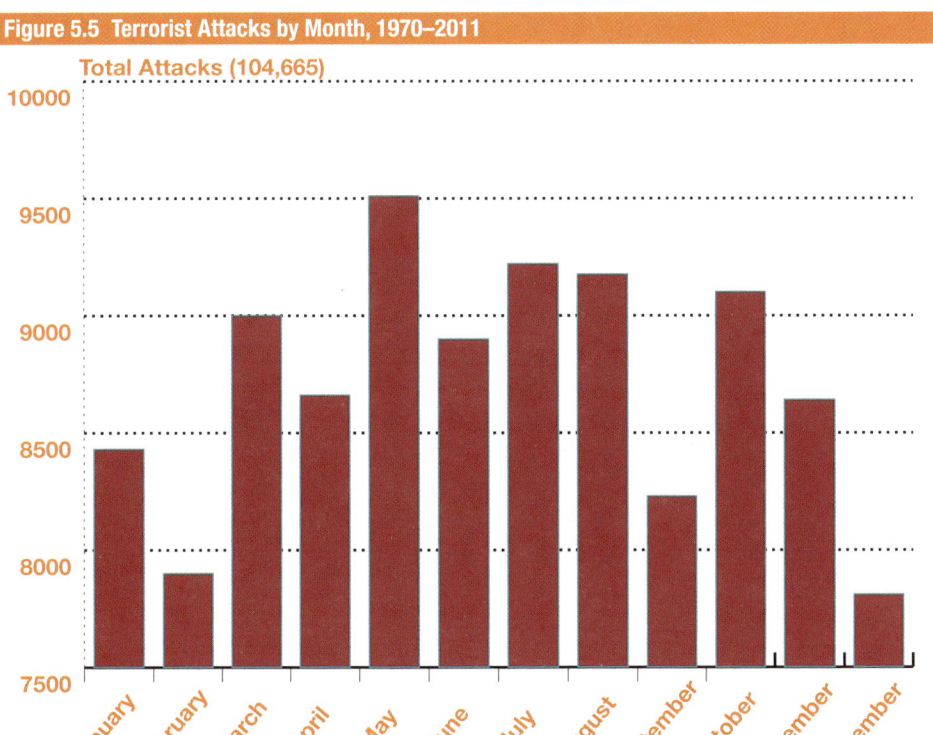

Figure 5.5 Terrorist Attacks by Month, 1970–2011

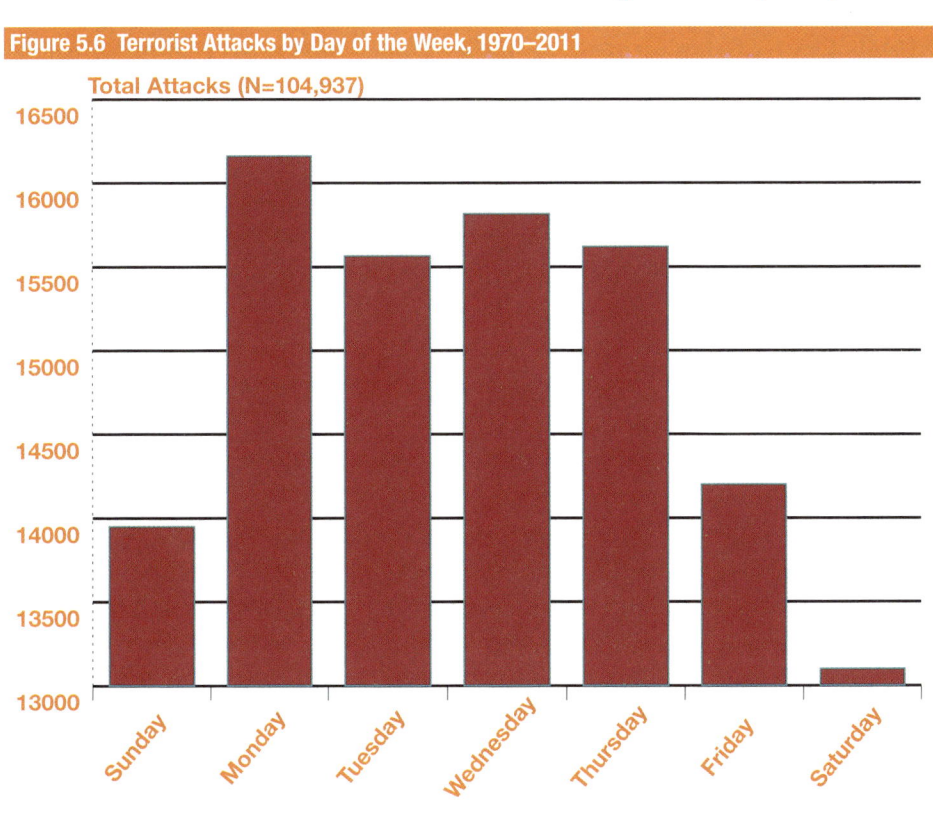

Figure 5.6 Terrorist Attacks by Day of the Week, 1970–2011

GLOBAL TRENDS IN TERRORISM, 1970–2011

Conclusion

This chapter examined the most recently available data on terrorist activity from the GTD, emphasizing changes in trends and characteristics before and after our last report on data through 2008. Our review suggests that both total terrorist attacks and fatalities increased dramatically from 1970 to the early 1990s, declined until about 2000–2002, and then increased again during the past decade. In 2011, fatalities were at their highest level since 1970, and total attacks were just short of the peak.

As in our earlier *Peace and Conflict* reviews (LaFree, Dugan, and Fahey 2008; LaFree, Dugan, and Cragin 2010; LaFree and Dugan 2012), the most common targets of terrorists continued to be private citizens and property—a pattern amplified from 2009–2011. Bombings and armed assaults remained the most common tactics, followed by assassinations, facility attacks, and kidnappings, and these patterns have also grown more pronounced since 2009. A majority of attacks involved readily available explosives or firearms, with the former increasing and the latter decreasing in share after 2008.

Over the past four decades, Latin America leads other regions in terms of both total attacks and fatalities. From 1970–2008, seven Latin American countries were in the top 25 in terms of terrorism. During the period from 2009–2011, however, the most active regions for terrorism were the Middle East/North Africa and South Asia, accounting for more than 72 percent of attacks recorded in the GTD. The decline in attacks in Latin America coincides with the collapse of the Soviet Union, which had important implications for leftist insurgencies and civil wars throughout the region. These results remind us that trends in terrorism do not occur in a vacuum. Rather, they interact with geopolitical circumstances and events. Meanwhile, the rapid increase in terrorist attacks in the Middle East/North Africa and South Asia since 9/11 also coincides with an emergence of civil conflict in these regions. Clearly, policies that address the sources of these conflicts may have meaningful consequences for the sources of terrorism.

> *From 1970–2008, seven Latin American countries were in the top 25 in terms of terrorism. During the period from 2009–2011, however, the most active regions for terrorism were the Middle East/North Africa and South Asia, accounting for more than 72 percent of attacks recorded in the GTD.*

The GTD can be a useful source of data on the microdynamics of conflict because it records the day on which attacks occurred and, for a subset of cases, the city or county (or province) where they occurred. We demonstrated the potential for spatial and temporal disaggregation of the GTD by showing terrorist attacks in the United States by county and by showing worldwide terrorist attacks by month and day of the week. In the case of the United States, the analysis and accompanying visualizations reveal that terrorist attacks are heavily concentrated in large cities, but have occurred in all US states at some point since 1970. We also show that the worldwide occurrences of terrorist attacks are more frequent in specific months and days of the week. In the future, we plan to undertake far more detailed analysis of GTD disaggregated by time and place.

SPECIAL THEME—DISAGGREGATION AND THE MICRODYNAMICS OF CONFLICT AND PEACEBUILDING: INTRODUCTION

David A. Backer

A substantial share of academic research on political conflict, especially in the subfield of international relations, has involved studies with country-year as the unit of analysis. In part, this reflects the traditional interest in interstate conflict and its causes, onset, duration, impact, termination, and recurrence. Also, statistical estimations to assess factors associated with forms of large-scale violence are enabled by the availability of comprehensive cross-national datasets with annual, country-level observations. Even revolutions, riots, and genocides are frequently examined in relation to states—considering risks and actual exposures—and as undifferentiated events with overall characteristics. Qualitative research tends to afford better insight into the underlying dynamics of these events, but with certain inherent shortcomings in the ability to investigate, understand, and compare instances, to test theories, and to generalize findings.

In response to these limitations, studying conflict and peacebuilding processes in a disaggregated manner, down to the micro level, has garnered increased attention over recent years. A basic premise is that the phenomena are complex and warrant greater detail in analysis. One aspect is to train attention at the subnational level, on regions, communities, and neighborhoods, across which circumstances and outcomes often vary in consequential ways. Another aspect is to move outside the confines of calendar years, especially to explore shorter periods. Processes can also be broken down into incidents and further into specific actions and interactions, each with spatial and temporal attributes. In addition, the events implicate numerous types of actors (individuals, households, groups, organizations, companies, institutions, etc.) in a range of roles. They can exercise a degree of agency, with attitudes and behaviors affected by dispositions, context, and constraints. Valuable empirical research is burgeoning on all these fronts, facilitated by novel data compiled via conventional (e.g., coding of documentation in government and NGO archives, surveys, experiments) and emergent (e.g., crowdsourcing, remote sensing) techniques, as well as geolocation tagging that permits the pairing of pertinent information from a diverse assortment of existing and new sources. Capitalizing on these resources is allowing more precise consideration of causality in relationships, with the benefit of refined knowledge about proximity and sequencing, and thus supplying distinctive, improved assessments of important, enduring questions and claims.

The special theme section of *Peace and Conflict 2014* features a set of perspectives from specialists on the disaggregation and microdynamics of conflict and peacebuilding. The chapters highlight developments in data collection and analysis and their significance for theory testing and applications to policy and practice. Some contributions have a global, long-term scope. Others focus on select countries and/or narrower time frames, while emphasizing comparative analysis of patterns and trends, including through the accumulation of findings from series of studies about the same topic. The blend of breadth and depth, spanning different angles and levels of analysis, illuminates the theme by juxtaposing a diversity of data, methods, and findings. A common thread throughout is pushing the boundaries of and learning from the evolving state of the art in the field.

6. DISAGGREGATING CONFLICT BY ACTORS, TIME, AND LOCATION

Karsten Donnay, Elena Gadjanova, and Ravi Bhavnani

Disaggregated studies of conflict, which are increasingly common, provide fine-grained renderings of the relevant actors, timing, and location of events. These studies look beyond the country-year as the unit of analysis, in lieu of research designs that focus on individuals, households, or groups, the heterogeneous characteristics, beliefs, and interests of these actors, and resulting variation in attitudes, decision making, and behavior. The shift toward the micro level also permits a more nuanced analysis of conflicts, with explanations that account for changes over time and across spatial units—spanning the range from villages, neighborhoods, cities, subnational administrative units, states, and regions—in the incidence, intensity, and duration of events. The ability to specify and test causal mechanisms, and thereby address a characteristic limitation of more highly aggregated large-N studies, constitutes a noteworthy advancement in conflict research.

Yet disaggregated approaches are not without limitations. One involves the trade-off in sacrificing greater external validity for internal validity—when variation is explored at the subnational level, within a single country or even several countries, as opposed to cross-national studies that yield broadly applicable findings. Also, there are uncertainties about design, measurement, and analysis: What is the appropriate level of disaggregation? What should be measured? What is observable in practice? How can studies that select different units of analysis be compared, given the known problems with changing the number of units under study and the shape and size of those units? In what ways can different datasets on conflict be linked to each other and to data on other factors? How can challenges associated with analyzing disaggregated data be addressed? In particular, what are the strengths and weaknesses of statistical inference from disaggregated analysis?

This chapter takes stock of the emerging research track by providing an overview of notable recent work that disaggregates conflict by its constitutive actors and the timing and location of events. We discuss select insights from these examples, why they challenge results from prior research or the conventional wisdom, and the associated implications for policy. Our concise review reveals a surge of rich context-specific research, which represents welcome progress, despite the rather limited communication across studies, the absence of data pooling, and the plethora of mixed findings.

Disaggregation by Actors

Micro-level research on conflict draws attention to actors who feature less prominently, if at all, in state-centered analyses that rely on country-year research designs (see Buhaug and Rød 2006; Humphreys and Weinstein 2006; Salehyan, Gleditsch, and Cunningham 2011). By disaggregating agency, these studies explicitly take individuals (Bhavnani and Backer 2000; Florez-Morris 2010; Annan et al. 2011; Bosi and Della Porta 2012), households (Justino 2009; Bozzoli and Brück 2009; Justino, Brück, and Verwimp 2013), and groups (Buhaug, Gates, and Lujala 2009; Cederman, Weidmann, and Gleditsch 2011; Gubler and Selway 2012; Staniland 2012; McCauley 2013) as units of analysis.

Micro-level research on conflict draws attention to actors who feature less prominently, if at all, in state-centered analyses that rely on country-year research designs.

Representative studies account for actors' heterogeneous characteristics, beliefs, and interests, underscoring variation in their propensity to engage in violence (Bhavnani and Backer 2000; Verwimp 2006; Humphreys and Weinstein 2008), join paramilitary groups (Muldoon et al. 2008; Bosi and Della Porta 2012), and stay put or flee (Steele 2009; Czaika and Kis-Katos 2009). An added benefit is the impetus to identify mechanisms and emergent structures that shape the attitudes, decision making, and behavior of actors. Influences include: the link between ethnicity and conflict during counter-insurgency operations, due to the identity of soldiers conducting sweeps and their prior experience as insurgents (Lyall 2010); individual decisions to migrate as a function of security considerations, police presence, and intimidation by rebels (Czaika and Kis-Katos 2009); flight patterns determined by community characteristics and the salience of ascriptive cleavages during a war (Steele 2009); and levels of violence against adversaries and civilians as determined by rewards and punishments used to foster intragroup cohesion (Bhavnani 2006; Humphreys and Weinstein 2006; Staniland 2012). The remainder of this section provides three detailed examples of sets of research on conflict that disaggregate by actors.

Targeting of Civilians

One focus of disaggregated analyses has been variation in the extent to which civilians are targeted, most notably within the same civil war. This topic has been examined with respect to violence committed by both state and non-state actors, differentiated into factions and even assessed at an individual level.

Kalyvas (2006) emphasizes the distinction between selective and indiscriminate violence during civil war as a function of territorial control. Selective violence against civilians is predicted to be highest where control is hegemonic but incomplete, whereas the use of indiscriminate violence is greatest in zones completely under rival control. Building on this distinction, Herreros and Criado (2009) use the case of the Spanish Civil War to advance two separate logics to account for civilian victimization during civil war. One is strategic violence targeting potential political entrepreneurs. The other is indiscriminate violence as a consequence of the breakdown of the state. While the link between state collapse and the onset of civil war is well established in the literature, Herreros and Criado (2009) demonstrate that temporal variation in the recovery of public services better accounts for patterns of abuse against civilians.

Humphreys and Weinstein (2006) focus instead on warring factions, hypothesizing that internal structures and oversight of members are critical factors in determining whether civilians are abused during civil wars. The authors use data from a novel survey of ex-combatants to show that the absence of in-group policing within rebel groups leads to indiscriminate violence against civilians. Similarly, Balcells (2010) finds, based on the analysis of municipal-level data on violent events during the Spanish Civil War, that pre-war political competition between rival political factions is a factor in the degree of violence committed against civilians. Subsequently, Balcells (2011) shows that varying levels of violence against civilians within the same conflict are affected by prewar political support for enemy groups and wartime political parity within a locality.

All of this research highlights the advantages of not analyzing conflict as an aggregate, generic event. Taking the specific nature of violence seriously—and seeking to explain variation in type and severity, in this case with respect to the targeting of civilians—has prompted scholars to look more carefully at different actors. The findings demonstrate that the characteristics of those actors and how they are constituted and operate matters greatly for inferences regarding conflict. In addition, there is strong evidence to suggest that treating groups as monolithic and unified tends to be a poor assumption, since myriad interests, cleavages, and disputes are evident in conflicts. It is clear that the historical context and current environment exert influence, but also that both of these effects are not constants, as they depend on the specific situations of actors.

Rebel Group Dynamics

Another line of research seeks to understand the capabilities and actions of rebel groups, which affect the duration and severity of civil wars. Studies have yielded crucial awareness of conflict as typically comprised of complex interactions among a number of separate groups, rather than merely a dyadic interaction between a government and challenger.

Of particular importance is the finding that rebel in-fighting and side-switching may result in the proliferation of numerous local disputes, prolong the tenure of weak governments, and complicate settlement in the face of conflicting allegiances and grievances. Staniland (2012) demonstrates that lethal competition among insurgent factions can result in ethnic defection, with some groups joining the government. This mechanism is used to explain the rise of pro-state paramilitaries in Kashmir and Sri Lanka. Bakke, Cunningham, and Seymour (2012) draw attention to rebel group fragmentation as a function of the degree of internal institutionalization, the number of organizations within a movement, and the internal power structures. These factors determine the cohesion of rebel movements and affect the duration and intensity of fighting.

Recent studies also delve into rebel motivations. A noteworthy example is Lyall (2013), which employs a novel geocoded dataset of 23,000 air strikes and shows of force in Afghanistan between 2006 and 2011. The analysis demonstrates that shows of force are associated with more insurgent violence, insofar as they create incentives for insurgents to establish and maintain their reputations with the local population. Lyall's finding provides unusual insight into the relative effectiveness of different counter-insurgency tactics, with a degree of rigor and precision that is facilitated specifically by the disaggregated nature of the data and the ability to examine events and their consequences in proximity.

Clearly, overlooking the full extent of what happens among and within rebel groups risks a mischaracterization of conflict, by oversimplifying what are actually complex dynamics. The latest research tackles those dynamics head on, capitalizing on new data, and provides a more nuanced understanding about how conflict unfolds.

Inequality and Violence

A further theoretical advance made possible by disaggregating agency in conflict pertains to the relationship between inequality and civil war. A decade ago, Fearon and Laitin (2003: 85) remarked that: "The poor quality of the inequality data, available for only 108 countries, does not allow us to go beyond the claim that there appears to be no powerful cross-national relationship between inequality and onset." The constraint they identified has, to a large extent, been relaxed with the availability of detailed subnational data on inequality across countries.

Buhaug et al. (2011) find that civil wars are more likely to break out in areas with low absolute income or high deviations from the national average, regardless of a country's aggregate level of economic development. Further research in this vein indicates that one of the principal drivers of violence is grievances arising from the unequal distribution of resources and resulting in resentment along group lines. Cederman, Weidmann, and Gleditsch (2011) use geocoded data on ethnic group settlement patterns and income to show that relatively richer or poorer groups fight more compared to those with incomes near the country mean (see also Chapter 9). McCauley (2013) suggests that when economic inequalities overlap with ethnic identities and few provisions are made to include or compensate marginalized groups, the likelihood of violence increases. Sekulic, Massey, and Hodson (2006) examine the causal link between ethnic intolerance and conflict, drawing attention to the importance of elite political mobilization. Pappas (2008) shows that elite exclusion from government creates incentives to capitalize on resentment and increases the salience of identity categories. Gubler and Selway (2012) find, however, that the likelihood of civil war decreases when ethnic cleavages crosscut class, regional, and religious ones.

Taken together, studies examining the ethnic bases of income inequality in a disaggregated fashion effectively challenge the notion that greed or opportunity override grievances as explanations for civil war, as has been claimed (Collier and Hoeffler 1998; Azam 2002; Fearon and Laitin 2003). The micro-level research underscores the intricate interactions between the behavior of key actors and broader social structures that can either enable or restrict such behavior.

Taken together, studies examining the ethnic bases of income inequality in a disaggregated fashion effectively challenge the notion that greed or opportunity override grievances as explanations for civil war.

Disaggregation by Time

The increasing availability of detailed information on the timing of conflict events enables analysis at monthly, weekly, daily, and even hourly time scales. From a theoretical standpoint, temporal disaggregation permits researchers to study mechanisms at more natural or appropriate time scales, thereby closing the gap between concepts and data (Kalyvas 2008). Consider, for instance, cycles of escalation and de-escalation in the Israeli-Palestinian conflict, which typically last for days or weeks and are obscured by data reporting violence for calendar years (Jaeger and Pasermann 2006, 2008; Haushofer, Biletzki, and Kanwisher 2010; Bhavnani and Donnay 2012). With the same logic, Strauss (2007) uses temporally disaggregated data to study the relationship between the broadcast of "hate radio" messages and the onset of genocidal violence in Rwanda during 1994. Because the violence was concentrated in a period of about 100 days, and its onset around the country varied by weeks, calendar-year data is again inadequate. Taking proper account of this compressed timing, with respect to the sequence of events, Strauss' analysis rejects the popular narrative that hate radio was the primary driver of the genocide.

Temporal disaggregation also lends itself to addressing the endogeneity of conflict: the notion that previous conflict shapes factors such as actors' preferences, which then influence the potential for ongoing and future conflict (Kalyvas 2006, Voors et al. 2012). Bhavnani and Backer (2000), in a study of ethnic conflict and genocide in Rwanda and

Burundi, show that temporal variation in the scale of violence is best explained by a combination of individual-level factors such as the propensity to engage in violence, form independent beliefs about others, and react to public messages about current levels of ethnic aggression, and genocidal norms enforced by group leaders. In their model, these factors both influence and are influenced by ensuing violence. Justino (2009) also highlights the self-reinforcing nature of endogenous dynamics. She suggests that poorer households in conflict areas support armed groups for protection and are in turn preyed upon, increasing the duration of conflicts independent of other explanatory factors.

Two examples that follow illustrate the utility of temporal disaggregation in studying civilian agency in conflict and the value of social media as a novel data source.

Civilian Agency

During the ongoing conflicts in Iraq and Afghanistan, civilians are often caught in the line of fire. Recent research by Condra and Shapiro (2012) sheds light on how violence against civilians—perpetrated both by insurgent and coalition forces—shapes the dynamics of conflict. Using weekly time-series, district-level data from 2004–2009, the study finds that civilian casualties caused by coalition forces led to an increase in the level of insurgent attacks, whereas civilian casualties caused by insurgent attacks dampened insurgent violence. As the authors explain, support for coalition troops among civilians increases when the latter are targeted by insurgents, and declines when targeted by coalition forces. Greater levels of civilian support for the coalition, in turn, tend to reduce insurgent violence. The study illustrates the value added of temporal disaggregation, given that Condra and Shapiro's analysis requires a precise tracing of what transpires following incidents resulting in civilian casualties—something that is impossible with more aggregated data. The research bolsters a literature that highlights the role of individual civilian agency in civil war (see also Kalyvas 2006; Lyall and Wilson 2009). It also sheds light on how the interactions between civilians and military actors shape violence.

Using Crowdsourced Data

Understanding the dynamics of short-duration military conflicts, in which events unfold over a matter of days or even hours, has traditionally been a challenge because of a lack of data with sufficiently high temporal resolution. This constraint has recently been overcome, thanks in part to the advent of social media and its exploitation as an information resource, greatly improving the prospects for relevant analysis.

One of the earliest examples of such research focuses on the conflict in Gaza from late 2008 to early 2009, the most deadly escalation between Israelis and Palestinians following the second Intifada, which was both rapid and intense. Zeitzoff (2011) generated hourly, dyadic conflict-intensity scores from Twitter and a number of other social media sources. He then analyzed these detailed time series to find an endogenous relation between current and future levels of violence. The results revealed a tendency for violence to escalate immediately after attacks by the rival side, as well as responses sensitive to international reactions. Zeitzoff's work demonstrates how social media sources can be used creatively, with great depth and a relatively fast turnaround, to study political violence in ways that were normally infeasible in the past.

Other "crowdsourced" data collection efforts have attracted broad attention. One that stands out is the deployment of the online platform Ushahidi, which was first developed to track the violence that broke out after the disputed 2007 election in Kenya.

This particular platform has since been used in numerous other conflict settings, as well as in response to natural disasters, such as with the coordination of humanitarian relief after the devastating 2010 earthquake in Haiti. Similar crowdsourcing initiatives related to conflicts and disasters have been implemented elsewhere (see also Chapter 11).

Through the work of organizations such as ICT4Peace, crowdsourced "big data" tools have been readily embraced by various UN agencies. Their general utility for conflict research, however, remains to be established. In this respect, a key issue is data quality, which inevitably affects the confidence in the results that can be obtained. The underlying idea is simple: thousands of discrete, small pieces of information supplied by local witnesses more accurately reflect a situation on the ground than any expert observer possibly could. Nonetheless, there are valid concerns that these data have limitations (e.g., selective availability of geolocations) and even biases (e.g., those with the means to access technology and an inclination to report what they see are disproportionately represented). Of course, conventional datasets on conflict are hardly immune to analogous issues, especially given their reliance on mainstream media as data sources.

Disaggregation by Location

The burgeoning micro-level approaches to the study of conflict have directed far greater attention to the location of violence. The use of geographic information systems (GIS) permits researchers to combine spatial and statistical data to examine existing problems in novel ways (Cederman and Gleditsch 2009). In particular, GIS simplifies integration of data from other existing sources, including covariates like GDP, elevation, and population.

Some conflict studies that use locations are based on data collection by individual scholars or small teams. These typically focus on a single case or a select number of cases. They may employ a combination of intensive field research (e.g., Ibáñez and Velásquez

The use of geographic information systems permits researchers to combine spatial and statistical data to examine existing problems in novel ways.

2009; Staniland 2012), existing surveys, data collected by NGOs, official statistics and/or newspaper reports (e.g., Lyall 2010; Bhavnani, Miodownik, and Choi 2011). Other studies draw upon large-scale institutional initiatives, such as the Uppsala Conflict Data Program's Georeferenced Event Dataset (UCDP GED) (Sundberg et al. 2010) and the Armed Conflict Location and Event Dataset (ACLED) (Raleigh et al. 2010).[1] Such initiatives generally involve more expansive data collection spanning many countries, with standardized coding procedures to maximize precision and minimize error.

Among the research at the subnational level, some focuses on centers of population such as villages and cities and administrative units such as districts and regions (Kalyvas 2006; Czaika and Kis-Katos 2009; Steele 2009; Østby, Nordas, and Rød 2009; Balcells 2011), while others employ grids composed of cells of an equal predefined area (Hegre, Østby, and Raleigh 2009). The specific research question typically determines the choice of spatial unit for the analysis. Studies then seek to explain variation across or within units, controlling for variations in unit characteristics (Buhaug, Gates, and Lujala 2009; Do and Iyer 2010; Lujala 2010). Examples include analyses of variation in

---

[1] For more details on ACLED, see Chapter 7.

civilian abuse (Humphreys and Weinstein 2006), the incidence of indiscriminate versus selective violence as a function of territorial control (Kalyvas 2006), the number and relative capacities of rivals in shaping the use of selective violence (Bhavnani, Miodownik, and Choi 2011), the role of in-group policing and segregation in reducing violence in civil wars (Weidman and Salehyan 2013), and local wealth differentials as determinants of conflict onset (Buhaug et al. 2011).

We discuss two examples of research using spatially disaggregated units of analysis to study reactive dynamics and segregation. These examples further highlight the breadth of methodological approaches used in micro-level studies on conflict.

Reactive Violence Dynamics

The increased availability of disaggregated event data has renewed interest in the relationship between conflict events. Studies examine what is broadly referred to as "reactive" dynamics—the circumstances under which violence perpetrated by one group elicits a reaction from the targeted group, resulting in the escalation (or de-escalation) of the conflict. Locations and their characteristics are logically important factors when examining the relationship between events. For instance, an attack in one ethnic enclave might be expected to generate a retaliatory attack on the rival group's stronghold. Such topics can be studied properly only if the necessary details—such as where groups are based and commit acts of violence—are available. The latest research has made that leap, using data disaggregated by actor-group, as well as temporally and spatially. For instance, Linke, Wittmer, and O'Loughlin (2012) investigate the "tit-for-tat" dynamics between insurgent and coalition forces in Iraq. Applying autoregressive techniques, after aggregating event counts to small spatial grid cells, they find evidence for a "reactive" dimension to violence.

Of note, there are specific methodological challenges associated with disaggregating data spatially, in particular when conflict events are not confined to natural units of analysis, such as cities or villages. As in the study discussed earlier, researchers frequently aggregate data to arbitrary cells in order to apply standard econometric techniques to the resulting discrete spatio-temporal series (see also Raleigh and Hegre 2009; and Buhaug et al. 2011). The resulting inferences may be biased, however, given the selection of artificial grid sizes. In the geography literature, this issue is referred to as the "modifiable areal unit problem" or "MAUP" (Openshaw and Taylor 1979). A number of disaggregated studies address this problem. Schutte and Weidmann (2011) introduce an innovative technique for the study of conflict diffusion processes in civil wars that overcomes the MAUP. Braithwaite and Johnson (2012), who examine the relationship between insurgent attacks and coalition counterinsurgency operations in Iraq, provide another example in which the inferences about spatial and temporal patterns are unaffected by the MAUP.

To achieve robust causal inferences, others prefer field experiments. For example, Lyall (2009) uses a natural quasi-experimental design to study reactive violence in Chechnya. Using shelled and unshelled villages as units of analysis and a statistical matching design for pseudo-random assignment, he demonstrates that indiscriminate violence produces a significant decrease in subsequent insurgent attacks. In this study and Linke et al. (2012), disaggregated data is essential for the detection of reactive dynamics, which are entirely obscured by data at higher levels of aggregation.

Segregation and Violence

The new data resources have also sparked interest in "bottom-up" agent-based modeling (ABM) techniques. This approach is well suited to studying dynamic interactions among agents on natural (i.e., realistic geographic) and artificial landscapes and to relating hypothesized micro-level processes to observed macro-level outcomes. Seeded with geographic and population data, ABM affords a high degree of empirical validity.

Recent studies demonstrate the utility of empirically grounded ABMs for analyzing the relationship between individual-level interaction and violence. Weidmann and Salehyan (2013) analyze ethnic violence in Baghdad following the US troop surge in Iraq. Their ABM is seeded with detailed empirical data on the topology and ethnic geography of the city, as well as the location of violence. In a similar vein, Bhavnani et al. (2013) examine the case of Jerusalem between 2001 and 2009 using a realistic representation of the city based on the population structure and location of dwellings within each neighborhood. The study aims to reconcile competing perspectives on the effect of intergroup contact on violence. The first assumes that intermixed group settlement patterns reduce violence, with more frequent interactions enabling rivals to overcome their prejudices towards each other and become more tolerant. The second suggests just the opposite: that group segregation more effectively reduces violence given less frequent contact and fewer possibilities for violent encounters to occur.

Both studies make significant methodological advances and contribute to the long-standing debate on the relationship between residential settlement patterns and violence. The combination of formal models with rich, spatially disaggregated data enables the systematic study of alternative scenarios, with possible implications for policy makers and practitioners.

Contributions to Policy and Practice

By employing a disaggregated, micro-level approach to study the roots of conflict, the research surveyed in this chapter has illuminated, with considerable rigor and precision, the assortment of factors that contribute to violence. In the past, many of these drivers were consigned to a black box, or rendered as rough assumptions or post-hoc explanations for conflict phenomena. In contrast, the latest empirical analyses tackle these factors head on as hypotheses and are better able to detect the presence and absence of correlations and even causal relationships down to the level of groups (and segments thereof), communities, and individuals, accounting for spatial and temporal variation in dynamics. Next, we briefly consider the applications of this research to policy and practice, paying particular attention to several key issues: participation, victimization, migration, segregation, governance, and reconstruction.

Participation

The question of who participates in violence is complicated, given that violence lacks a single root cause and is driven by a mixture of grievance and opportunity. Individual studies point to a wide assortment of factors: the salience of religious and political identification, communal responsibility, patriotism, social status, reputation, and peer pressure (Muldoon et al. 2008); interactions between individual motivations, group networks, and state repression (Bosi and Della Porta 2012); poverty, a lack of access to education, and political alienation (Humphreys and Weinstein 2008); personal dependence on an organization, shared values with other recruits, the appeal of a clandestine lifestyle, and self-valuation (Florez-Morris 2010); and age, gender, the size of rented land, and household income and investment (Verwimp 2005).

> *What emerges from these studies is that the motives for participation in violence are heterogeneous, as are the characteristics of those who volunteer or are recruited for military and other groups.*

What emerges from these studies is that the motives for participation in violence are heterogeneous, as are the characteristics of those who volunteer or are recruited for military and other armed groups. This insight may not be surprising, let alone revolutionary. The real contribution of the disaggregated approach has been to provide a growing accumulation of compelling evidence of the influences that matter, with ample room for exploring and understanding nuances, conditions and contradictions. This work underscores the need for evidence-based policy measures that are tailored to address the local topography of conflict—i.e., the relevant actors and their motivations and behavior.

Victimization

A conventional approach to studying vulnerability to conflict at the macro level is to focus on structural variables, some of which exhibit strong correlations to outcomes. A natural question is whether parallel relationships are observed at the micro level—e.g., do individual manifestations of structural conditions, like poverty, have the same relationship to vulnerability?

From various studies, different conclusions emerge. Local conflict is positively correlated with unemployment, inequality, natural disasters, changes in sources of incomes, and clustering of ethnic groups within villages (Barron, Kaiser, and Pradhan 2004); with inequality and group polarization (Nepal, Bohara, and Gawande 2011); with poverty (Do and Iyer 2010); larger group shares and more densely populated locales (Dabalen, Kebede, and Paul 2012); and wealth (Hegre, Østby, and Raleigh 2009). Such detailed awareness is crucial to devising and deploying targeted, effective measures of conflict prevention that identify those at maximal risk.

Migration

A major consequence of violence is the movement of individuals, households, and groups to locations—including segregated enclaves—that ostensibly offer a greater degree of safety. What drives individual flight, and who is most likely to flee?

Compared to a cruder analysis of country-year data, such as on populations of refugees and IDPs, disaggregated research offers more revealing insights. Studies highlight the salience of conflict clashes, socio-economic factors, and local ethnic composition (Czaika and Kis-Katos 2009); violent events as drivers of increased migration, with political events displaying the opposite effect (Williams et al. 2012); and the type of community (urban or rural) and the characteristics of the conflict (the existence of some ascriptive cleavage) (Steele 2009). Improving the ability to anticipate flight—especially in large numbers—and understand the composition, motivations, and concerns of populations that flee are important for the planning and logistics of humanitarian relief efforts, the implementation of which can also have repercussions for the course of conflicts.

Segregation

A high-stakes consideration for policy makers is whether members of nominally rival social groups ought to be kept apart, more closely integrated, or at least encouraged to interact in various formal and informal settings. Conflicting arguments and evidence exist about which of these strategies achieves the best results in avoiding and mitigating conflict, as well as contributing to post-conflict peacebuilding. On the one hand, studies using disaggregated data suggest that ethnic avoidance and the establishment of relatively homogenous enclaves result in declining violence by reducing contact (Field et al. 2008; Blair, Blattman, and Hartman 2012; Weidmann and Salehyan 2013). On the other hand, the opposite conclusion—pointing to a correlation between violence and ethnically segregated residential patterns—emerges in different contexts (Kingoriah 1980; K'Akumu and Olima 2007; Kasara 2013). While findings are mixed, the latest research also suggests that the effects of segregation and mixing on conflict are critically dependent on the nature of intergroup relations, as gauged by indicators such as social distance (Bhavnani et al. 2013). The implication is that more fine-grained empirical research can help to inform what approach ought to be favored, and when.

Governance

What effect do specific state policies have on violence? Of note, disaggregated studies have focused on spending priorities, land tenure, and access to state power. One set of findings indicates that increased government spending on education, health, and social security mitigates civil conflict, albeit with little or no effect attributed to non-targeted public spending and military expenditures (Taydas and Peksen 2012) or to the absolute level of state wealth (Bohlken and Sergenti 2010). Another study shows that absolute poverty and inequality increase conflict risk (Buhaug et al. 2011). Additional research reveals that secure property rights feature among the most significant drivers of long-term income (Voors and Bulte 2008) and by association, given the relationship between income and conflict, conflict mitigation (Butler and Gates 2012). These results suggest a number of policy goals that governments could emphasize, including to reduce violence in locations with certain contributing characteristics.

Reconstruction

Policy makers and practitioners often strive to successfully navigate the aftermath of conflict and maximize the potential for sustained peace. A portion of the recent literature has evaluated the effects of targeted reform efforts in post-conflict societies. Studies examine the impact of promoting the adoption of specific crops on household welfare per capita (Bozzoli and Brück 2009); the relation between subjective perceptions of violence, consumption expenditure, land use intensity, and the adoption of more risk-taking crop mixes (Badiuzzaman, Cameron, and Murshed 2011); individual exposure to violence, altruistic behavior, risk seeking, and high discount rates (Voors et al. 2012); the relationship between gender, reintegration and resilience (Annan et al. 2011); and the link between pre-conflict wealth and post-conflict economic growth at the provincial level (Justino and Verwimp 2013).

In contrast to more aggregate studies of outcomes like conflict recurrence and their relationship to structural political, economic, and social characteristics of countries, the fine-grained results of disaggregated and especially micro-level research provide detailed assessments of policy successes and failures from the perspective of individuals, households, and groups. These findings offer concrete guidance to development agencies and organizations that are seeking to allocate programs and resources in a more targeted, calibrated, and efficient manner.

> *In contrast to more aggregate studies of outcomes like conflict recurrence and their relationship to structural political, economic, and social characteristics of countries, the fine-grained results of disaggregated and especially micro-level research provide detailed assessments of policy successes and failures from the perspective of individuals, households, and groups.*

Conclusion

The various theoretical, methodological, and policy contributions reviewed in this chapter follow a common logic: new, more rigorous, accurate, and subtle insights are generated and overall understanding is improved by studying conflict and violence at the level at which the hypothesized mechanisms actually operate. This means gathering the necessary data on (1) actors, including individuals, households, and groups; (2) the timing of events of different kinds; and (3) their location, including neighborhoods, cities, municipalities, and provinces, as well as exact geographic coordinates. Disaggregation has shed light on previously unexplained issues, clarified or rectified findings from previous analyses, and in the process, uncovered new considerations and questions.

Moving to data with greater geographic and/or temporal resolution typically increases sample size, with obvious benefits for statistical inference. Shortcomings may arise, however, from inadequately disaggregated variables:

> These practices lead to the reproduction of problems encountered in the macro-literature such as the absence of clear microfoundations, the distance gap between theoretical constructs and proxies, and the inability to adjudicate between observationally equivalent causal mechanisms. (Kalyvas 2008: 398–399)

In particular, Shellman, Hatfield, and Mills (2010) show that inadequate actor disaggregation may affect inferences and lead researchers to commit both Type I (i.e., false positive) and Type II (i.e., false negative) errors. The problem of finding the "right" unit of actor aggregation is often complicated by the fact that the coding or identification of actor groups varies over time and across regions—a long-standing challenge recognized in the literature on cross-national studies (see, for example, Hug 2003). Nonetheless, the ability to account for subnational variation, both over time and across space, has yielded important insights on the dynamics of violence, its reactive dimensions, and its relation to patterns of territorial control and ethnic settlement patterns, as was discussed with respect to the examples provided earlier. Designs that continue to use the country-year as their unit of analysis miss relevant action at finer temporal and geographic scales.

Meanwhile, the expansion of new media has been opening up productive avenues for policy-relevant analysis. Most notably, data collection relying on social media, including crowdsourcing and big-data approaches, is distinguished by the ability to cover conflict in close to real time. The opportunity for rapid, contemporaneous analysis represents a vast improvement relative to traditional approaches, which involve lags—often lengthy—between when conflict events occurred, information was collected from archives of mainstream media, datasets were made available, and studies were conducted. Now, up-to-date, detailed profiles and maps can be assembled on the course of conflicts all around the world in a matter of days or even hours, with information derived exclusively from new media sources.

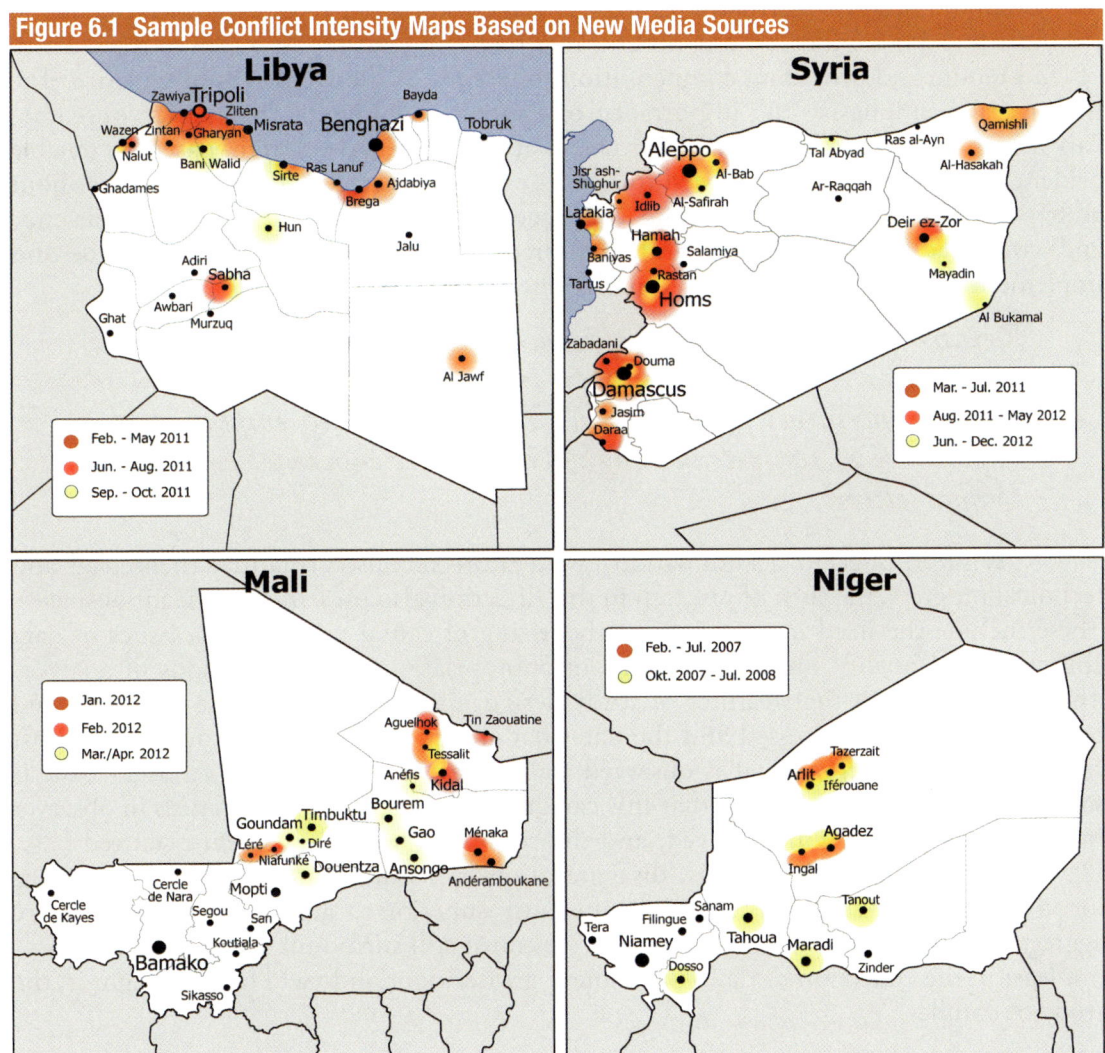

Source: Compiled by authors.

Figure 6.1 presents the results of one such exercise, yielding visual timelines of the distribution, progression, and severity of violence during recent civil conflicts in Libya, Syria, Mali, and Niger. Different colors mark the areas affected in different phases of the conflicts in each of these countries; the darker the shading, the more intense the conflict. The conflicts and other aspects of these countries differ in consequential ways. Moreover, the settings present challenges to traditional data collection, such as difficult security environments and limited infrastructure, including low availability of

DISAGGREGATING CONFLICT BY ACTORS, TIME, AND LOCATION   55

technology and free media. Yet the patterns of violence in each country can be examined via content available on social media. Such capabilities, if employed effectively, enable more current, informed assessments of conflict risks and events, as well as faster, more targeted and otherwise better calibrated responses by a wide range of actors, including intergovernmental organizations, states, and civil society.

With respect to policy, research using disaggregated approaches highlights a need for systemic solutions to structural inequality, inclusion, and representation to dampen the incentives for conflict, among other things by paying greater attention to the security of land tenure and providing compensation to victims in the aftermath of violence. The findings also emphasize the importance of context and suggest that policy outcomes vary across conflict settings. It remains true that disaggregated research, based on reliable evidence, where available, is needed to ask the critical "what if" types of questions about addressing the causes, dynamics, and consequences of violence. Yet greater consistency and comparability across studies are required to facilitate the choice, design, and implementation of successful peacebuilding measures.

Research using disaggregated approaches highlights a need for systemic solutions to structural inequality, inclusion, and representation to dampen incentives for conflict.... The findings also emphasize the importance of context and suggest that policy outcomes vary across conflict settings.

While the recent accumulation of literature reveals substantial theoretical and technical progress, the turn of research in this direction also presents significant obstacles. These include the need for appropriate theorizing of causal mechanisms, issues of data collection and quality, and decisions about appropriate units and methods of analysis. The findings suggest that features of study design, including the specific questions and hypotheses that are addressed and the data that are gathered, could account for at least some of the variation in what is observed across the country contexts. Another issue is source bias. Studies have shown that this can arise as a function of differences in observer interest, the type of event observed, and the context in which the event occurred (e.g., Davenport and Ball 2002). Thus, disaggregation is not immune to the issues evident in other existing research, much less inherently superior to anything done at a more aggregate level. Instead, disaggregated analyses must still surmount significant hurdles—not least in the collection of data—to achieve greater rigor and yield better insight in the study of conflict.

7. THE POLITICAL GEOGRAPHY OF CLIMATE VULNERABILITY, CONFLICT, AND AID IN AFRICA

Joshua W. Busby, Clionadh Raleigh, and Idean Salehyan

Over the past five years, the number and types of datasets on conflict have grown considerably. Perhaps the most significant development is a "disaggregation revolution," involving the collection and dissemination of information with greater spatial and temporal detail. This includes continent-wide (e.g., the Armed Conflict Location and Event Dataset, or ACLED) and country-specific datasets (e.g., Nigeria Watch), as well as event-based datasets of various specifications (e.g., Crisis Mappers, Ushahidi). Many datasets begin coverage in the mid-1990s, coinciding with increased digitization of source material. In addition, recent innovations in data collection and management have dramatically reduced the lag between the occurrence of events and the compilation and release of related datasets. The increased availability of geocoded subnational data has opened up innumerable research opportunities, allowing scholars to move beyond state-level analysis to think about local properties of politically important phenomena.

As the revolution was occurring, the US Department of Defense announced a Minerva Initiative to support social science research. One of the first initiatives funded was the five-year Climate Change and African Political Stability (CCAPS) program led by the University of Texas-Austin. Entering its final year in 2013–2014, the mission of CCAPS is to (1) assess causal connections between climate indicators and security outcomes, including the location of vulnerable areas, (2) examine government capacity to withstand and recover from shocks, including climate ones, and (3) identify patterns of climate adaptation assistance to better serve vulnerable areas.[1] As part of that effort, CCAPS has pioneered new datasets, indices, and data platforms to display and analyze the political geography of climate vulnerability, conflict, and aid in Africa.

This chapter reports on those efforts, focusing on ACLED, the Social Conflict in Africa Database (SCAD), and the Climate Security Vulnerability Model (CSVM), with reference to efforts to map climate adaptation aid. We describe the datasets and relevant indices and discuss some of their applications, paying attention to how the diverse data can be analyzed together, particularly through our online dashboard (http://ccaps.aiddata.org/), created in partnership with Development Gateway. We conclude by summarizing valuable findings and insights and expected future payoffs as more work is completed.

The Armed Conflict Location and Event Dataset (ACLED)[2]

ACLED, the product of the Armed Conflict Location and Event Project, is the most comprehensive dataset on political violence presently available.[3] It was created to address the deficit of disaggregated data on political violence and analyses of conflict. ACLED

---

[1] See http://www.strausscenter.org/ccaps/. This material is based upon work supported by the US Army Research Office contract/grant number W911-NF-09-1-0077 under the Minerva Initiative of the US Department of Defense.

[2] This section presents work of Clionadh Raleigh and her various collaborators on ACLED, including Andrew Linke, Håvard Hegre, Joakim Karlsen, Catriona Dowd, and Lee Macias.

[3] ACLED is accessible online at http://www.acleddata.com/. The website provides a comparison between ACLED and other event data sources (http://www.acleddata.com/wp-content/uploads/2012/08/Dataset-Typology-Overview.pdf).

covers all African states from January 1997 to the present with updating in near-real time—coding lags behind events by only a month.[4] More limited coverage is offered for select unstable states, including Haiti, Myanmar, and Pakistan. As of 2013, information on over 75,000 discrete events has been collected. Extensions to all of South Asia and the Middle East are planned for 2014. The data are derived from a variety of sources, concentrating on reports from war zones, humanitarian agencies, and research publications.

Methodology

ACLED is designed to present a realistic assessment of violent political activity within a state, depicting as closely as possible what kind of conflict is happening on the ground. Although conflict data projects apply increasingly consistent frameworks and methodologies to the collection of data, the data are not always directly comparable. For that reason, ACLED is likely to look different, due primarily to three innovative features: the use of atomic data structures, the types of groups that are included, and the multiple ways in which it quantifies conflict rates.

> *ACLED is designed to present a realistic assessment of violent political activity within a state, depicting as closely as possible what kind of conflict is happening on the ground.... The structure of ACLED, using standardized collection and coding procedures, enables meaningful, direct comparative analysis of the intensity and dynamics of political conflict and violence across conflict types, actors, time periods, and locations, while also permitting the greatest number of aggregation options.*

With an atomic data structure, the scale and parameters of units are consistent across each entry. An ACLED event is defined as a "single altercation where often force is used by one or more groups for a political end" (Raleigh, Linke, and Dowd 2012). Each altercation is coded as a discrete event between identified actors of particular types (rebels, governments, militias, armed groups, protesters, civilians), at a specific georeferenced location, on a single day, which is generally the lowest level of disaggregation possible based on source material. Events are also differentiated by type, according to whether an altercation is between armed groups (battles), an armed group and unarmed civilians (violence against civilians), or the state and demonstrators protesting peacefully or with force (protests/riots). An example would be a battle between Al Shabaab and the forces of the Transitional Federal Government of Somalia and the African Union Mission to Somalia on August 23, 2010, in Mogadishu. In addition, the dataset contains details on recruitment activities of the actors involved, outcomes such as fatalities and changes in territorial control, and the sources of information.

The structure of ACLED, using standardized collection and coding procedures, enables meaningful, direct comparative analysis of the intensity and dynamics of political conflict and violence across conflict types, actors, time periods, and locations (Raleigh et al. 2010), while also permitting the greatest number of aggregation options (e.g., all acts of violence against civilians, all acts by a particular group or type of group, all events that occurred in March 2005, all events in an administrative zone). For example, conflict and

---

[4] ACLED predates CCAPS, but was expanded with CCAPS support to have Africa-wide coverage.

post-conflict violence rates in specific regions (e.g., Kivu, DRC) can be directly compared, as can rates of activity across different actors (e.g., LRA vs. M-23). Such comparisons are critical when assessing trends and patterns within a conflict, as well as phenomena like diffusion and contagion.

ACLED takes a wide view of political violence: the dataset encompasses all actors who use force for a political motivation or purpose, regardless of the number of events in which they engage or the number of fatalities that result. Political violence is changing across Africa as civil war has decreased in prevalence and activity by other non-state (e.g., militias) and civic actors (e.g., rioters) is more common. These actors often have organizational structures that are less formal, elite ties, local and regional political goals, and patterns of activity suited for their specific contexts. Integrating these events into conflict data creates a more complete picture of political violence as it is experienced in localities. It also does not bias the collection of data by focusing on events with arbitrary characteristics, such as the role of government or a threshold of fatalities. By coding along a political violence spectrum, the progression of violence among actors can be accurately measured and analyzed.

Another distinguishing premise of ACLED is that richer knowledge of the characteristics of conflict events is crucial to allow for various ways to quantify violence. The standard approach, reflected in resources like several of the datasets of the Uppsala Conflict Data Program, has been to measure conflict-related battle deaths. Yet information on fatalities tends to be subject to a greater degree of uncertainty, inaccuracy, and even bias —shortcomings of what is and is not reported in the sources—than information on the type of activity, the location, the date(s), and the actors involved. ACLED does include fatality statistics, from which rough estimates of the intensity of violence—per year, actor, etc.—may be calculated. At the same time, ACLED provides alternative proxies of the frequency and scale of violence, including the proportion of affected locations within a state, the number of active conflict actors within a state, and the number and proportion of conflicts that involve the military. These and other features of ACLED greatly increase the ability to address a variety of questions of empirical and theoretical interest.

Applications

The data and interface are designed to be accessible and relevant to the academic and policy communities and the general public. Of course, the applications are not mutually exclusive: many opportunities exist to develop research agendas and conduct analyses that have value to multiple communities—e.g., merging academic and policy interests.

The geocoding of ACLED allows users to visualize the locations of conflict activity in a manner that is both detailed in terms of the level of precision and broad in comparative scope.

A basic descriptive use is assembling summaries of the event data, which improve comparative understandings of conflict over time and across space. Of note, the geocoding of ACLED allows users to visualize the locations of conflict activity in a manner that is both detailed in terms of the level of precision and broad in comparative scope.

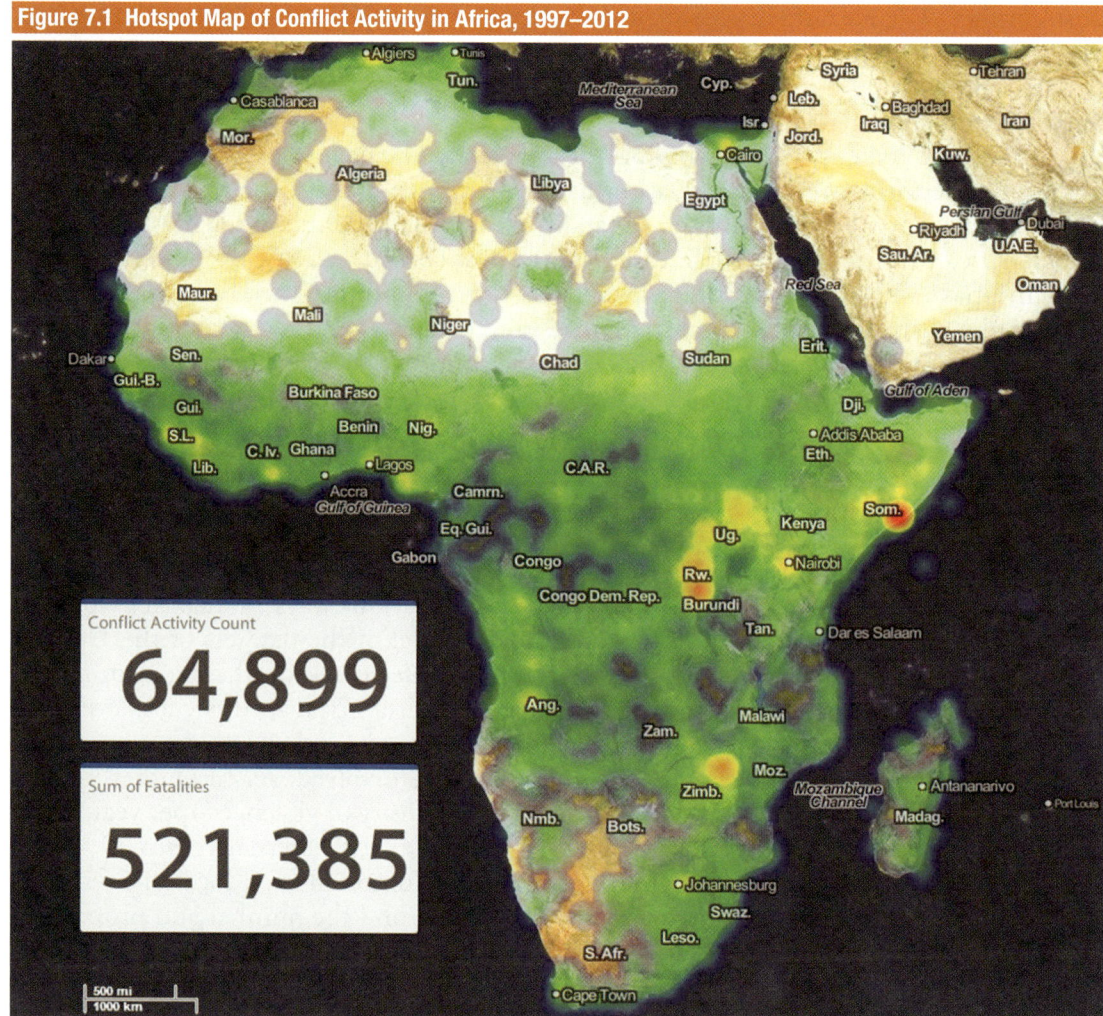

Figure 7.1 Hotspot Map of Conflict Activity in Africa, 1997–2012

Source: Compiled by authors.

For example, Figure 7.1 maps the overall distribution of conflict events across Africa from 1997–2012. The relative frequencies of events are represented by different colors: blue for minimal, green for low, yellow for medium, orange for high, and red for very high. This depiction clearly identifies the worst hotspots of violence: in particular, large sections of Eastern Congo, Rwanda, and Burundi, the areas around Mogadishu, Somalia and Harare, Zimbabwe, and to a somewhat lesser extent Northern Uganda. Many other areas across the continent are affected, to varying degrees, while a limited number of areas—typically, places with low population densities, such as most of the Sahara Desert—are less exposed. The results corroborate what is generally known about conflict in Africa. The difference is that ACLED affords an expansive, reliable view of patterns, with the ability to draw more careful distinctions about frequency and intensity and to drill down into the data to look at specific aspects and locations of conflict.

Researchers involved in the Armed Conflict Location and Event Project produce monthly trend reports that highlight the evolving patterns of political violence across the

African continent in near-real time. By tracking recent activity in conflicts and comparing the locations and actors involved to what was observed in the past, using the full range of data from 1997, new patterns and sites can be detected and studied. Such analysis can also discern emergent trends that may indicate important shifts in security conditions—e.g., a rise in Islamist groups or unidentified armed groups.

Knowing who is most responsible for political violence has major implications for policy prescriptions by the international community, individual governments, and NGOs. ACLED provides a handle on this question. Figure 7.2 displays the variation in participation in conflict events by different categories of actors over the last 15 years. Early in this time period, rebel activity spiked, before tailing off through 2005. Subsequently, militia activity surged. All categories exhibited far more activity in 2011–2012, an effect largely attributable to the Arab Spring.

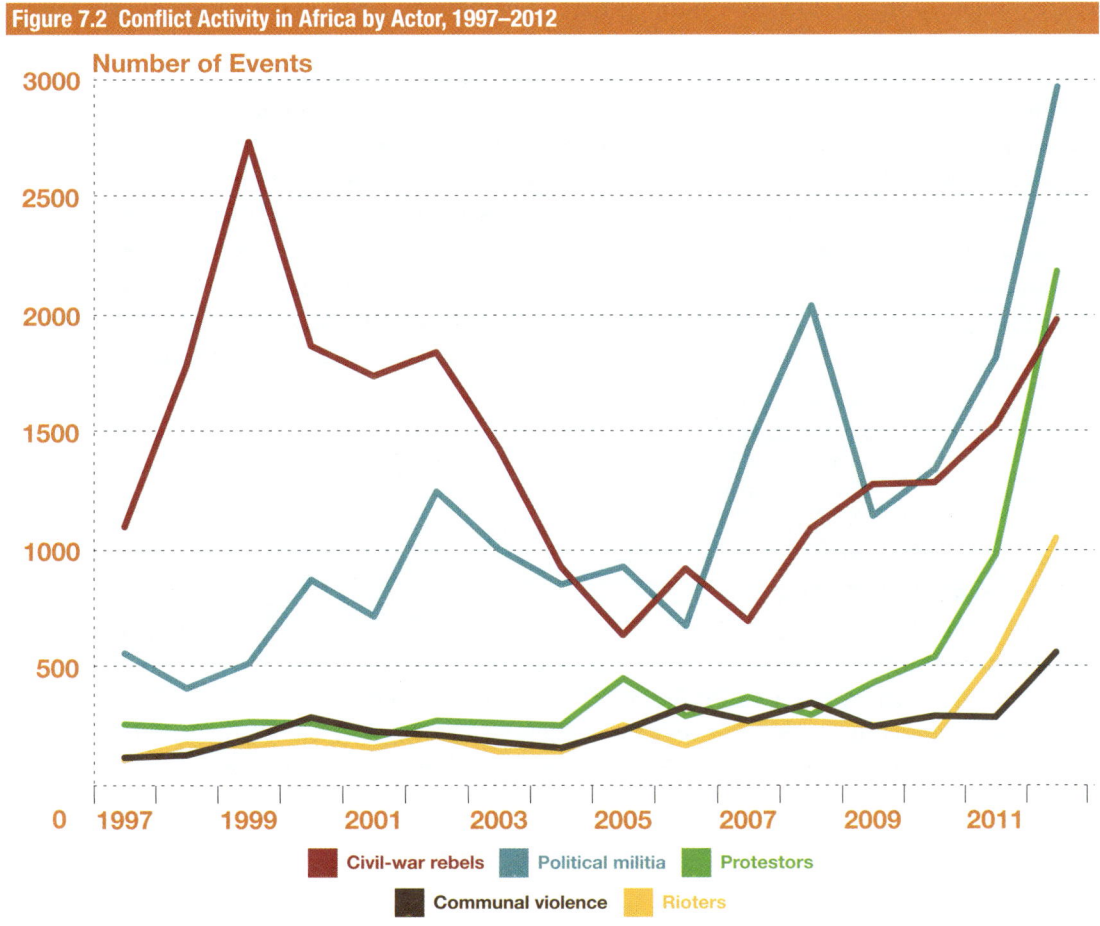

Figure 7.2 Conflict Activity in Africa by Actor, 1997–2012

Source: Compiled by authors.

In addition, policy makers are often interested in exploratory, prospective applications. One example is the integration of ACLED in the design and targeting of peacebuilding and conflict mitigation programming. For this purpose, assessments of risks—especially those associated with different interventions—are essential. ACLED provides relevant insight by itself and can be combined with other information to produce more contextualized understandings of complex issues that are known to have interactive elements. In particular, the data are often used to model the volatility and diffusion of conflict during periods of increased vulnerability, such as elections, natural disasters, and food shortages. The overlap between conflict hotspots and political (e.g., borders of states and administrative units), socio-demographic (e.g., population centers, ethnic groups), environmental (e.g., natural resource deposits, rivers), and technological features (e.g., availability of electricity and cell phone service) can also be studied. These analyses present concrete evidence that international organizations, governments, officials, and civil society practitioners can use when seeking to plan appropriately and develop actionable scenarios taking account of the near- and long-term security environment. For instance, ACLED reports have examined the vulnerability of civilians to violence in Northern Uganda and Eastern DRC, a topic with obvious implications for establishing policy and funding priorities, as well as for the implementation of specific programs. At a later stage, ACLED enables evidence-based evaluations of the efficacy of interventions via the use of baselines and control cases.

A primary application of conflict data is to study the nature, drivers, and impact of violence. Of note, ACLED has been used to observe patterns of violence against civilians (Raleigh 2012). The available information permits other fine-grained descriptive analysis, such as whether the number of cattle raids differs across wet and dry seasons. In addition, ACLED is employed regularly in testing hypotheses from theoretical frameworks about political violence, with the level or onset of conflict serving as either dependent or independent variables. For example, researchers have investigated how inequality may contribute to conflict (Hegre, Østby, and Raleigh 2009), whether rioting increases before organized group violence (Krause 2011), and how violence affects elections and democratic transitions (Daxecker 2012; Weidmann and Callen 2013). Such findings can also be used for forecasting and to anticipate likely future trends.

Applications of ACLED data in the research as part of the CCAPS program include studies of how multiple types of conflict co-occur within the same state (Raleigh 2013a), institutional forms are associated with predominant forms of conflict (Choi and Raleigh 2013), and militias are becoming the dominant agent of political violence (Raleigh 2013b), as well as the spatial properties of militia movements (Raleigh and Hegre 2009; Raleigh 2010; Raleigh and Kniveton 2012; Dowd 2013). Researchers have also observed and modeled the emergence of new actor subtypes (Dowd 2013), as well as instability across specific areas (Dowd and Raleigh 2013b). The Sahel belt, in particular, has garnered significant attention as the site of a "complex emergency" (Dowd and Raleigh 2013a; Raleigh and Dowd 2013). In addition, ACLED has featured in other research that relates to the mandate of the CCAPS programs, including prominent studies on the relationship between climate change and conflict (O'Loughlin et al. 2012; Raleigh and Kniveton 2012; Scheffran, Link, and Schilling 2012; Busby, Smith, White et al. 2013), migration and conflict (Raleigh 2011), urban vulnerability (Raleigh 2013c), land use change in vulnerable settings (Alix-Garcia, Bartlett, and Saah 2012), and Somalia's recent climate and conflict crises (Maystadt, Ecker and Mabiso, 2013; Checchi and Robinson 2013).

Raleigh and Kniveton (2012) is illustrative of the depth and intricacy of analysis that ACLED facilitates. The authors focused on small-scale conflict in East Africa, where the link between resource availability and conflict is assumed to be more immediate and direct, since residents practice subsistence agriculture and pastoralism and are therefore highly dependent on climatic conditions. The analysis showed that in locations experiencing rebel or communal conflict events, the frequency of these events increases in periods of extreme rainfall variation, irrespective of the direction of the change. Furthermore, the results lend support to both a "zero-sum" narrative, where conflicting groups use force and violence to compete for ever-scarcer resources, and an "abundance" narrative, where resources spur rent- or wealth-seeking and the recruitment of people to participate in violence. Amid the current context of uncertainty regarding the future direction of rainfall change over much of Africa, these findings imply that small-scale conflict is likely to be exacerbated by increases in rainfall variability if the mean climate remains largely unchanged; higher rates of rebel conflict will tend to be observed in

> *The analysis showed that in locations experiencing rebel or communal conflict events, the frequency of these events increases in periods of extreme rainfall variation, irrespective of the direction of the change. Furthermore, the results lend support to both a "zero-sum" narrative, where conflicting groups use force and violence to compete for ever-scarcer resources, and an "abundance" narrative, where resources spur rent- or wealth-seeking and the recruitment of people to participate in violence.*

anomalously dry conditions, while higher rates of communal conflict will be expected in increasingly anomalous wet conditions.

Another significant development, as alluded to earlier, is that the interaction between ACLED and the research mandate of CCAPS has stimulated new avenues in research on complex emergencies. Until recently, the label of "complex emergency" has largely been a reference to the complexity of devising a response to a large-scale, difficult crisis. Complex emergencies are better understood, however, as multiple, interactive crises overlapping within—and sometimes across—states over time, such as famines that occur within conflict zones and increases in food within cities affected by rioting. ACLED is being used to delineate the common types and document the hotspots of complex emergencies (Macias 2013).

The Social Conflict in Africa Database (SCAD)[5]

SCAD is designed to provide the academic community and policy analysts with a tool for studying non-violent and violent contentious events across Africa.[6] All countries with a population of one million or greater are included. This is not the first data resource on conflict events in Africa. Others have looked at protest behavior (Scarritt and McMillan 1995; Bratton and Walle 1997), communal violence (Meier, Bond, and Bond 2007), coups d'état (McGowan 2003), armed conflict (Raleigh et al. 2010), and other distinct conflict types. While these resources are quite useful, SCAD has several advantageous features. One is comprehensive information on a wide variety of conflict types, encompassing both violent events, including riots and armed clashes between actors at a level of severity short of civil war, and peaceful events, such as mass demonstrations and strikes. A second is a transparent data collection methodology. The third is an intuitive framework for understanding the who, what, when, where, and why behind an event.

---

[5] This section is based on the collaborative work of Idean Salehyan and Cullen Hendrix.

[6] SCAD is accessible online at http://www.scaddata.org.

Methodology

Currently, SCAD (version 3.0) contains nearly 8,000 social conflict events in Africa spanning the period from 1990–2011; the dataset is updated on an annual basis. To identify events, the SCAD research team conducts keyword searches of Associated Press (AP) and Agence France Presse (AFP) newswires. AP and AFP were selected because of their English and French language coverage, wide geographic reach, the quality of the reporting, and online accessibility in the Lexis-Nexis archives. Relying instead on local sources has benefits, but the team decided against doing so, since cross-national comparisons would be difficult. Of particular concern, countries such as Eritrea and Zimbabwe do not have a free press and are not likely to report accurately on contentious politics. This circumstance, in addition to uneven availability of news through online archives, would mean better reporting on some cases relative to others. By comparison, AP and AFP are more transparent, and original stories are easier to consult when learning about an event. A filtering of events is conducted using five keywords: *protest, riot, strike, violence*, and *attack*. Based on several analyses, these keywords are sufficient to capture the most significant events, while making the task of manually sorting through thousands of articles manageable. The search results are then sifted to identify valid events (e.g., "attack" often appears in stories about sporting events, but those items are usually immaterial to SCAD). Relevant information on the events is coded by research assistants. Intercoder reliability checks are conducted by double-coding 10 percent of the country-years.[7]

Each record in SCAD is a unique conflict event (unlike in ACLED, where each record is a day of an event). While most events last a single day, some can persist for weeks or even months. A conflict is classified as a single event if the issues, actors, and targets are the same and the action in question occurred in a chronologically continuous manner. For example, the "Arab Spring" protests in Tunisia lasted for several weeks before President Ben Ali resigned, but these protests are considered to be a single, sustained protest event for purposes of SCAD. By contrast, a series of strikes in 1996–1997 by the Swaziland Federation of Trade Workers targeting the central government is coded as multiple events, because of long gaps in the group's activities.

SCAD is intended as a resource for information on *social* conflict. As such, cases pertaining to interstate (i.e., two sovereign states engaging in violence against one another) and intrastate (i.e., an organized group using violence to challenge government authority) armed conflict are excluded. To accomplish this, the SCAD coding procedure screens out events that were part of organized armed conflicts, as defined by the Uppsala Conflict Data Program's Armed Conflicts Database (ACD), which requires at least 25 battle-related deaths in a calendar year (Gleditsch et al. 2002).[8] SCAD does contain some information on anti-government attacks by organized actors, so long as these attacks do not meet the criteria for inclusion in the ACD (e.g., violence did not reach 25 deaths).

---

[7] Specifically, Cohen's Kappa statistics are computed on each of the variables. The results indicate substantial agreement among independent codings of the data. When the protest, riot, and strike subcategories are collapsed into three (rather than six) types, however, intercoder reliability increases significantly.

[8] For periods of armed conflict, as defined by the ACD, SCAD contains a placeholder row, indicating that a conflict was underway. The start and end dates are provided, along with summary information about the conflict, as well as the ACD event ID number, to facilitate data mergers. For most purposes, users can treat the ACD civil wars listed in SCAD as a distinct type of event, to be included in analyses, as these are made to conform to the SCAD data structure. Reports of individual battles are not included, unlike with ACLED (Raleigh et al. 2010). Users wanting more information about armed conflicts are advised to consult the ACD.

SCAD contains several pieces of information about each event. Start and end dates are listed. The type of action is coded as one of the following: 1) organized demonstration; 2) spontaneous demonstration; 3) organized riot; 4) spontaneous riot; 5) general strike; 6) limited strike; 7) pro-government violence; 8) anti-government violence; 9) extra-government violence; 10) intragovernment violence. Descriptions of these types can be found in the SCAD Codebook. SCAD contains a column for escalation, which indicates whether or not the type of action changed during the course of the event (e.g., peaceful protests turn into violent riots). Next, the actor(s) and target(s) involved in the event are listed as a text field. Actors can be specific if identified with a particular group (e.g., Inkatha Freedom Party) or generic (e.g., "students"). SCAD provides the number of participants, in categories, along with the number of deaths during the event. A repression field indicates the use of lethal or non-lethal force against the actors. Location information is also given, including the particular town(s) or village(s) name, the type of location (urban, rural), and latitude and longitude coordinates based on standard gazetteers, which can be used in geospatial analyses. SCAD classifies the issues at stake in the event, relying on a 14-point scheme.[9] Finally, a short event narrative is provided.

Applications

Because of its diverse contents, SCAD is a versatile resource that enables quantitative analyses, qualitative case studies, and geospatial analyses. In particular, SCAD has been used to study the determinants of social conflict (Hendrix and Salehyan 2012; Hendrix 2013; Salehyan 2013; Smith 2013). Other questions that can be examined include the frequency and outcomes of violent and non-violent events in a given country, the use of repression by government actors, and contentious issues like elections and food prices.

As described earlier, a major advantage of SCAD is the availability of geospatial data. The applications of this data can be illustrated by examining how the patterns of conflict shifted during the recent era of democratization in Nigeria. During the military rule of Sani Abacha, violence was relatively contained by the repressive nature of the state. Many authors note that after democratization, the incidence of rioting and communal conflict rose significantly (Bolaji 2010; Ikelegbe 2005; Ukiwo 2003). This explosion of visible forms of social unrest has been attributed to democratization coupled with weak state institutions, long-standing ethnic cleavages, and competition over Nigeria's natural resources, at least in the short term. First, electoral competition at the federal and state level has led to conflict and intimidation during election campaigns (Bratton 2008). Second, ethnic antagonisms, fuelled by local politicians and armed militia groups—such as the Oduduwa People's Congress, based among the Yoruba—have been on the rise, as communal groups compete for power and influence (Ukiwo 2003; Ikelegbe 2005; Eifert, Miguel, and Posner 2010). In this regard, one of the most significant cleavages in Nigeria has been between Christian and Muslim populations. Decentralization under democratic rule provided room for many northern states to enact shari'ah law, exacerbating religious tensions that have resulted in deadly riots (Bolaji 2010). The post-military government has not demonstrated the will or capacity to contain violence in the north, including by the militant group Boko Haram. Third, the Niger Delta has become increasingly violent

---

9 The issue codes are (1) elections; (2) economy, jobs; (3) food, water, subsistence; (4) environmental degradation; (5) ethnic discrimination/issues; (6) religious discrimination/issues; (7) education; (8) foreign affairs/relations; (9) domestic war, violence, terrorism; (10) human rights, democracy; (11) pro-government; (12) economic resources/assets; (13) other; (14) unknown, unspecified.

as militia groups attack government forces, sabotage oil facilities, and kidnap oil workers (Oyefusi 2008). Finally, climate change, increasing aridity, and shifting settlement patterns have deepened competition over water and land resources, particularly in the north (Obioha 2008). Disputes over land use rights are especially apparent between sedentary farmers and nomadic pastoralists.

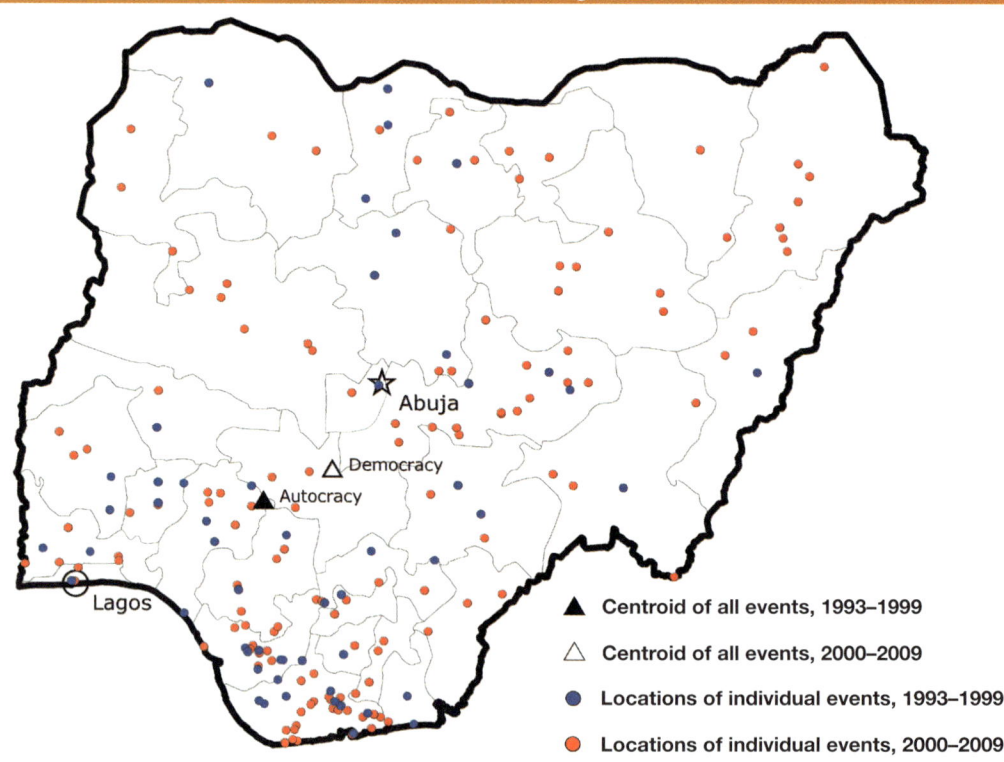

Figure 7.3 Conflict Events in Nigeria—Autocratic vs. Democratic Regimes

Source: Compiled by authors.

Figure 7.3 displays a map that overlays the locations of events of social conflict—including peaceful protests and violent unrest—across Nigeria during the Abacha era (1993–1999) and the subsequent period of democracy (2000–2009).[10] Several interesting patterns emerge from an analysis of the two periods, providing systematic quantitative evidence that confirms many of the arguments in the existing literature. First, the frequency of events increases, with an average of 31 events (violent and non-violent) per year during the Abacha regime and 61 events per year afterward.[11] In addition, the spatial distribution of events has also shifted. During the period of military rule, conflicts were mostly confined to the southern part of the country. Only a handful of northern states (e.g., Kaduna, Kano, Katsina) experienced notable unrest. After democratization, however, a significant cluster of events around the Niger Delta was offset by a major expansion of

---

[10] Abacha died in 1998, and Olusegun Obasanjo was inaugurated on May 29, 1999. Since 2000 was the first full calendar year during which Nigeria was under democratic rule, this is used as the dividing line. The maps display Nigerian federal states under the latest (1996) specifications of federal borders.

[11] Further analysis of SCAD reveals that the average number of violent events was just 13 events per year during the 1990s, compared to 35 per year during the 2000s.

conflict among the northern states. For instance, Borno state, in the far northeastern corner, experienced no significant social unrest during the 1990s, but exhibited several conflicts during the 2000s. Indeed, all of Nigeria's 37 states have experienced overt conflict in the latter period, unlike in the earlier period. Figure 7.3 also shows the centroid—or geographic centerpoint of all events—for the recent periods of autocracy and democracy in Nigeria. As can be seen, the center shifts to the north and east in the 2000s, consistent with the observation that the Muslim-Christian divide has been the basis for significant conflict in recent years. The ability to document and visualize these sorts of patterns, with greater rigor and precision, represents a major benefit of geolocated data such as SCAD.

In connection with the Minerva-funded CCAPS project, SCAD has also been used to study environmental influences on conflict. For example, Hendrix and Salehyan (2012) examine how deviations from normal rainfall patterns (e.g., drought, extreme rain) affect social conflict. Rainfall is positively related to civil war, with wetter years more likely to suffer from violence as resources become more available to militant organizations. Abnormally dry and wet years are associated with all types of political conflict, including non-violent unrest, violent conflict, and anti-government conflict. Understanding such factors in the timing and location of violence can yield better forecasts about where unrest may occur, enabling policy makers to develop better intervention strategies.

The Climate Security Vulnerability Model (CSVM)[12]

Similarly, CSVM focuses on the security consequences (including the risk of conflict and violence) of climate change throughout Africa at the subnational level.[13] The aim is to identify locations of chronic vulnerability, with as fine-grained resolution as possible, so that decision makers can anticipate potential trouble spots and direct attention and resources accordingly. Areas within Africa are ranked relative to the rest of the continent, rather than the rest of the world. The sources of physical exposure used in the model are based on historic data on climate-related hazards. The findings are triangulated by comparing projections of future climate change (Busby, Gulledge et al. 2012), as well as collaborating directly with climate scientists on future projections of climate exposure (Cook and Vizy 2012; Vizy and Cook 2012; Busby, Cook, Vizy et al. 2013). In addition, CSVM is externally validated through extensive groundtruthing with local experts (Berenter 2012a; Berenter 2012b), plus comparisons with other models. The model has been updated twice as better subnational data have become available and project directors reflected on comments from local experts in and on Africa.[14]

Understanding Vulnerability

Vulnerability is not purely a function of physical exposure to climate-related hazards, but also depends crucially on the number of people living in a given area, what resources they have to protect themselves, and whether their governments are willing to help them in times of need. The analysis using CSVM focuses on situations where large numbers of people could be subject to death from exposure to climate-related hazards, while recognizing that

---

[12] This section reports on work of Joshua Busby in collaboration with Todd Smith, Nisha Krishnan, and Mesfin Bekalo.

[13] The methods underlying this model are detailed in Busby, Smith, Krishnan et al. (2013a, 2013b).

[14] The first iteration is examined in Busby et al. (2010), while the second set of iterations is discussed in Busby, Smith, White et al. (2013); Busby, Smith, and White (2011); and Busby, Smith et al. (2012).

such situations may or may not escalate to armed conflict. The research can therefore be distinguished from traditional climate security studies that focus exclusively on climate and armed conflict, as well as other approaches that focus more on livelihoods.[15]

Methodology

The diverse sources of vulnerability are gauged by indicators, which have been grouped into four baskets: (1) climate-related hazard exposure, (2) population density, (3) household and community resilience, and (4) governance. Each basket is reduced to an index. The four baskets, their components, and the calculation of the indices are described in the next subsection. Different types of vulnerabilities coincide in some locations but not others, as is evident when the four indices are reduced to a composite index.

A key decision in this subnational work is the unit of analysis. Previous work on this topic relied on shapes of subnational units, using the data from Global Administrative Areas (GADM) dataset.[16] Other available options include data from the Global Administrative Unit Layers (GAUL) and Map Library.[17] An exploration of the USAID Demographic and Household Surveys (DHS) data, seeking more subnational indicators for this third iteration of CSVM, revealed that DHS shapes do not always neatly coincide with GADM and that GADM does not always have the latest political divisions for some countries. Therefore, a new master shapefile was created for all level-one administrative boundaries across Africa, typically corresponding to regional boundaries of states or provinces, based on the latest shape files that are available from various sources.[18]

Findings

The first basket consists of indicators of physical exposure to climate-related hazards, including historic data on the frequency and intensity of cyclone winds, the frequency of wildfires, the presence of chronic aridity, the frequency of rainfall anomalies, and the potential for coastal inundation.[19] Each indicator is converted to a unit scale. An index for the basket is created by giving each indicator a 20 percent weight, except for chronic aridity and rainfall anomalies, which share a 20 percent weight equally, since they are meant to capture similar phenomena. The results show that the most vulnerable areas extend in a wide swath across the continent from Equatorial Guinea to Somalia, with additional pockets in North Africa, coastal Mozambique, and Madagascar. They represent the areas with the greatest historic exposure to these climate-related hazards.

Another primary concern is where large numbers of people are at risk of death from exposure to climate-related hazards. Therefore, the CSVM incorporates a measure of ambient population density—i.e., the average over 24 hours, measured at a 1 km by 1 km resolution. The data are derived from the 2011 version of LandScan, which is produced by Oak Ridge National Laboratory. The data are normalized into percentiles on a unit scale. Population concentrations are found along the Nile River in Egypt, in western Ethiopia,

---

15 For example, Maplecroft (2012) has produced a global climate vulnerability ranking at the subnational level. See also Wheeler 2011.

16 The GADM website is http://www.gadm.org/.

17 The GAUL website is http://www.fao.org/geonetwork/srv/en/metadata.show?id=12691. The Map Library website is http://www.mapmakerdata.co.uk.s3-website-eu-west-1.amazonaws.com/library/.

18 See Smith, Busby, and Agnihotri (2013).

19 Busby, Smith, Krishnan et al. (2013a, 2013b) provide further detail on these indicators, their scale, the sources of data, and the temporal coverage.

throughout Nigeria and coastal West Africa, in and around the Great Lakes region, along Lake Malawi, and along the Mediterranean coastline from Morocco to Tunisia. Luckily, only some of these areas are also locations that have historically exhibited high climate-related hazard exposures. Meanwhile, a number of the least populated areas—especially in the Sahel and parts of Central Africa—are locations of high climate-related hazard exposure, which is a major reason people avoid living in these areas. From a security perspective, this circumstance is fortunate.

The next basket reflects sources of resilience at the household and community levels: those that are better educated and healthier and have greater access to services, all else equal, will be more capable of withstanding and recovering from exposure to climate hazards that can pose risks to security. In fact, these same attributes are often viewed as vital as part of a more general resilience to conflict. This basket contains pairs of indicators for four categories: education, health, daily necessities, and access to health care. In this iteration of the model, updated infant mortality data was obtained and normalized to the year 2008 from the Environmental Indications and Warnings Project from the Central Intelligence Agency. In addition, new subnational data for literacy and school enrollment were derived from the USAID DHS and the UNICEF Multiple Indicator Cluster Survey (MICS). Data on underweight children and access to improved water sources were also updated to take advantage of new DHS and MICS data. Finally, some subnational information for mothers' delivery in a health facility was obtained from the DHS and MICS data. This means that subnational data are now used for six of eight indicators in this basket. All of these indicators were converted into percent ranks and normalized on a zero to one score. All four categories—and each of the constituent indicators—received equal weight in the index.[20] North Africa and Gabon are found to be the most resilient areas, whereas the least resilient areas are in northern Mozambique, Somalia, and a band that stretches from West Africa into the Sahel. A broader point is that large portions of the continent exhibit heightened vulnerability, but many of these locations overlap with lower levels of population density.

The final basket concerns governance. Since some hazards exceed the capacity of households and communities to respond, whether or not governments are willing and able to provide support can be crucial. The basket includes six indicators in five categories: government responsiveness, government response capacity, openness to external assistance, political stability, and presence of violence.[21] The indicator of the presence of violence is the only one measured at a subnational level. It encompasses all types of ACLED events for the period 1996–2012, with more weight placed on recent events.[22] Events are aggregated to the level-one administrative unit, again corresponding to subnational regional boundaries in most cases. Areas with poor governance scores include most of Somalia and Libya, half of Zimbabwe, and pockets of South Sudan, Sudan, the Democratic Republic of the Congo, and the Central African Republic. Significant portions of southern Africa have relatively favorable scores.

---

20 In the event a particular indicator was missing data, the other indicator would take on the full category weight.

21 Government responsiveness and capacity are captured through a diminishing weighted-average of data from the Worldwide Governance Indicators for 2008–2011. The indicator for openness to external assistance, which likely changes slowly, is obtained from the 2009 KOF Index of Globalization. Two indicators reflect the volatility of governance in a country, derived from the Polity IV data.

22 Events in 2012 get a full weight of 1, then the weight diminishes by 1/16 each year through 1997.

The indices for the baskets can be combined using various functional forms. In the analysis presented here, the physical exposure index is multiplied by the sum of the other three indices. To preserve the clarity of the unit scale, the composite index is renormalized, dividing each value by the total possible score. Values are then subtracted from 1, such that 1 represents the most vulnerable and 0 the least vulnerable.

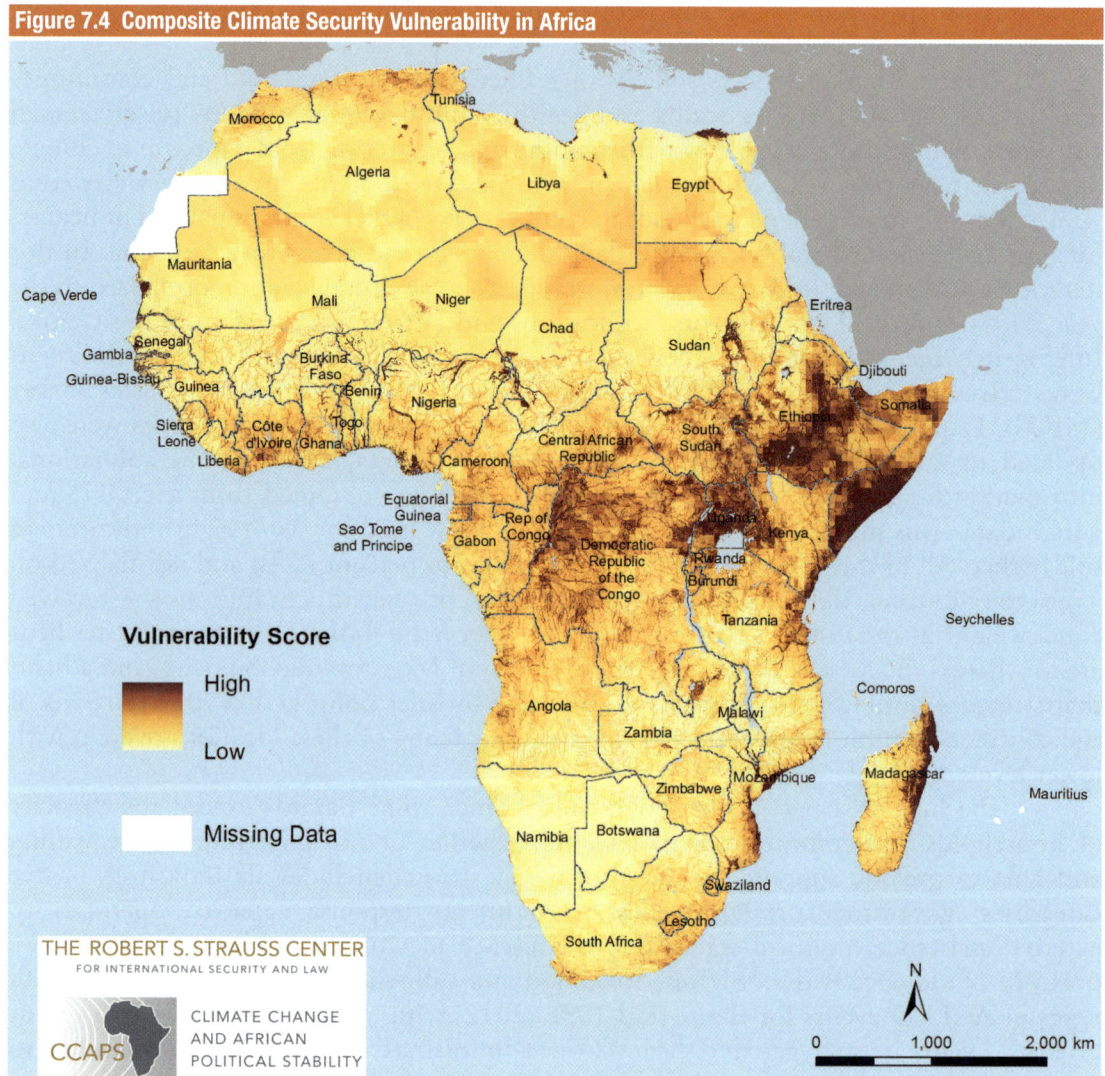

Figure 7.4 Composite Climate Security Vulnerability in Africa

Figure 7.4 displays the map of this composite index of climate security vulnerability. Extreme levels are found across the Horn of Africa, with the maximum being in Somalia (0.85). Other areas of high vulnerability are concentrated in central and eastern Ethiopia, Uganda, pockets in the DRC, Nigeria, Egypt along the Nile, and the eastern coasts of Mozambique and Madagascar. Parts of southern Africa and North Africa rate as less vulnerable, due among other things to higher living standards and better governance compared to other parts of the continent. The lowest level of vulnerability (0.00) is observed in northwestern Ethiopia.

> *Extreme levels [of climate security vulnerability] are found across the Horn of Africa, with the maximum being in Somalia (0.85). Other areas of high vulnerability are concentrated in central and eastern Ethiopia, Uganda, pockets of the DRC, Nigeria, Egypt along the Nile, and the eastern coasts of Mozambique and Madagascar.*

An advantage is that CSVM backs characterizations with multi-dimensional, systematic evidence that affords greater rigor and precision. The significant elements of disaggregation in the calculations and presentation of results represent a major advance, allowing finer-grained assessment that is superior to crude national-level assessments. Refinement of the model, to achieve ever more reliable statistics that improve the value as a tool for guiding research, policy, and practice, remains an ongoing process. As part of work in progress, these maps are being validated by comparing the observed patterns of vulnerability to other similar indicators such as the EM-DAT International Disaster database of climate-related disasters (CRED 2011). This dataset has limited, low-quality geographic information, but as part of the CSVM project, all climate-related disaster events over the period 1997–2011 have been geocoded (Busby et al. 2013a, 2013b).

Applications

CSVM has been used primarily to identify hot spots of chronic concern. The model has other important applications, especially when analyzed in conjunction with additional geolocated data. Indicators of interest can be overlaid on top of the map of climate-related security vulnerability to assess the extent of co-location. For example, one study assessed the extent to which foreign assistance is being delivered to the most vulnerable areas (Busby, Smith, and White 2012). Active World Bank and approved African Development Bank projects in Africa were geocoded across all sectors.[23]

As Figure 7.5 reveals, some of the areas of greatest vulnerability, such as Somalia, received little foreign assistance from multilateral lending institutions in 2009 and 2010. Of course, the absence of a competent or even functioning government, together with widespread insecurity, heighten vulnerability and produce a setting where foreign assistance is too risky and thus discouraged. Such analysis raises questions about whether funding should be directed to countries most capable of successful implementation (e.g., Kenya and Tanzania were major beneficiaries of multilateral assistance in East Africa) or to the most vulnerable areas. These issues have been examined with respect to East Africa (Busby, Smith, and White 2012) and North Africa (Busby, White, and Smith 2010).

> *Some of the areas of greatest [climate security] vulnerability, such as Somalia, received little foreign assistance from multilateral lending institutions in 2009 and 2010.*

Another notable angle is the intersection between climate vulnerability and US strategic interest. This has been studied by incorporating data on terrorist attacks, piracy, oil wells, minerals, and embassies. Here, preliminary findings suggest that Nigeria and Somalia in particular possess both high climate vulnerability and relatively high strategic importance (Busby et al. 2013).

---

[23] See http://ccaps.aiddata.org/aid. Other CCAPS colleagues are pioneering the coding of adaptation-specific projects (Weaver and Peratsakis 2011; Ackerson et al. 2013).

Figure 7.5 Development Projects and Climate Security Vulnerability in Africa

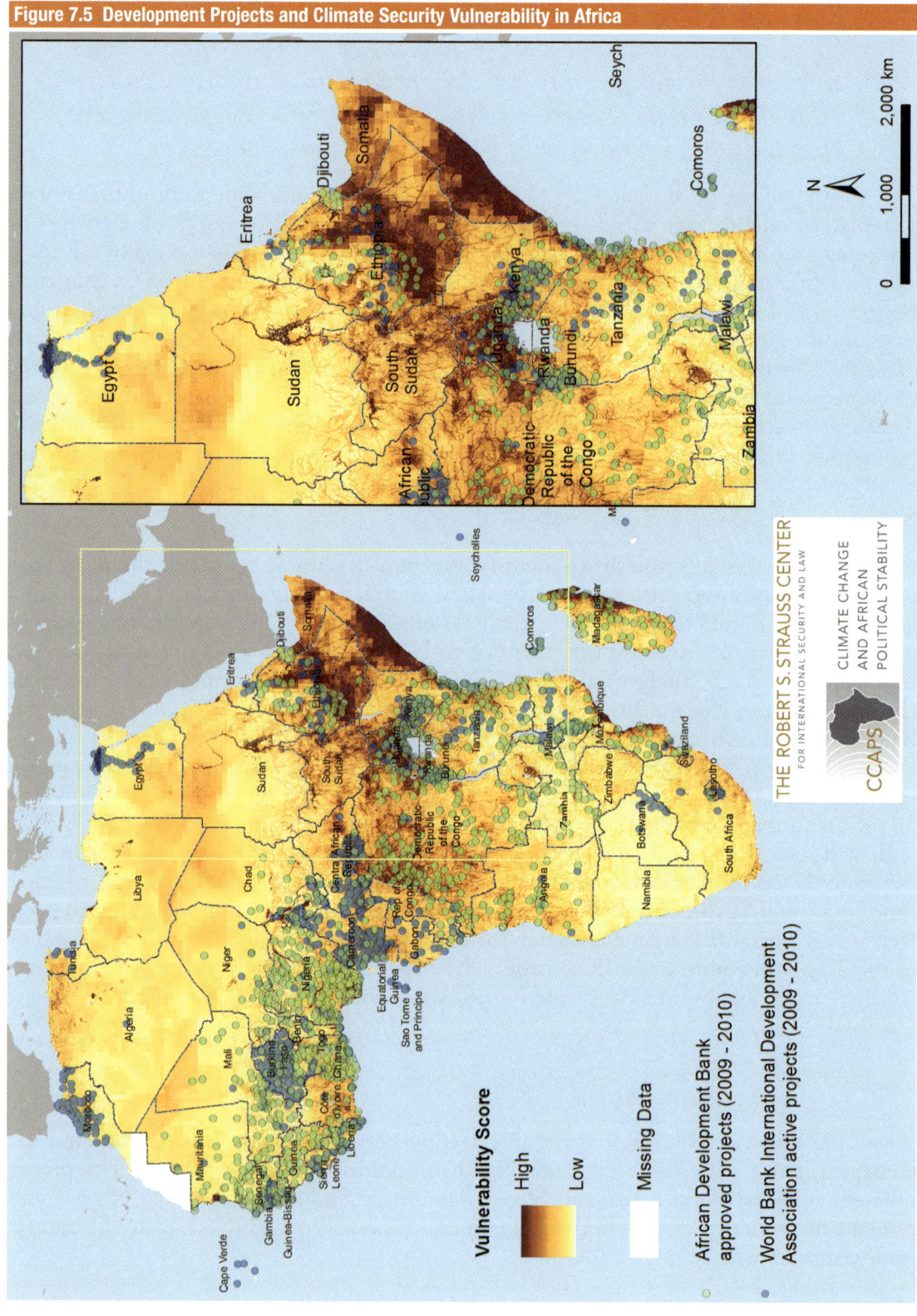

CSVM also has potential to be used as a simulation tool for exploring "what-if" counterfactuals. Scenarios can be conceived that reflect a range of alternative values of the constituent indicators for particular locations. The range might encompass things such as future development objectives (e.g., increased literacy), specific interventions (e.g., deployment of peacekeeping forces), or changes in conditions (e.g., drought).

In addition, this project has generated new information resources that facilitate cross-sectoral analyses. For example, data on subnational administrative units in Africa, subnational educational attainment, and access to improved water sources are available from Smith, Busby, and Agnihotri (2013). Geocoded data on terrorism and disasters in Africa are expected to be made publicly available in 2014.

Conclusion

The diverse data sources described in this chapter enable the examination of questions related to climate change and security outcomes. More fine-grained geolocated data is essential to that enterprise since environmental variables like precipitation typically do not have a uniform distribution over national units. While conflict does not always take place proximate to where local drivers originate, the datasets described here enable scholars to assess the extent to which subnational variation matters. ACLED, SCAD, and CSVM can also be used to address topics well beyond the climate change debate. These datasets further open the door to a rich research agenda that integrates subnational geographic data into the study of security and international politics.

While subnational studies of political phenomena are gaining in popularity, methods and analysis are still at early stages. Maps of these phenomena can be compelling, but hinge on many underlying decisions, such as how to classify data, what are appropriate divisions between categories, and how many different colors or shades should represent these categories. Maps usually say little about statistical significance—they do not come with error bars—or the quality of input data. Some outputs, such as the composite maps of vulnerability described in this chapter, may be difficult to test and externally validate using econometrics, because of data limitations. ArcGIS, the leading software of mapping geospatial data, now includes more tools for geospatial analysis and econometrics. Yet much of the work in this domain still relies on simple overlays of indicators.

Even statistical analysis that takes advantage of new geospatial data sources and uses subnational units faces difficult modeling choices. The politically salient divisions are administrative regions, which vary in size within and across countries, complicating comparative analysis. Some analyses instead employ equally sized grid squares, which have the drawback of being artificial and not reflecting actual political units (Theisen 2011; Busby and Hazen 2011; O'Loughlin et al. 2012; Theisen et al. 2012). A related problem is how to ascribe event data with X,Y coordinates to larger geographic units, particularly in instances where battles, disasters, or complex emergencies affect multiple towns, provinces, or regions—but not all of them. Also, beyond the fact that news reports may have biased counts of deaths and casualties, trying to apportion these guestimates to different geographic units is potentially fraught with even greater error.

In sum, analysts have to be clear about their assumptions when using geospatial data. Ultimately, none of the work using the new data sources, methods, and mapping tools is a substitute for close and nuanced understandings of particular situations on the ground and strong foundations for theorizing and testing causal relationships.

8. EXPLORING INEQUALITY AND ETHNIC CONFLICT: EPR-ETH AND GROW^{up}

Lars-Erik Cederman, Luc Girardin, and Julian Wucherpfennig

This chapter discusses the Ethnic Power Relations (EPR) family of datasets. These resources are available through the online data portal GROW^{up} (Geographic Research On War, unified platform), which is provided by the International Conflict Research (ICR) group at ETH Zürich (see http://growup.ethz.ch). This platform allows users to gain easy access to data on ethnic groups' political power and conflict behavior around the world from 1946 through 2009. After describing the motivations, development, and design of the data and the portal, we turn to their research applications.

Introducing the Research Area and the Need for Data

In response to the surge of ethnic conflict in the early 1990s, systematic data collection on ethnic groups and their roles intensified. Previous datasets, such as the Atlas Narodov Mira (Bruk and Apenchenko 1964), were primarily anthropological or focused on linguistic differences alone. The new wave of empirical research was led by Gurr's Minorities at Risk (MAR) project, which introduced a series of political indicators recording grievances and inequalities focusing on exposed minorities (Gurr 1993a, 1993b, 2000). Based on this evidence, Gurr concluded that members of politically, economically, and culturally disadvantaged groups are more likely to stage protest and rebellion against incumbent governments than those who enjoy a more secure position in society. The MAR dataset quickly became the standard source of systematic data on ethnic groups. Thanks to its comprehensiveness, in terms of geographic coverage and the number of variables, the new data resource has spawned an entire research program that analyzes various aspect of ethnic conflict (Hug 2013).

Despite these impressive achievements, there was considerable reluctance in the literature to accept grievance-based explanations of the outbreak of civil war. Arguing that grievances are both ubiquitous and irrelevant as predictors of internal conflict, leading scholars introduced accounts based on material incentives and opportunities, such as warlords' rent seeking, rebels' opportunity costs, and state weakness in peripheral regions (Fearon and Laitin 2003; Collier and Hoeffler 2004).

One major reason why these scholars have been reluctant to embrace Gurr's grievance perspective is empirical limitations associated with the MAR dataset. By focusing on the notion of minorities "at risk," that is, minorities already discriminated against or otherwise disadvantaged, this dataset breaks new ground on political relevance, but unfortunately at the cost of introducing potential selection bias. The sample includes some "advantaged" minorities, yet remains incomplete since Gurr and colleagues exclude many powerful groups, some of which may decide to challenge the incumbent government (Cederman, Wimmer, and Min 2010). These difficulties have often been overstated as inherent flaws of the MAR dataset. After all, selection bias and endogeneity can only be defined in relation to specific research questions. As such, this data resource is perfectly appropriate for many inquiries (Hug 2013). To the extent group-level data are used to explain conflict onset coded at the same level, however, the MAR data can be incomplete and should not be used naively without further correction (Birnir et al. n.d.). There is much to be said for such a disaggregated level of analysis, not the least because the use of highly aggregated ethnodemographic measures of fractionalization and polarization is far removed from specific conflict mechanisms (Cederman and Girardin 2007). As we will discuss later, both political and economic inequality at the group level have been linked directly to civil-war violence.

The Ethnic Power Relations Dataset

The EPR dataset was introduced as a way to circumvent the difficulties associated with apolitical or incomplete samples of ethnic groups. The original version of the dataset identifies all politically relevant ethnic groups and their access to state power, where political relevance is defined by including groups that are active in national politics and/or directly discriminated against by the government (Cederman, Wimmer, and Min 2010). This corresponds closely to MAR's definition of political relevance, but without restricting the sample to minority groups. Ethnicity itself is conceptualized as a subjectively experienced sense of commonality based on the belief in common ancestry and shared culture (Weber 1978: 385–398; Cederman 2013: 533). According to this general definition, ethnic groups can be based on any combination of linguistic, religious, or somatic markers.

In the initial round of coding, carried out as a joint venture between the ICR group at ETH and collaborators at UCLA, around 100 country and regional experts participated in an online survey. The survey asked each expert to judge whether ethnicity is relevant in the country in question and, if so, to identify power relations between all politically relevant ethnic groups and the government. The most recent version, EPR-ETH, includes ethnic groups around the world from 1946–2009.[1]

The dataset allows access to power and ethnic identities to vary over time, such that political relevance or identification may move from one level to another. For each group and time period, the demographic weight and access to power are provided as absolute, rather than relative, measures. Power access is based on the influence over the country's executive, whether in terms of cabinet seats or control of the army in military regimes. The dataset divides power status into three main categories, depending on whether a group controls power alone, shares power, or is excluded from power. Groups that fall into the two first categories are classified as included, whereas those that belong to the last category are excluded. Each of the three categories encompasses several subcategories:[2]

1. Included groups that rule alone can be either in monopoly or dominant, depending on whether the control is total or allows for "token" representation.

2. Included groups that share power play either a senior or junior role, measured by their absolute influence over the cabinet.

3. Excluded groups are powerless (access to power is blocked), discriminated against (exclusion is systematic and targeted), autonomous (granted regional autonomy), or separatist (unilaterally secured regional autonomy).

Thus, the coding reflects meaningful qualitative differentiation about the nature of power.

---

[1] The EPR project manager is Manuel Vogt. For a list of coders, see http://www.icr.ethz.ch/data.
[2] For further details on the coding, see Cederman, Wimmer, and Min (2010).

Figure 8.1 The EPR-ETH Coding of Iraq, 1946–2009

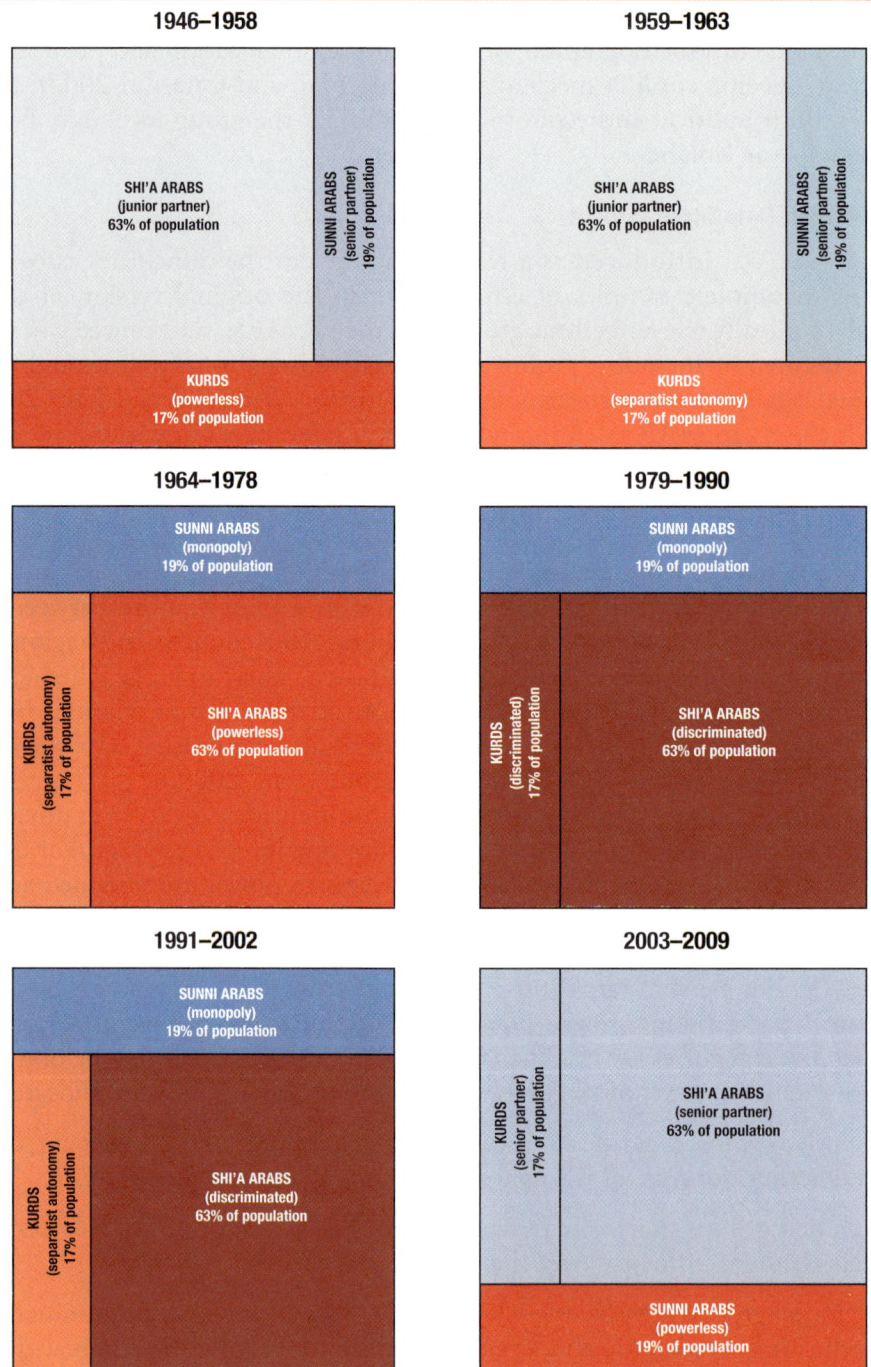

The example of Iraq demonstrates the time-sensitive coding.[3] EPR-ETH identifies three politically relevant ethnic groups in Iraq: Shi'a Arabs, Sunni Arabs, and Kurds. For the period from 1946–2009, EPR-ETH records six intervals during which the ethnopolitical constellation remained relatively constant (see Figure 8.1).

---

[3] This discussion draws on Min, Cederman, and Wimmer (2012).

Following the end of WWII, Iraq continued to be ruled as the reinstated Hashemite Kingdom of Iraq, drawing heavily on support by ex-Sharifian officers and descendants of the old Ottoman elite in Baghdad who were mostly of Sunni extraction, including Prime Minister Nuri al-Said and King Faisal II. There was considerable Shi'a representation, mostly at the ministerial level. Sunni Arabs are coded *senior partners* and Shi'a Arabs as *junior partners*. Kurds were *powerless*, after a failed attempt to establish an autonomous state on Iranian soil in 1946. Subsequently, a Kurdish separatist movement, under the leadership of Mustafa Barzani, gained control over the northern parts of Iraq, taking advantage of the weakness of Abd al-Karim Qasim's regime, which came to power in the revolution of 1958. Kurds are therefore coded as having *separatist autonomy* for the period 1959–1974. In 1963, Iraq witnessed the Ramadan Coup, which led to the installment of the Sunni-dominated Baathist government. Shi'a Arabs are coded as *powerless* from 1964–1978. In the late-1970s, Saddam Hussein's regime launched a campaign of "Arabization" against the Kurdish community, involving repression, forced deportation, and the use of chemical weapons against civilian populations. Widespread incidents of severe political discrimination also afflicted the Shi'a Arabs. The end of the first Gulf War brought about the creation of a UN-guaranteed safe haven, which allowed Kurdish nationalists to regain control over the north. Sunni domination of Iraqi politics came to an end with the 2003 invasion that toppled Saddam Hussein's regime, producing another major shift in the ethnopolitical power distribution. The new federal constitution, imposed by the United States, formally aimed at power sharing among all three groups. Yet electoral boycotts and ethnic voting, as well as an insurgency by Sunni fundamentalists and former members of the Baath regime, led to ineffective representation and political marginalization of Sunni Arabs.

Table 8.1 Status of Groups in EPR-ETH as of 2009

Category	Number	Share
Rule Alone		
Monopoly	26	3.8%
Dominant	41	5.9%
Power Sharing		
Senior Partner	80	11.6%
Junior Partner	144	20.9%
Excluded		
Regional Autonomy	117	17.0%
Separatist Autonomy	11	1.6%
Powerless	201	29.1%
Discriminated	70	10.1%

For the period from 1946–2009, EPR-ETH contains a total of 827 ethnic group identities, some of which are composites of lower-level groups. In 2009, the most recent year of observation, 690 groups were classified as politically relevant. As Table 8.1 shows, 57.8 percent of groups were excluded from power, 32.5 percent of groups enjoyed shared access to executive power, and 9.7 percent of groups ruled alone. The most frequent subcategory is *powerless*, which encompasses almost a third of all groups.

> *In 2009…57.8 percent of [politically relevant ethnic] groups were excluded from power, 32.5 percent of groups enjoyed shared access to executive power, and 9.7 percent of groups ruled alone.*

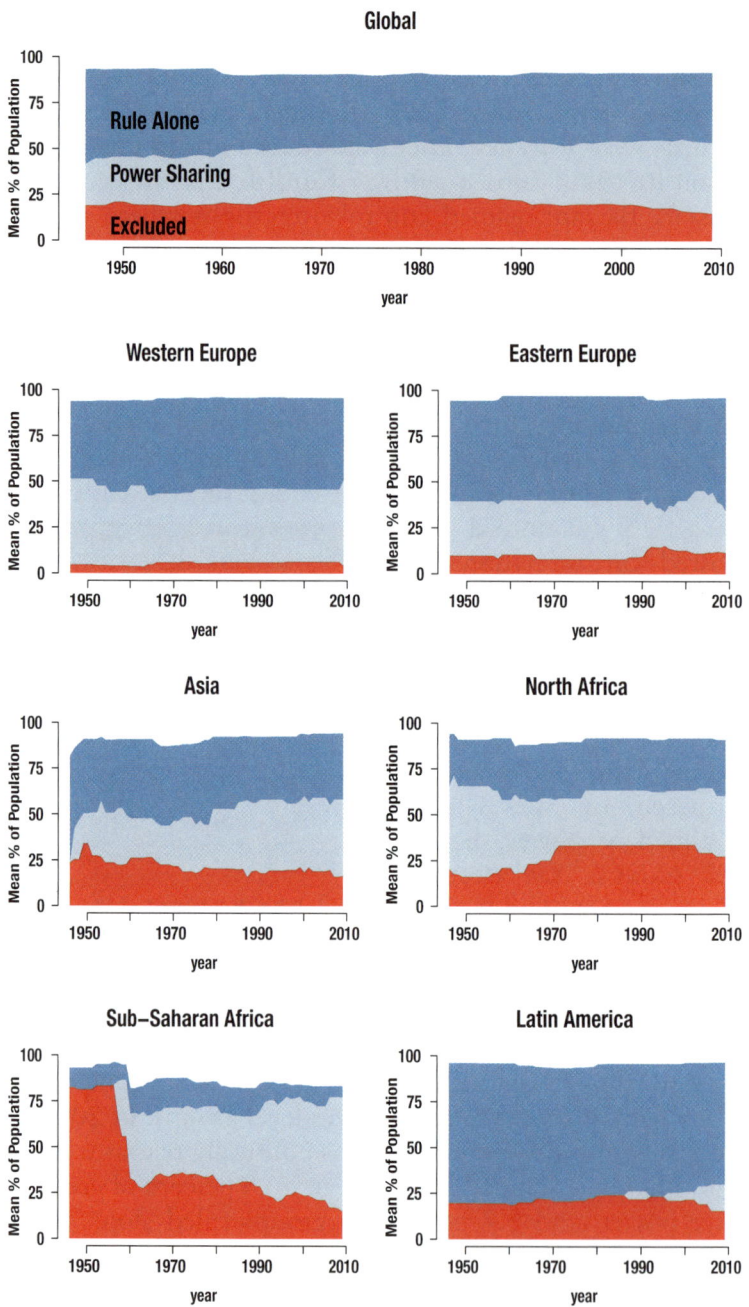

Figure 8.2 Trends in Power Status of Politically Relevant Ethnic Groups

Source: Compiled by authors.

Figure 8.2 presents the relative frequency—measured as the average share of population—over time of the three major categories of power status for politically relevant ethnic groups. The upper panel depicts the trends for the entire world. Monopolistic and dominant groups experienced considerable decline across the entire sample period. Exclusion has also declined since the 1980s. Meanwhile, power sharing increased throughout the post-Cold War period. The other panels reveal that the trends vary considerably by region. The largest declines in exclusion were recorded in Asia and Sub-Saharan Africa, followed by Latin America. By contrast, exclusion has edged up in Eastern Europe since the end of the Cold War. North Africa and the Middle East remains the region with the highest level of exclusion, despite a slight decline over recent years. Meanwhile, significant shifts toward greater involvement in ethnic power sharing were observed in both Asia and Sub-Saharan Africa. Latin America exhibited little power sharing until the late 1980s, but has recorded more cases since then.

Extensions of the EPR-ETH Dataset

The most elaborate addition to the EPR family of datasets is GeoEPR-ETH, which offers geocoded data on settlement patterns of ethnic groups that can be used in geographic information systems (GIS) for various analytical purposes (Wucherpfennig et al. 2011).[4] Geography plays an explicit role in many theories of civil war. The geocoded settlement patterns can also be used to overlay and indirectly extract other non-spatial information.

GeoEPR-ETH builds directly on the Geographic Representation of Ethnic Groups (GREG) dataset (Weidmann, Rød, and Cederman 2010), a geocoded version of Atlas Narodov Mira (ANM), which provides a series of maps by Soviet ethnographers charting ethnic groups across space (Bruk and Apenchenko 1964). Rather than being limited to the now dated list of groups in the ANM, GeoEPR-ETH is fully compatible with EPR-ETH. The dataset was created through an expert survey based on various types of map material, including the ANM. Subsequently, GIS experts geocoded this information by using GREG data directly or digitizing other maps.

For example, Figure 8.3 shows a map of the results of the GeoEPR-ETH coding for Iraq. Each of the three ethnic groups predominates in certain areas of the country. The data are sufficiently fine-grained to permit detailed visualizations at a subnational level, which are not limited to the boundaries of administrative units.

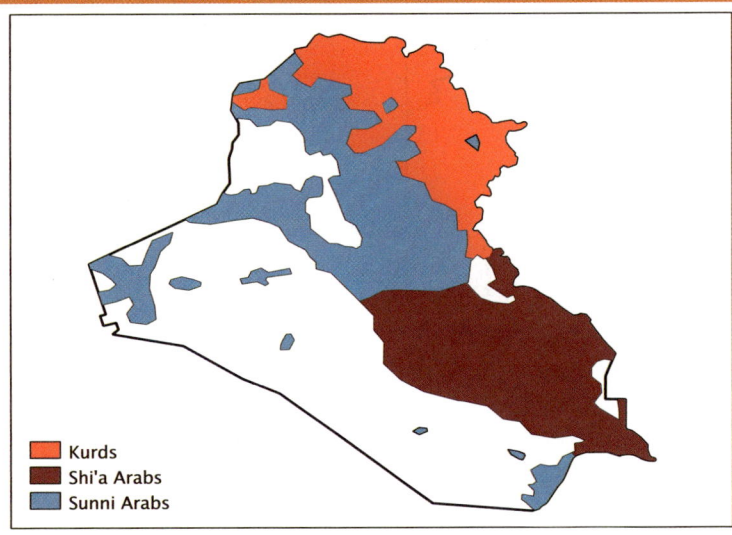

Figure 8.3 Settlement Areas of Ethnic Groups in Iraq

Source: Adapted from Wucherpfennig et al. (2011).

---

[4] Nils-Christian Bormann managed the data collection of GeoEPR-ETH. For a list of the coders, see http://www.icr.ethz.ch/data.

GeoEPR features the following assortment of settlement types: (1) regionally based,[5] (2) urban,[6] (3) regional and urban, (4) migrant, (5) dispersed, and (6) aggregated.[7] Explicit information about regional bases is provided only for groups of types (1), (3), and (6). Groups that are exclusively settled in urban areas (type 2) are not geocoded due to limited data availability. Migrant groups (type 4), by definition, do not have a permanent regional base. For dispersed groups (type 5), the regional base corresponds to the country borders as a whole (see details in Wucherpfennig et al. 2011).

Figure 8.4 Changes of Settlement Areas in Bosnia-Herzegovina

1946-1991

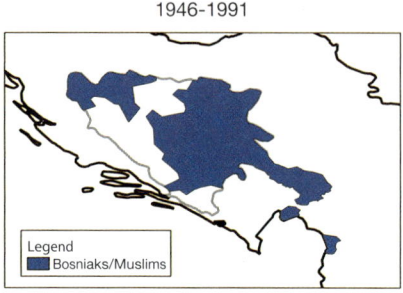

1992-1995

1996-2009

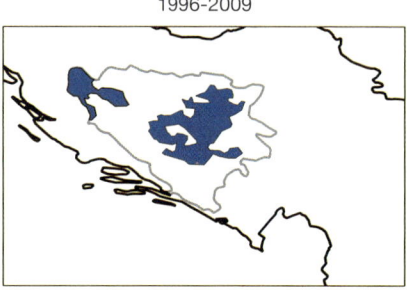

Source: Adapted from Wucherpfennig et al. (2011).

Like EPR-ETH, GeoEPR offers time-varying information, although with less precision. In particular, the geocoding records important changes in settlement patterns caused by things such as ethnic cleansing, large-scale migration, and varying state borders. For example, Figure 8.4 depicts how the settlement areas of Bosniaks/Muslims in Bosnia-Herzegovina evolved during the war in the former Yugoslavia and in its aftermath. Meanwhile, gradual, incremental changes—for example, those driven by long-term trends in urbanization—are not captured.

To test propositions about ethnic conflict, knowledge of the behavior of groups is necessary. For this purpose, the ACD2EPR dataset codes the linkages between ethnic groups and rebel organizations (Wucherpfennig et al. 2012).[8] This project integrates the core EPR dataset on politically relevant ethnic groups with the Non-State Actor dataset (Cunningham, Gleditsch, and Salehyan 2009),

---

5 Groups are coded as regionally based if group members reside in one or more particular regions that are easily distinguishable on a map.

6 Groups are coded as urban if more than 60 percent of their members are located primarily and on a permanent basis in urban areas and not in a particular region or regions.

7 Aggregated groups are those that involve mergers of multiple groups and exist as coalitions during particular periods. Codings are based on the component groups, provided their ethnic geography remains constant.

8 See http://www.icr.ethz.ch/data for a list of coders and other information on the dataset.

which builds directly on the UCDP/PRIO Armed Conflict Dataset (Gleditsch et al. 2002). The mapping is "many-to-many," since a rebel organization can be linked with multiple ethnic groups and an ethnic group can be linked to multiple rebel organizations.

The ACD2EPR data address two crucial properties of the linkage between ethnic groups and rebel organizations: recruitment and claim. These criteria, interpreted as necessary conditions, correspond closely to an intuitive definition of ethnic civil war. The first criterion assesses the ethnicity of the fighters by indicating from which ethnic groups, if any, a particular rebel organization recruits. A significant number of the group members must participate actively in the organization's combat operations for such a linkage to apply. Recruitment along ethnic lines is, by itself, insufficient because this may be merely the result of local availability, rather than a deliberate strategy or related to an organization's actual agenda. Therefore, the second criterion addresses whether a given rebel organization publicly claims that it is operating on behalf of the ethnic group in question—i.e., pursues an objective that is directly linked to the group's fate. We label this an exclusive claim because the stated objective is to provide selective benefits for groups. If recruitment and claim occur jointly, we code a rebel organization as "ethnic."

To illustrate, consider the case of Liberia. Rebel organizations fighting in the first Liberian civil war (1989–1996)—for example, the National Patriotic Front of Liberia (NPFL) and the Independent National Patriotic Front of Liberia (INPFL)—meet both criteria of ethnic recruitment and claim involving the Gio, Mano, and other indigenous groups. LURD fighters in the second Liberian civil war (2000–2003) were predominantly recruited from the Mandingo and Krahn (Guere), but the organization's sole stated purpose was to remove Charles Taylor from office. Thus, the ACD2EPR dataset codes this rebel organization as nonethnic (see Wucherpfennig et al. 2012 for details).

The ACD2EPR data allow us to differentiate between organizations that pursue an ethnic agenda and those that do not, including within the same conflict.

With this information, some problems in previous subjective assessments of whether a given conflict is ethnic can be avoided. In particular, the ACD2EPR data allow us to differentiate between organizations that pursue an ethnic agenda and those that do not, including within the same conflict. Also, by drawing on information included in EPR-ETH, it is possible to determine whether the ethnic groups within a rebel organization are subject to state-induced exclusionary policies, which allows us to establish the ethnopolitical context of particular rebel organizations.

The GROWup Online Data Portal

Most research relying on the EPR datasets also employs complementary data. To facilitate these efforts, the online portal GROWup (Geographic Research On War, unified platform) supports the integration of data, as well as their creation, maintenance, storage, analysis, and dissemination.[9] GROWup is effectively a federation of sources, offering convenient and easy access to complex conflict data, rather than a new dataset. The system is built

---

[9] Luc Girardin directs the development of GROWup with support from members of the ICR group. Sebastian Schutte has contributed to the raster dataset and system programming. Philipp Hunziker designed and documented the RFE. Nils Weidmann played a key role in the design of the system.

around the EPR-ETH datasets, but includes data from other sources as well. Among these are the partner institutions of the ICR group at ETH Zürich, which is currently taking the lead in the European Network of Conflict Research (ENCoRe), an EU-funded COST initiative that links together conflict researchers in Europe who contribute to the data portal or conduct related quantitative conflict research.[10] The main building blocks of GROW^{up} are joined together in a structure that corresponds to the workflow of database generation. A Coding Front End (CFE) allows researchers to feed data into the Database Back End (DBE), which processes them and makes them available to end users through a Public Front End (PFE) and a Research Front End (RFE).

The CFE is a standardized online interface that allows researchers to edit the component datasets. A generic online tool facilitates large-scale coding efforts, including support for GIS-based data. Thanks to multiuser functionality and project monitoring features, data collection tasks can be distributed to a team of coders.

The DBE is a relational database that ties together the datasets in a fully consistent, non-redundant way. The database is constituted by linked component data tables that are populated through a procedure that checks for coding mistakes and inconsistencies. Placed on the servers of the ICR group at ETH Zürich, the DBE can be queried by SQL calls—i.e., commands that extract complex information from layers of the database.

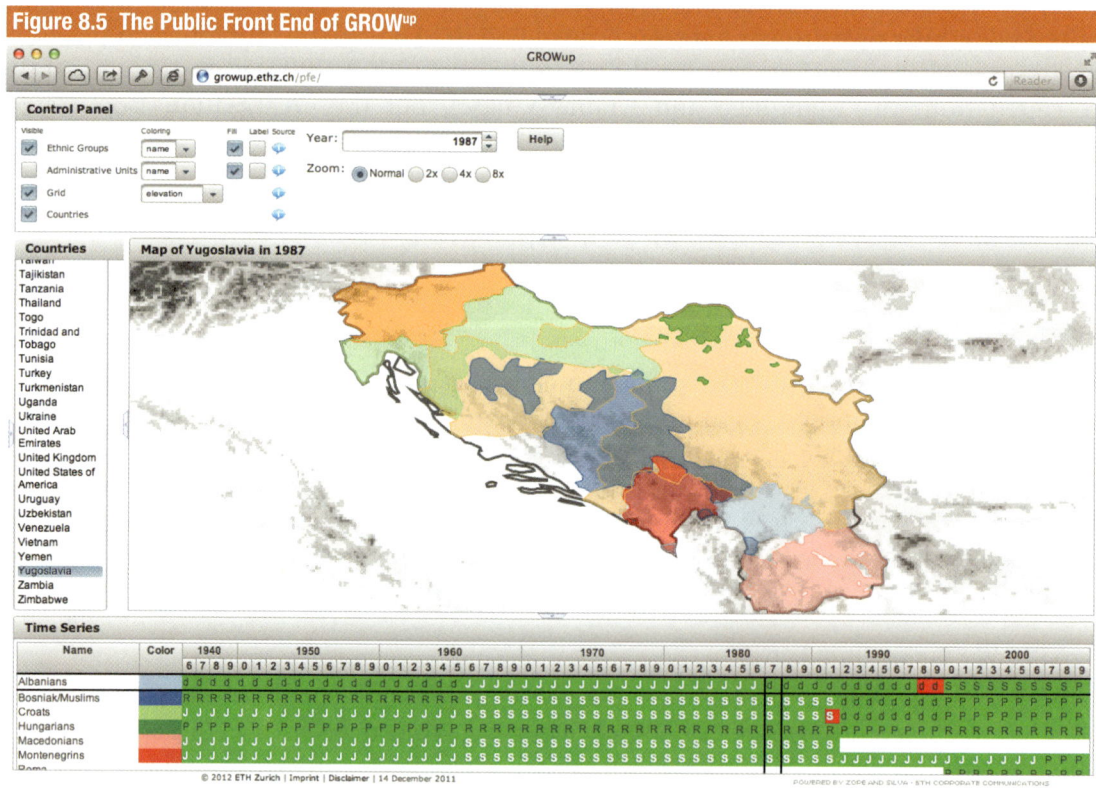

Figure 8.5 The Public Front End of GROW^{up}

Figure 8.5 shows a snapshot of the PFE (http://growup.ethz.ch/pfe/), an online visualization tool that displays combinations of data in time and space, affording the most direct and intuitive access to information from the underlying sources. This tool makes it

---

10 See http://www.encore.ethz.ch.

possible to zoom in and click on regions and groups within countries, thereby retrieving data directly from the DBE. A slider enables users to browse the history of countries, organizations, and groups, thus tracing changes in their boundaries and various key properties, such as political institutions, ethnic configurations, and conflict activities. The PFE has also been adding maps showing the spatial distribution of various features, such as terrain, environmental conditions, communication networks, wealth, natural resources, demographics, and synthesized risk estimates.

> *[The Public Front End of GROW^{up}] enables users to browse the history of countries, organizations, and groups, thus tracing changes in their boundaries and various key properties, such as political institutions, ethnic configurations, and conflict activities.*

Figure 8.6 shows a snapshot of the RFE (http://growup.ethz.ch/rfe/), another online tool, which facilitates the generation of customized merged datasets, including for replication purposes (Hunziker 2011). The interface allows users to register and select data for analysis via a wizard. This tool is primarily designed to serve researchers who want to download popular datasets with countries and ethnic groups as the standard units of analysis. Future updates will provide access to data on other types of subnational groups (e.g., rebel organizations, social movements, political parties), as well as conflicts.

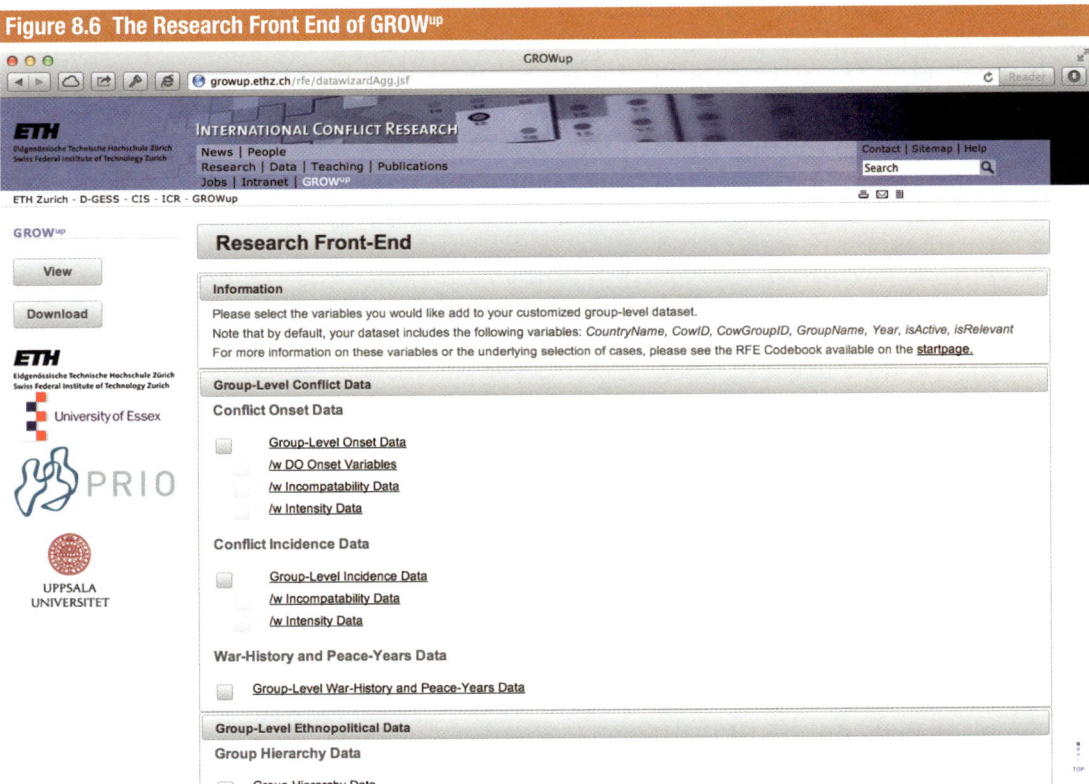

Figure 8.6 The Research Front End of GROW^{up}

Overview of Research Findings Based on the EPR Family of Data

The EPR family of datasets is a recently developed resource, but has already generated a series of publications. The original aim was to evaluate hypotheses about the impact of inequalities among politically relevant groups on internal conflict. EPR-ETH data has enabled research positing that such group-level inequalities, also referred to as horizontal inequalities (Stewart 2008), engender grievances, which in turn increase the probability of ethnic civil war. The latest study in this vein examines the effects of horizontal inequalities on conflict onset (Cederman, Gleditsch, and Buhaug 2013).

One aspect of inequality is the political exclusion of ethnic groups. Standard theories of nationalism anticipate that situations of ethnic domination and exclusion will be associated

Table 8.2 Conflict Propensities of Ethnic Groups, by Power Status

Power Status	Group Years	Onsets
Group Included	8,951	29 (0.32%)
Group Excluded	20,582	178 (0.86%)

with heightened conflict risk because they violate basic principles of political legitimacy. In particular, "alien rule" can be expected to lead to ethnonationalist grievances. Following in the footsteps of Gurr and his team, Cederman, Wimmer, and Min (2010) relied on the first version of EPR to establish that political exclusion, especially recent loss of power, is strongly linked to the outbreak of ethnonationalist civil wars, controlling for groups' demographic size and conflict history. Using more recent data drawn from both EPR-ETH and ACD2EPR, Cederman, Gleditsch, and Buhaug (2013) come to the same conclusion, while finding that the group-size effect applies to excluded groups only. Table 8.2 displays the main result of this study, which reveals a clear disparity in relative frequencies of conflict onset: the rate among excluded groups is nearly three times that for included groups, and the difference in rates is statistically significant ($p < 0.001$). This is compelling evidence that access to power reduces the frequency of conflict. Multivariate regression analysis controlling for a number of variables yields consistent conclusions.

Political exclusion, especially recent loss of power, is strongly linked to the outbreak of ethnonationalist civil wars.... The rate [of conflict onset] among excluded groups is nearly three times that for included groups.

The relative wealth of ethnic groups also influences the probability of internal conflict. Grievances can emanate from resentment linked to backwardness and governmental neglect, or, in the case of relatively affluent groups, frustration with having to support less effective parts of the state. A challenge is that data on relative wealth at the group level has been notoriously difficult to find. A solution to this problem is to adopt a spatial approach that estimates regional income based on geographic data on economic wealth provided in grid-cell format by the G-ECON map (Nordhaus 2006). As we have demonstrated, GeoEPR, offers a bird's eye view of ethnic settlements around the world that builds directly on the EPR dataset. Using the settlement areas as "cookie cutters," Cederman, Weidmann, and Gleditsch (2011) computed the relative wealth of ethnic groups since 1990. This is achieved by summing the gross cell products provided through G-ECON for those grid-cells located inside the ethnic group's settlement polygon.

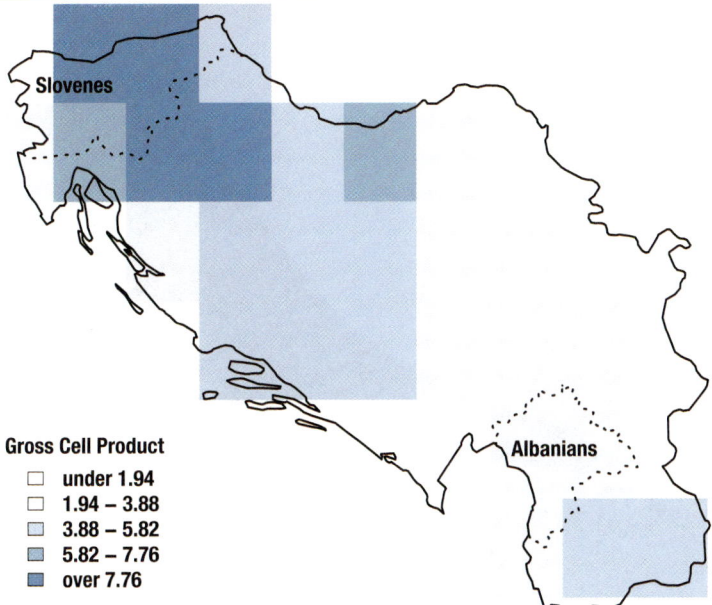

Figure 8.7 Estimated Income per Capita of Ethnic Groups in the Former Yugoslavia

Source: Adapted from Cederman et al. (2013).

Figure 8.7 shows how the settlement areas of selected groups in Yugoslavia in 1990 can be used to estimate their relative wealth. Darker blue areas, from the G-ECON grid, correspond to higher levels of economic production (gross cell product is the subnational equivalent of gross domestic product). In turn, horizontal inequality can be measured as the ratio of the per capita income of the group to that for the country as a whole. Such calculations indicate that groups poorer than the country average, such as the Kosovo Albanians, are at significantly higher risk of getting involved in civil wars. This effect is also present for those groups that are wealthier than the average, such as the Slovenes and Croats, although the evidence is somewhat weaker in this case.

> *Groups poorer than the national average...are at significantly higher risk of getting involved in civil wars. This effect is also present for those groups that are wealthier than the average.*

The former relationship relating to groups that are economically disadvantaged can be illustrated with a simple graph depicting the annual conflict probability of different levels of inequality. Figure 8.8 shows that the conflict propensity increases rapidly with greater inequality, measured in terms of the "low ratio"—i.e., the number of times poorer the group is compared to the national average.

Although these two sets of results do not test directly whether grievances are felt by the respective ethnic groups, they are consistent with grievance-based interpretations. If those theoretical perspectives are correct, both political and economic inequality will be associated with a higher probability of conflict outbreak.

In other research, Cederman, Gleditsch, Salehyan, and Wucherpfennig (2013) study the influence of transborder ethnic kin (TEK), building on an extension to EPR-

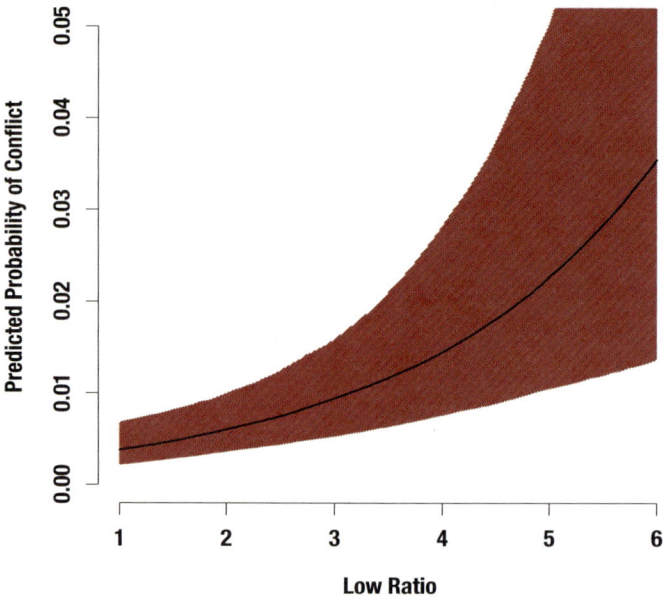

Figure 8.8 Effect of Economic Inequality Between Ethnic Groups on the Likelihood of Conflict

Source: Adapted from Cederman et al. (2013).

ETH that records transnational ethnic links.[11] They postulate a curvilinear relationship between a group's relative size and conflict onset. The results confirm that the risk of conflict is higher within the middle range of the group size spectrum. Large TEK groups have a conflict-dampening effect, provided they control their own state, while excluded groups are not associated with lower conflict probabilities. These findings shed light on why the post-Soviet republics have experienced relatively little conflict, whereas greater violence is observed in other cases (e.g., the former Yugoslavia).

> *Large [transnational ethnic kin] groups have a conflict-dampening effect, provided they control their own state, while excluded groups are not associated with lower conflict probabilities.*

Wucherpfennig et al. 2012 draw on the ACD2EPR dataset to show that civil wars last longer if rebel organizations linked to excluded ethnic groups are active in the fighting.[12] This research reiterates the value of deviating from an apolitical, mostly demographic approach to ethnicity. Evidently, it is not ethnicity per se that prolongs fighting, as argued by authors relying on essentialist assumptions, but rather its relationship to political institutions. These results suggest that the concept of "sons of the soil" (Weiner 1978),[13] which has been cited as a major driver of civil-war duration (Fearon 2004), should be seen as a special case of ethnic exclusion, rather than a unique conflict configuration.

---

[11] In addition, see Chapter 6 in Cederman, Gleditsch, and Buhaug 2013. For an overview of previous studies on transnational ethnic kin and conflict, see Saideman and Jenne (2009).

[12] In addition, see Chapter 8 in Cederman, Gleditsch, and Buhaug 2013.

[13] Sons of the soil conflicts involve a peripheral, geographically concentrated ethnic minority facing migration to its perceived homelands that is initiated by the central state under the control of a dominant ethnic group.

Another significant application of EPR data is Roessler's (2011) study of coups in Africa, which demonstrates that leaders may in some cases prefer to fight peripheral insurgencies, rather than exposing themselves to the risk of being toppled by power-sharing partners in the capital. Similarly, Wucherpfennig (2011) draws on the EPR dataset to analyze the conflict-preventing impact of power sharing, while taking endogeneity into account. This research, implemented through strategic estimation, shows that power sharing has a net positive effect after incorporating into the analysis the reasons why such arrangements are invoked in the first place. Cederman, Gleditsch, and Hug (2013) apply EPR data to the question of whether elections in multiethnic states increase the risk of conflict. Their findings suggest a sore-loser effect among large ethnic groups. Relying on GeoEPR, Fjelde and Hultman (forthcoming) employ GIS-based techniques to study the influence of ethnic links on the outbreak of one-sided governmental violence in Africa. They find that governments are more likely to target ethnically distinct rebel populations with repressive means, compared to other populations.

Conclusion

The EPR family of datasets fills an important gap in contemporary conflict research. In recent years, a growing number of scholars have reacted to overly aggregated research by disaggregating analysis down to the micro level, focusing mostly on individuals and small groups. This shift has left the intermediate level of ethnic groups relatively understudied. Fortunately, the MAR dataset continues to be updated and improved, but it does not satisfy all needs of research on ethnic conflict (Hug 2013). The EPR-ETH dataset spans a narrower set of variables, compared to MAR, but offers a more complete global selection of ethnic groups, including those that are in the majority and not at risk. This breadth enables firmer conclusions concerning the influence of inequality on conflict behavior of ethnic groups. As we argue, the evidence strongly supports grievance-based interpretations, without dismissing the influence of material factors. These grievance mechanisms relate to collective—not individual—reactions to injustice and inequality.

The next major update of EPR-ETH, which will extend the coverage from 2009 to 2013, is scheduled to be released in 2014. In the near future, we also plan to release new extensions to EPR-ETH. One is a global dataset of transborder links and refugee flows (Rüegger 2013). Another is a dataset drawing on anthropological information, which reveals what ethnic dimensions characterize the EPR-ETH groups (Bormann, Cederman, and Vogt 2013), including linguistics, religious, and racial cleavages. Furthermore, work is underway to improve—in particular, to render more precise—the coding of both governmental and territorial power sharing. Over the longer term, major efforts will be devoted to broadening the organizational coverage of the group-level coding by extending the link from ethnic groups beyond rebel organizations to include both political movements and parties in peacetime. Further areas of expansion could include types of violence other than civil war, as well as more precise (geo)coding of conflict events. To the extent possible, we will include these new data structures through GROW^{up}, as a way to integrate them with the core of EPR-ETH. Important new data layers will include improved information on group-level inequalities, natural resources, and road networks, among others.

9. DESCRIBING AND UNDERSTANDING SEXUAL VIOLENCE IN ARMED CONFLICT: THE ROLE OF DISAGGREGATION

Amelia Hoover Green

What counts as "conflict-related sexual violence?" How much of it happens in a given conflict? What kinds of people suffer conflict-related sexual violence? What kind of people perpetrate it, and under what circumstances? What explains variation in levels of conflict-related sexual violence across time, space, conflicts, and individuals? Research into conflict-related sexual violence (CRSV) has attempted to answer all these questions. In doing so, this area aligns with a more general trend toward disaggregation and micro-comparison in the social sciences.[1] Several scholars have produced studies that problematize the category of CRSV, much as other research has sought to problematize the over-aggregation of "violence" more generally (Ron 1997, 2000; Wood 2008; Steele 2011; Hoover Green 2011). While research specific to sexual violence is still a relatively small part of the overall study of conflict-related violence, this literature has advanced considerably in the past several years.

This chapter discusses key findings on CRSV, as well as ongoing controversies in this area of inquiry. In particular, I examine the challenges of measuring CRSV in the context of a broader trend toward studies that emphasize disaggregation and analysis of micro-level variation. This trend is vital to theory-building on wartime sexual violence. Yet the nuance of causal theories—and, hence, the specificity of hypotheses—has, in many cases, outstripped the ability to reach accurate descriptive inferences. This issue is mirrored in the policy world. For example, in Resolution 1889 (2009), the United Nations Security Council sought the creation and analysis of data on "patterns and trends" in CRSV, both within and across countries and groups. The quality of these data varies considerably over time, space, and other dimensions. Thus, in a context of growing global awareness of CRSV, efforts to prevent, mitigate, or prosecute CRSV are often built on an inconsistent (and at times conflictual) informational foundation.

What Is "Conflict-Related Sexual Violence"?

Sexual violence is an especially difficult object of study, in both wartime and peacetime. The first and most basic issue concerns the identification of the phenomenon. CRSV research in the social sciences follows, to some extent, the path of research on wartime and war-related "violence" more generally. Scholars, often responding to episodes in which sexual violence was evidently deployed massively and strategically, have identified CRSV as a distinct phenomenon from other forms of violence against civilians (Stiglmayer 1994; Allen 1996; Seifert 1996; Sharlach 2000; Skjelsbaek 2001; Wood 2006; Alison 2007). Yet significant debates remain about the definitions of sexual violence and conflict-relatedness.

---

[1] In the context of this chapter, "micro-comparison" means comparison across sub-units of a larger unit. For example, a common analytical strategy in contemporary comparative politics research has been to conduct micro-comparative research across time, space, or actors within a single country (or, in the case of conflict research, within a single conflict). "Disaggregation," as it is commonly used, is a broader category that encompasses both micro-comparison (e.g., breaking countries into departments or municipalities) and the separation of broad phenomena into sub-phenomena (e.g., violence into types of violence, sexual violence into separate forms of sexual violence).

Kalyvas (2006), in work about lethal violence against civilians, points out that killings are frequently studied because they have the dubious distinction of being (relatively) easy to identify. By contrast, sexual violence can encompass a number of acts. Researchers have sought to list and theorize various forms of sexual violence that appear most frequently during wartime, identifying rape, gang rape, sexual torture, sexual slavery, genital mutilation, sexual humiliation, sexual slavery, forced abortion, forced sterilization, and trafficking as distinct phenomena with (potentially) distinct causes (e.g., Wood 2006b; Leiby 2009a). Some definitions include verbal or psychological violence as an element of the broader phenomenon (e.g., Johnson et al. 2008, 2010; Oxfam/Casa de la Mujer 2010). In addition, definitions of sexual violence and understandings of specific acts often vary across regions, cultures, and individuals, even within the same context, which has important implications for assessing prevalence, causes, and consequences.

> *Definitions of sexual violence and understandings of specific acts often vary across regions, cultures, and individuals, even within the same context, which has important implications for assessing prevalence, causes, and consequences.*

Consider, for example, two recent survey-based studies of sexual violence during armed conflict in the Democratic Republic of the Congo (DRC). Johnson et al. (2010: 555) define sexual violence as follows:

> Any physical or psychological violence carried out through sexual means or by targeting sexuality and includ[ing] rape and attempted rape, molestation, sexual slavery, being forced to undress or being stripped of clothing, forced marriage, and insertion of foreign objects into the genital opening or anus, forcing individuals to perform sexual acts on one another or harm one another in a sexual manner, or mutilating a person's genitals.

In turn, the research team asked a large number of specific behavioral questions in order to provide a disaggregated estimate of sexual violence as it affected Congolese women and men. By contrast, Peterman et al. (2011) relied on a simple question with no embedded operational definition: "Has anyone ever forced you to have sexual relations with them against your will?"[2] Perhaps unsurprisingly, the two studies reached quite different conclusions about the prevalence of sexual violence.

This chapter casts a broad net, following the International Criminal Court's (ICC) definition of sexual violence: a perpetrator commits an act of sexual violence when s/he "commits an act of a sexual nature against one or more persons or cause[s] such person or persons to engage in an act of a sexual nature by force, or by threat of force or coercion… or by taking advantage of a coercive environment or such person's or persons' incapacity to give genuine consent" (2010: 30). This definition includes rape, the most commonly researched form of sexual violence, but also gang rape, non-penetrative sexual assaults, sexual harassment, sexual torture, sexual slavery, forced marriage, sexual humiliation, forced undressing, forced prostitution, and other acts that target the victim's sexuality.

---

[2] This question wording was from the Demographic and Health Survey for the DRC, on which the findings of Peterman et al. (2011) were based.

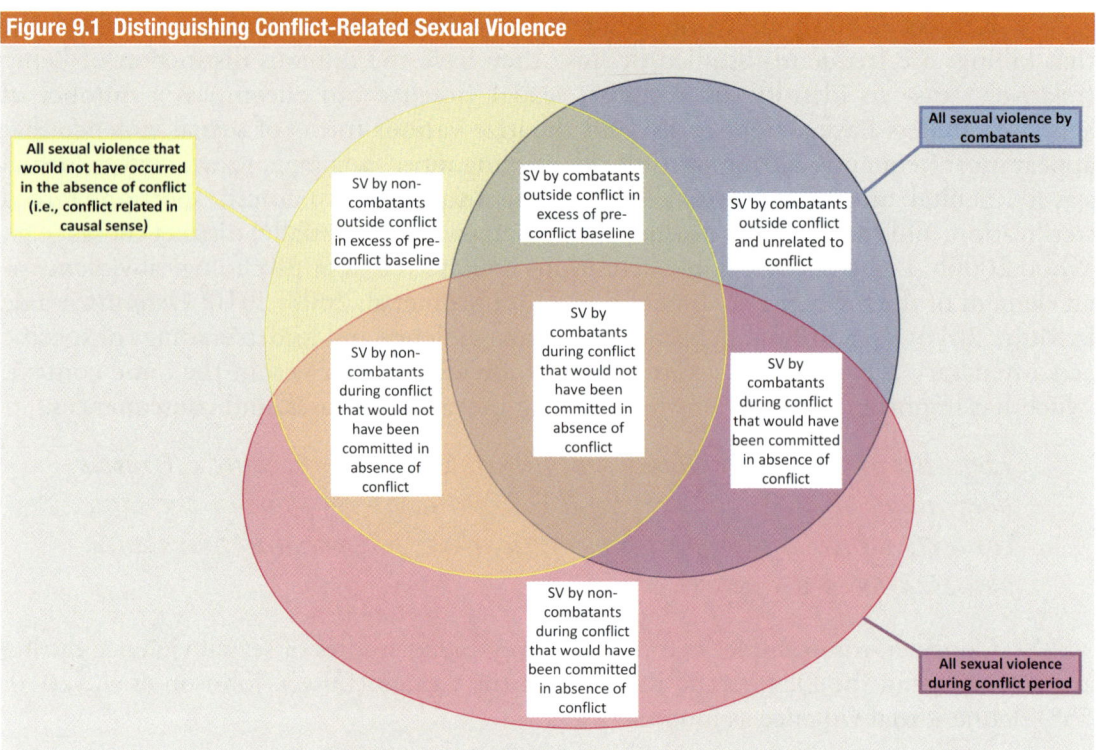

Figure 9.1 Distinguishing Conflict-Related Sexual Violence

This definition of sexual violence does not include assumptions about the sex of the victim or the perpetrator. As documented in a number of cases, males frequently fall victim to sexual violence, and females frequently perpetrate it (e.g., Sivakumaran 2007).

In defining CRSV, researchers must also clarify the meaning of conflict-relatedness. In this respect, it is useful to distinguish among sexual violence that (1) happens because of a conflict, (2) occurs during a conflict, and/or (3) is committed by conflict actors.

Social scientists are often inclined to employ a causal definition of conflict-relatedness, which encompasses all acts of sexual violence that would not have occurred absent conflict. Unfortunately, this definition is effectively impossible to operationalize, because it requires accurate knowledge of a pre-conflict baseline level of sexual violence. Scholars must therefore turn to rough proxies for the theoretically interesting, but practically infeasible, causal definition. Some identify as conflict-related only those acts of sexual violence that are committed by combatants (e.g., Leiby 2009a; Cohen 2013). Others include all acts of sexual violence that occur during a period of conflict (e.g., Peterman, Palermo, and Bredenkamp 2011; Cohen, Hoover Green, and Wood 2013).

As Figure 9.1 shows, these definitions overlap in complex ways. Sexual violence that occurs during a war may not be caused by war. Many cases are part of the baseline level of this endemic social ill (represented by the pink and purple regions). These might include episodes of intimate-partner violence, by civilians or combatants. Similarly, members of armed groups may perpetrate sexual violence that neither occurs during war nor is caused by it (blue region).[3] This is particularly true in countries with significant peacetime military populations. Well after a war ends, it may also lead to sexual violence,

---

3 For the purposes of this chapter, "armed group" is a general term that refers to any state or non-state armed organization that is party to an armed conflict.

including by perpetrators with no relationship to any armed group. This outcome could ensue if conflict alters social norms about violence or the state's capacity to enforce prohibitions on violence (e.g., Wood 2008), prompting changes in the level or pattern of sexual violence by civilian or military perpetrators (yellow and green regions, respectively).

Thus, the set of acts considered to be conflict related may not be fully clear, either conceptually or empirically. Rather than arguing for or against a given operationalization, I consider all operationalizations of conflict-relatedness, while noting the extent to which different operationalizations suggest different conclusions.

Regardless of what definition is used, the benefits of disaggregating sexual violence, like the benefits of disaggregating conflict violence more generally, are considerable. Rape of individual civilians by individual soldiers, under cover of night, when not ordered though perhaps tacitly condoned, represents a very different dynamic than a public gang rape (see discussion of gang rape in Cohen 2013). Both types of violence seem to differ considerably from practices such as sexual torture, which frequently occurs in the context of detention and in many conflicts is targeted across genders, as well as other types of sexual violence. Information about the relative prevalence of different types of sexual violence over time and space would provide much-needed evidence to distinguish between competing explanations. As I discuss later, however, sufficient data to examine fine-grained patterns of sexual violence simply do not exist for most armed conflicts.

Measurement Difficulties

The difficulty of measuring wartime sexual violence can hardly be overstated and should be a key point of discussion in any investigation of this topic. This is particularly true because most social-scientific testing of causal hypotheses assumes the accuracy of descriptive inferences. In the context of data on human rights, though, such an assumption is implausible. Data on violence are socially produced; that is, observed patterns of human rights violations depend heavily on cultural, linguistic, political, geographic, and logistical factors, any or all of which may (or may not) produce selection bias in the resultant data (Davenport and Ball 2002; Roth, Guberek, and Hoover Green 2011; Krüger et al. 2013).

Quantitative CRSV research has typically been based on three key types of data: (1) systematic, population-based samples, (2) convenience samples, and/or (3) indices. Each type is based on—and all ought to be supplemented by—detailed qualitative data.

Data from systematically sampled, population-based surveys provide the best chance at an accurate, population-level view of CRSV, particularly when it occurs on a large scale...[but] frequently are not designed for disaggregation or micro-level comparisons.

Data from systematically sampled, population-based surveys provide the best chance at an accurate, population-level view of CRSV, particularly when it occurs on a large scale. Of the types of data discussed here, only systematic survey data can be used to create estimates that apply at the population level. Of course, surveys differ in methods, focus, and overall quality. A number of high-quality survey estimates have reached rather different conclusions regarding CRSV, often due to differences in question working or enumeration methods, as shown in Table 9.1.

Table 9.1 Overview of Select Survey Research on Conflict-Related Sexual Violence

Reference	Country	Year of Survey	Region	Reference Population	Definition of CRSV	Key Finding(s)
Swiss et al. (1998)	Liberia	1994	Capital city	Women 15–70	"Forced sex" (question references "physical force," but no further definition given).	49% of respondents reported experiencing at least one act of physical or sexual violence by a soldier or fighter. - 17% beaten, tied up, or detained in a room under armed guard; - 32% strip-searched (32%); - 15% raped, subjected to attempted rape, or sexually coerced
Amowitz et al. (2002)	Sierra Leone	2002	Three internally displaced persons' camps and one town	Internally displaced women, 18+	"Sexual violence included rape and other forms of sexual assault, such as molestation, sexual slavery, being forced to undress or being stripped of clothing, forced marriage, and insertion of foreign objects into the genital opening or anus…. War-related prevalence of sexual violence included experiences of sexual assault committed by combatants during the past 10 years of war. Lifetime prevalence of non-war-related sexual violence included experiences of sexual assault committed by family members, friends, or civilians at any time in a woman's lifetime. These two prevalence rates did not overlap since the perpetrator categories were mutually exclusive."	9% of respondents and 8% female household members reported war-related sexual assaults Lifetime prevalence among respondents of non-war-related sexual assault committed by family members, friends, or civilians was 9% Lifetime prevalence increased to 17% with addition of war-related sexual assaults (excluding 1% of respondents who reported both war-related and other sexual assault)
Amowitz et al. (2004)	Iraq	2003	Three cities in southern Iraq	Women and men, 18+	"Sexual assault included rape and other forms of sexual assault, such as molestation, sexual slavery, being forced to undress or being stripped of clothing, forced marriage, and insertion of foreign objects into the genital opening or anus."	0.4% respondents reported a regime-related rape or sexual assault of a family member since 1991 2% reported a personal account of a non-regime-related sexual assault in their lifetime 6% knew of someone who had experienced sexual assault
Vinck et al. (2007)	Uganda	2005	Northern Uganda	Women and men, 18+	"Sexually violated" (no further definition given).	7% of respondents (male and female) report ever being "sexually violated" 25% reported witnessing a sexual violation

Table 9.1 Overview of Select Survey Research on Conflict-Related Sexual Violence

Source	Country	Year	Regions	Population	Definition	Findings
Uganda Bureau of Statistics and Macro International (2007)	Uganda	2006	All regions	Women and men, 15–49	"Forced to have sexual intercourse or perform any other sexual acts against one's will" (multiple questions; no further definition given).	39% of women and 11% of men reported ever experiencing any form of sexual violence 7% of women and 18% of men reported sexual violence by a "police/soldier," "stranger" or "other"
Vinck et al. (2008)	Uganda	2007	North Kivu, South Kivu, Ituri	Women and men, 18+	"Survey asked respondents several questions regarding 'sexual violence,' purposely leaving the term 'sexual violence' undefined."	16% of respondents reported exposure to sexual violence during the period of war Reports of sexual violence are approximately equal between men and women (authors note that men may report experiencing sexual violence when it occurs to women in their families)
Johnson et al. (2008)	Liberia	2008	All regions	Women and men, 18+	"Lifetime sexual violence was assessed by asking a respondent if they had experienced sexual violence to include molestation, forced undressing, forced intercourse, or other sexual acts.... Sexual violence was determined as any violence, physical or psychological, carried out through sexual means or by targeting sexuality and included rape and attempted rape, molestation, sexual slavery, being forced to undress or being stripped of clothing, forced marriage, and insertion of foreign objects into the genital opening or anus, forcing 2 individuals to perform sexual acts on one another or harm one another in a sexual manner, or mutilating a person's genitals."	42% of adult female former combatants experienced sexual violence at some point in their lifetime 9% of females who had not been combatants experienced sexual violence at some point in their lifetime 33% of adult female former combatants experienced sexual violence at some point in their lifetime 7% of females who had not been combatants experienced sexual violence at some point in their lifetime Soldiers were reported to be responsible for a majority of sexual violence against men, but not against women.
Ojeda et al. (2010) [ENDS data]	Colombia	2009	All regions	Women 15–49	"Raped or forced to have sexual relations" (no further definition given).	10% of women reported ever experiencing rape or forced sex by a husband or partner 6% of women reported rape or forced sex by someone other than a partner
NSD / MOF [Timor-Leste], and ICF Macro (2010)	Timor-Leste	2009	All regions	Women 15–49	"Forced to have sexual intercourse or perform any other sexual acts against one's will" (no further definition given).	3% of women reported ever experiencing any form of sexual violence

Table 9.1 Overview of Select Survey Research on Conflict-Related Sexual Violence

Stark et al. (2010)	Uganda	2009	Four internally displaced persons' camps in northern Uganda	Internally displaced women and men, 18+	Respondents were asked to report on their own, sisters', and closest neighbors' experiences of sexual violence. Marital rape was "defined as forced sex with an intimate partner through the use of physical violence, threat or other coercion" and rape as "sexual intercourse or attempted sexual intercourse, without consent, by someone other than a husband or an intimate partner."	41% of respondents reported forced sex by an intimate partner 22% of sisters and 25% of neighbors were reported to have experienced marital rape 5% of respondents reported an incident of rape by a non-domestic partner in the past year 4% of both sisters and neighbors were reported to have experienced an incident of such rape in the past year
Johnson et al. (2010)	Dem. Rep. of the Congo	2010	Eastern DRC	Women and men, 18+	Sexual violence included "any physical or psychological violence carried out through sexual means or by targeting sexuality" and included rape and attempted rape, molestation, sexual slavery, being forced to undress or being stripped of clothing, forced marriage, and insertion of foreign objects into the genital opening or anus, forcing individuals to perform sexual acts on one another or harm one another in a sexual manner, or mutilating a person's genitals."	40% of women reported sexual violence during war period 24% of men reported sexual violence during war period
Oxfam/Casa de la Mujer (2010)	Colombia	2010	407 municipalities affected by conflict	Women 15–44	Rape: "The act of forcing a person to have sexual relations or sexual contact, using violence or the threat of violence…whether or not that includes vaginal or anal penetration, oral sex, or penetration with objects." Other acts considered as sexual violence in this study include forced prostitution, forced pregnancy, forced abortion, forced sterilization, sexual harassment, forced domestic servitude, and regulation of women's social lives.	3% of women reported having been raped 18% of women report any form of sexual violence (as defined by the study)
Peterman et al. (2011)	Dem. Rep. of the Congo	2011	All regions	Women 15–49	"Forced to have sexual relations" (no further definition given).	22% of women reported ever experiencing intimate-partner rape 12% reported ever experiencing forced sex 3% reported forced sex in previous year Reported rates significantly higher in high-conflict provinces

For example, many survey investigations—including the Demographic and Health Surveys on which a significant amount of CRSV research is based—do not ask male respondents about their experiences of sexual violence. Yet males do suffer sexual violence, and the types suffered by male victims may differ systematically from those suffered by female victims (e.g., Sivakumaran 2007; Leiby 2009b; Johnson et al. 2010).

While there are exceptions to this rule, survey data frequently are not designed for disaggregation or micro-level comparisons. Most are designed to provide accurate information about the overall prevalence or incidence of some type of event in a given time period. Unless samples are extremely large, survey data frequently cannot be disaggregated to describe spatio-temporal patterns within a given population and reference period. For example, the survey data underlying an estimate of the last-year prevalence of rape among adult women in a particular country cannot be disaggregated to estimate the levels of sexual violence by municipality or month. Perhaps for this reason—and because such surveys are extremely costly in both time and resource terms—social science research attempting to explain variation in patterns of sexual violence generally does not rely on systematically sampled data.

Rather than systematically sampled data, many analysts rely on convenience data—i.e., data that are not drawn from a systematic sample and/or that lack a numerical estimate of uncertainty. Common sources of convenience data include media coverage, police reports, hospital records, NGO reports or case files, the archives of truth commissions, or combinations of these. Frequently, qualitative data such as testimony to truth commissions or interview data are coded to create convenience samples. Among researchers of CRSV and other conflict violence, the use of convenience data is common (e.g., Green 2006; Kalyvas 2006; Weinstein 2007; Leiby 2009a, 2009b; Albertus and Kaplan 2012; Hollenbach and Pierskalla 2013).

These data have a number of benefits: unlike many survey estimates and most narrative accounts, these collections offer large numbers of observations that can be coded and analyzed, producing fine-grained accounts of patterns of CRSV and other human rights violations. Frequently, analysts bypass the process of descriptive inference, drawing causal inferences from raw convenience data. However, the accuracy of these data cannot be determined and should not be assumed.

Convenience datasets on sexual violence often tell stories that conflict with one another and obscure true patterns of violence.

Convenience datasets on sexual violence often tell stories that conflict one another and obscure true patterns of violence. To take one recent example, data drawn from hospitals in war-affected regions of the DRC emphasize the plight of the most severely injured rape victims (e.g., Onsrud et al. 2008; Wakabi 2008; Mukwege and Nangini 2009). These victims, many of whom required surgery to correct genital fistulae, typically suffered their injuries at the hands of soldiers. These cases are sometimes (incorrectly) taken to be representative of CRSV in the DRC as a whole. Other, more representative data sources suggest that many, or perhaps most, rape victims in DRC do not suffer such severe physical injuries (e.g., Johnson et al. 2010, Peterman, Palermo, and Bredenkamp 2011). The difference between an epidemic of rape characterized by extraordinarily brutal violence and an epidemic of rape in which a minority of victims suffer brutally excessive violence is both practically and analytically significant.

Figure 9.2 Comparison of Surveys on Sexual Violence in Colombia

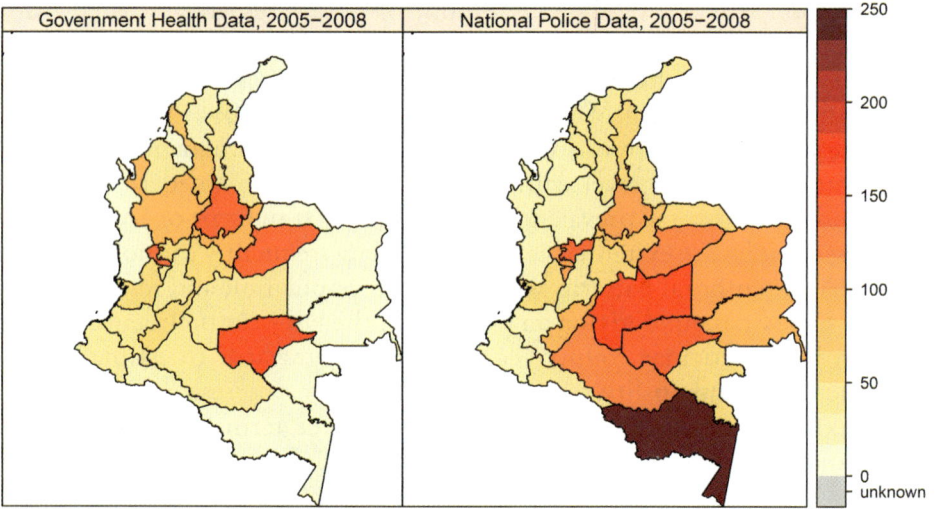

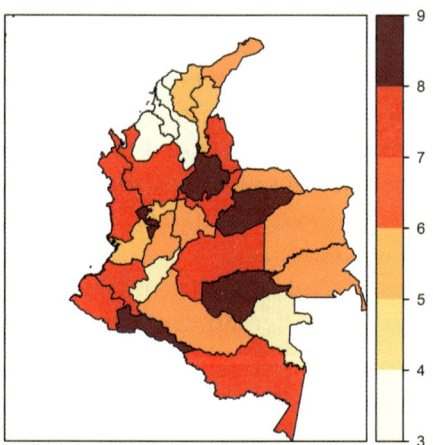

Source: Adapted from Roth, Guberek, and Hoover Green (2011); data used with permission.

Of course, civil war in the DRC is far from the only case in which convenience data have been misapplied to a wider population. For example, Figure 9.2 shows the results from two large convenience datasets and one population-based survey in Colombia, which reveal vastly different spatial and temporal patterns of violence. These disparities in the descriptive results also yield contrasting causal inferences. As this example suggests, the level of detail frequently included in convenience datasets may lend a misleading sense of specificity to numerical results based on these data.

A final type of data on CRSV is, like many other analyses, based on collated convenience data. A common measurement collapses specific qualitative assessments and/or raw numbers into broad, semi-quantitative categories. Cohen, for example, describes four levels of rape by government and rebel forces in civil wars between 1980 and 2009, each with specific definitions: no reported rape, isolated reports of rape, rape commonly reported, and widespread rape. Cohen's work is the first to create an index measuring wartime rape separately from other forms of violence, although it follows in the footsteps of a number of more general human rights or wartime violence indices, including the Political Terror Scale (Wood and Gibney 2010; Gibney et al. 2011) and various subscales of the Freedom House (e.g., Freedom House 2013) and Polity (Marshall, Jaggers, and Gurr 2002) projects. From a measurement perspective, indices can be seen as more cautious than convenience data. Index measures abandon claims to specificity, which are typically not supportable, in favor of more general categories that are, at least in theory, comparable across many conflicts, conflict actors, and years.

Cohen's (2013) data distinguishes between rape by rebel and government forces within each conflict-year. But it does not test micro-comparative hypotheses (e.g., spatiotemporal variation within conflict-years) and does not distinguish between individual rebel organizations. To do this work, and to illustrate the causal mechanism she proposes, Cohen relies on qualitative micro-comparative data from civil war in Sierra Leone. Qualitative information, including narratives about sexual violence from individual victims, perpetrators, and witnesses, provides rich contextual and interpretive detail, which may or may not be adequately represented in quantitative data. Frequently, narrative accounts place individual episodes of violence in context, supplying researchers with key details about who, what, when, where, and how—which, together, can yield useful hypotheses about why, and/or provide important "gut checks" about the accuracy of quantitative data.

Qualitative information, including narratives about sexual violence from individual victims, perpetrators, and witnesses, provides rich contextual and interpretive detail, which may or may not be adequately represented in quantitative data.

Given the extraordinary difficulty of gathering data on sexual violence that is accurate even in a limited sense, this type of multi-disciplinary investigation is not just salutary, but indispensible (Roth, Guberek, and Hoover Green 2011).

Key Findings

Despite a near-total lack of academic interest in CRSV as recently as the early 2000s, findings on CRSV have proliferated in recent years. Much is known now that was not known then, and new findings are frequently published. However, possibly because it is a young and interdisciplinary area of study, these findings frequently generate considerable controversy, both among academic researchers and among advocates and practitioners.

Many of these controversies are related, at least in part, to fundamental disagreements about the role of research into CRSV. Most researchers would agree that major goals include the eventual elimination of CRSV and—in the nearer term—more effective mitigation and reparation for victims of CRSV. Many academic social scientists argue that these goals are best served by developing theories that explain observable variation in patterns of sexual violence. Others argue that the development of a coherent legal and institutional framework to punish perpetrators is most valuable, that research into CRSV ought first and foremost to raise awareness among policy makers and the public, or that CRSV cannot be understood in the absence of its symbolic meanings.

In what follows, I focus primarily on the empirical social science literature, in which CRSV research flows from, and is influenced by, a research agenda on the dynamics of conflict and conflict-related "violence" (typically understood as lethal violence) more generally. As in that earlier literature, a primary goal is the identification of causes. What factors can explain variation in the incidence of CRSV? Scholars have put forth a number of different causal explanations, including armed group strategy (where specific "strategies" might include terror, punishment, or the destruction of communities), combatant opportunism, armed group socialization and culture, armed group discipline and hierarchy, and broader cultural factors such as the strength of patriarchy.

Little consensus has emerged about the causes of CRSV, in part because identifying the variation to be explained is difficult. Descriptive findings, which identify variation in CRSV and consequently provide important evidence about causal questions, have begun to emerge. I review three key findings before turning to an emerging causal consensus.

A Distinct Phenomenon

CRSV research challenges mainstream political violence investigations of political violence in a number of ways, none more fundamental than the increasingly confident assertion that the dynamics underlying variation in sexual violence are different from those underlying other forms of violence against non-combatants during armed conflict. In political science research, lethal violence has frequently been used as a proxy for "violence" more generally, but this over-aggregation, in assuming that "violence" is a single phenomenon, ignores significant amounts of violence and elides differences between perpetrating groups that may be fundamentally dissimilar. For example, during civil war in Peru, the Shining Path and the government committed very similar levels of lethal violence (Ball et al. 2003), but—with localized exceptions—very dissimilar levels of sexual violence (Comisión de la Verdad y Reconciliación 2003). While there are conflicts in which levels of sexual violence roughly track levels of other violence over time and space, there are many conflicts in which sexual violence appears unrelated to lethal violence and other forms of violence (e.g., Hoover Green 2011, on El Salvador; Wood 2009, on Sri Lanka).

> *There is little evidence to suggest that sexual violence follows similar patterns to lethal violence, or that all types of violence share similar underlying causes.*

In general, there is little evidence to suggest that sexual violence follows similar patterns to lethal violence, or that all types of violence share similar underlying causes. This assumption, however, was foundational to recent claims of global decline in CRSV, which generated considerable controversy in late 2012 and early 2013. Drawing on convenience data that attempts to tabulate global battle deaths, the Human Security Report (2012: 26) claimed that a measured decrease in overall fatalities indicated a decline in overall conflict intensity over time; they claimed, further, that sexual violence was likely in decline due to similar dynamics. It may be true that global battle deaths and/or global levels of CRSV are in decline, but there are, at this point, no convincing data regarding the latter claim (Hoover Green, Cohen, and Wood 2012). More generally, the Human Security Report flap illustrates the perils of over-aggregation (as well as the tenacity of the feminist scholars who have led attempts to consider CRSV as a phenomenon unto itself).

Not Ubiquitous

The difficulties of accurately measuring CRSV, and the initial tendency of researchers to focus on cases in which sexual violence was committed in widespread and systematic fashion, contributed, until relatively recently, to a persistent misconception that CRSV occurred in every armed conflict. Wood (2006), however, called for investigation of variation, particularly cases in which sexual violence, especially rape, was—or at least appeared to be—rare. Since then, in-depth studies have been conducted about a number of such cases, including the Tamil Tigers in Sri Lanka (Wood 2009), the FMLN in El Salvador (Hoover Green 2011), and the Israel/Palestine conflict.

A study of 48 African conflicts between 1989 and 2009...found that 64 percent of armed groups were not reported to have engaged in any form of sexual violence.

In addition to individual negative cases, recent cross-national research has demonstrated significant variation between armed groups, over time, and across space. In a study of 48 African conflicts between 1989 and 2009, researchers at the Peace Research Institute Oslo (PRIO) found that 64 percent of armed groups were not reported to have engaged in any form of sexual violence (PRIO 2013; see also Cohen, Hoover Green, and Wood 2013). Similarly, Cohen's (2013: 14) cross-national investigation of civil wars between 1980 and 2009 found considerable variation:

> Eighteen conflicts were coded as wars with widespread or systematic rape (with at least one conflict-year coded as 3), 35 as having many or numerous reports of rape (with at least one conflict-year coded as 2), eighteen as having isolated reports (with at least one conflict-year coded as 1), and fifteen wars had no reports of rape (all conflict-years coded as 0).... The data indicate that 62% of the conflicts (53 of 86) in the study period involved significant rape in at least one conflict-year (coded 2 or 3). This suggests that wartime rape is a major problem in many conflicts, but is not a ubiquitous feature of every conflict.

Variation is also observed during conflicts. Levels of CRSV are often asymmetric between parties to the conflict. Even within the same group, the use of sexual violence may vary considerably over space and time. For example, evidence suggests that Shining Path cadre committed little sexual violence during Peru's civil war (1980–2003), relative to the Peruvian armed forces (Comisión de la Verdad y la Reconciliación de Perú, 2003; Leiby 2009a). At some times and places, however, Shining Path cadre committed significant amounts of sexual violence against local civilian populations (e.g., Weinstein 2007).

The simple fact of variation in levels of CRSV—particularly within conflicts—suggests that some causal explanations, particularly those that focus on broad cultural factors such as patriarchy or ostensibly universal individual traits such as opportunism, cannot explain fully explain CRSV. Cohen, Hoover Green, and Wood (2013) point out that patriarchy may be a necessary but not sufficient condition for sexual violence in general and CRSV in particular. While theories of sexual violence rooted in patriarchy may not explain variation in levels of sexual violence, particularly at the micro-comparative level, it would be incorrect to say that patriarchy is not a cause of CRSV.

Perpetrators and Victims

In general, political science findings on sexual violence have focused on institutional perpetrators—i.e., armed groups that order, allow, or prohibit sexual violence. A number of recent findings, generally from outside political science, have affected understandings of which individuals commit or suffer sexual violence. Such findings challenge assumptions about sexual violence and invite re-evaluation of causal theories.

Perhaps the most important of these recent findings relates to the gender of victims and perpetrators. Conventional wisdom states that women suffer sexual violence and men commit it. Most survey investigations of CRSV did not ask male respondents about their experiences of sexual violence, and did not ask any respondents about the gender of the perpetrator(s). A number of studies that draw attention to male victims of CRSV have altered the conventional wisdom somewhat (e.g., Oosterhoff et al. 2004; Alison 2007; Sivakumaran 2007). A large household-based survey in DRC found that nearly as many male respondents as female respondents reported suffering some type of sexual violence, and that female perpetrators were reported in many incidents (Johnson et al. 2010).

Still, a lack of data hampers understandings of the gender breakdown of sexual violence victims and perpetrators across conflicts. For instance, some evidence suggests that male victims of CRSV are more likely to suffer sexual torture or humiliation than they are to suffer rape, but whether this signals a true difference in dynamics of violence or reflects a reluctance to report rape on the part of male victims is unclear. Findings that overturn conventional wisdoms regarding gender and CRSV must play a role in the design of future research on CRSV, but they should not be construed as evidence that sexual violence afflicts men and women equally or in the same ways.

> *Findings that overturn conventional wisdoms regarding gender and CRSV must play a role in the design of future research on CRSV, but they ought not be construed as evidence that sexual violence afflicts men and women equally or in the same ways.*

A second perpetrator identity question concerns sexual violence by non-combatants. Peterman, Palermo, and Bredenkamp (2011) found that women in the DRC were approximately 1.8 times as likely to report that a husband or partner forced them to have sex than to report that any stranger (including, but not limited to, combatants) forced them to have sex. As noted previously, not all sexual violence occurring during a conflict period is caused by conflict. For this reason, many researchers have chosen to focus on sexual violence by armed actors. Yet some sexual violence by non-combatants is undoubtedly conflict-related, as it would not have occurred in the absence of conflict. For example, here is some evidence that intimate-partner violence is exacerbated by conflict conditions and other complex emergencies (Stark and Ager 2011).

Not Always a "Weapon of War"

Early research into conflict-related sexual violence often focused on one of two conflicts in which sexual violence was both widespread and systematic (and, indeed, genocidal): the Balkan civil wars of 1992–1995 and Rwanda's 1994 genocide (e.g., Benard 1994; MacKinnon 1994; Stiglmayer 1994; Allen 1996; Salzman 1998; Snyder et al. 2006). In both cases, rape was systematized and highly violent; it frequently accompanied mass killings, and it was directed at both members of targeted ethnic groups and those who failed to comply with the violence. Accounts of wartime sexual violence from this period often frame rape as a top-down strategy specifically intended to break community taboos, "destroy the social fabric" of a community (see, e.g., discussion in Henry 2011 at p. 4), or impregnate members of the outgroup with the children of the ingroup (Fisher 1996).

In regards to non-genocidal conflicts, some scholars theorize that rape serves as a "weapon of war" (Card 1996, Diken and Lauststen 2005). Armed group leaders order or encourage sexual violence as spoils of war, as punishment for defection, as a mode of forced displacement, or as a message to opposing combatants, via "their" women. Both advocacy discourse and conventional wisdom now frequently assume that sexual violence caused by conflict must be a "weapon" or "strategy of war" (e.g., United Nations Office of the High Commissioner for Human Rights 2008; Amnesty International 2013).

Cases in which rape and other forms of CRSV are employed as an element of military strategy likely exist, but a large share of this behavior appears to stem from other causes. Empirical studies suggest that purely strategic understandings of sexual violence are insufficient in many contexts. Sexual violence may be quite widespread without being systematic. In particular, Wood (2006, 2008, 2009) highlights sexual violence that occurs as a practice, rather than a strategy. A practice, in Wood's terms, is a behavior that diffuses through a group in a bottom-across, rather than a top-down, manner. That is, rather than ordering or encouraging sexual violence, armed group leaders simply fail to halt it.

> *Cases in which rape and other forms of CRSV are employed as an element of military strategy likely exist, but a large share of this behavior appears to stem from other causes.... Sexual violence may be quite widespread without being systematic.*

Recent studies at the sub-national (e.g., Gutierrez Sanín 2004; Wood 2009; Hoover Green 2011) and cross-national (e.g., Cohen 2013) levels suggest that armed group institutions, including those for recruitment, training, and discipline, may play crucial roles in determining whether sexual violence plays a role in an armed group's repertoire of action. Both Wood (2009) and Hoover Green (2011) emphasize the importance of command and control institutions within armed groups: they exert a disciplining effect in cases where sexual violence is limited, whereas they are lacking in cases where violence is more prevalent. Cohen (2013) emphasizes socialization within armed groups, arguing that rape—particularly gang rape—serves as a means of bonding among combatants who otherwise lack social cohesion. Of these accounts, only Cohen's is a causal account in the sense that it specifies a particular mechanism that leads to sexual violence. Wood and Hoover Green remain agnostic, to an extent, about the cause or causes of sexual violence. Instead, they focus on mechanisms that restrain sexual violence. Each finds that strong armed group leadership was necessary to successfully prohibit sexual violence.

Unresolved Questions

Despite significant recent advances, a number of basic questions about CRSV remain unanswered. Of particular note, the overall prevalence of CRSV is unknown. Statistically valid survey results for a number of populations have been published. Yet the multiple definitions of sexual violence employed in studies diminish their comparability. Also, the limited extent of high-quality societal-level estimates precludes global estimates. For many conflicts, not to mention all the distinct armed groups as well as locations and moments within conflicts, no rigorous estimates have been compiled. The convenience data that do exist are valuable, including as documentation of an ongoing human rights emergency and clues to broader patterns. Absent strong arguments that such data are representative in a given case, however, no population-level descriptive or causal inferences can be drawn.

> *Despite significant recent advances, a number of basic questions about CRSV remain unanswered. Of particular note, the overall prevalence of CRSV is unknown.... At an even more basic level, it is unclear whether best practices for measuring sexual violence, at either the individual or population level, are similar in peacetime and wartime.... Finally, many causal theories about sexual violence have been proposed, and much evidence for and against these theories considered, but it remains unresolved whether one or a few key causal dynamics underlie variation in sexual violence, or instead a shifting multitude of factors is at play.*

At an even more basic level, it is unclear whether best practices for measuring sexual violence, at either the individual or population level, are similar in peacetime and wartime. Several survey methods have been shown to produce higher reporting rates, but these studies generally concern college women in non-conflicted countries with relatively less serious taboos surrounding premarital sex and rape. Whether such methods, particularly the sorts of extremely direct and specific behavioral questions that have been investigated with American college women (Fisher 2009), would be equally effective—or ethical—in conflict-affected areas is uncertain. Women known to have participated in surveys about violence, including sexual violence and intimate-partner violence, may experience retaliatory violence or other negative outcomes (Swiss and Jennings 2006). Alternatively, people in conditions of extreme scarcity who believe that reporting sexual violence makes them more likely to receive aid may falsely report sexual violence (e.g., Utas 2005; Cohen and Hoover Green 2012).

For policy makers, unanswered questions concerning the magnitude and patterns of CRSV are, in effect, unanswered questions about resource allocation and program effectiveness. Without accurate, disaggregated data that describe the scale and dimensions of the problem, policy makers—particularly those whose remit is regional or national, rather than highly localized—cannot effectively plan interventions for survivors of CRSV. Many survivors may need emergency medical attention. Others may not be seriously physically injured but instead may require assistance rebuilding their lives, particularly where one's identity as a victim of sexual violence leads to social isolation. These services might include education, job training, financial assistance, or mental health interventions. Here again, the importance of specific, disaggregated data about both victims and perpetrators is clear.

Finally, many causal theories about sexual violence have been proposed, and much evidence for and against these theories considered, but it remains unresolved whether one or a few key causal dynamics underlie variation in sexual violence, or instead a shifting multitude of factors is at play. Advocates, researchers, and policy makers all prefer preventing CRSV to mitigating its damages; prevention ultimately requires understanding.

Conclusion

CRSV research has made significant advances toward explaining variation over the past decade. In that time, data on CRSV has moved from case studies of individual conflicts to comparative studies, incorporation of negative cases, cross-national data collection and micro-level comparisons. While both cross-national and micro-comparative accounts are important to our understandings of broad patterns, each approach faces considerable measurement difficulties. Efforts to analyze sexual violence at the cross-national level, via index measures (e.g., Cohen 2013), face all the difficulties of comparability and over-aggregation common to cross-national analyses more generally. Micro-comparative accounts, on the other hand, may be falsely precise, making inferences far beyond what the data support.

Solutions to these difficulties lie in several directions. First and most generally, CRSV researchers—particularly those from disciplines that prize causal inferences over descriptive accounts—must consider seriously the limits of their descriptive inferences and develop tools to consider the extent to which available data on sexual violence are likely to represent the underlying population. Second, researchers whose ultimate goal is causal inference would benefit immeasurably from partnerships with those whose work is fundamentally concerned with descriptive inference at the population level—statisticians, demographers, and epidemiologists, to name a few. This type of collaboration, if properly supported, could produce data that are simultaneously representative and disaggregable. Third, if systematic survey data ought to underlie our descriptive (and, ultimately, causal) inferences about CRSV, then it follows that researchers should consider the extent to which best practices in survey construction and enumeration may vary across contexts. Fourth, given the reality that valid, survey-based estimates sufficiently disaggregated to answer micro-comparative questions are unlikely to materialize in the near future, collaborative investigations, relying on multiple data types and sources (including assessments of potential data biases), must become the norm in this research area.

Much of the variation [in conflict-related sexual violence] occurs at the level of the armed group; consequently, policies that focus on differences among armed groups—rather than differences among conflicts, cultures, or countries—appear most likely to effectively prevent or control sexual violence.

Despite the continuing difficulties of collecting and analyzing CRSV, this research area has already yielded significant policy implications. First, as Cohen, Hoover Green, and Wood have written, "the high level of variation in sexual violence across conflicts and armed organizations implies that sexual violence in wartime is far from inevitable—and therefore that policy interventions can be effective at preventing or mitigating it" (12). Much of the variation occurs at the level of the armed group; consequently, policies that focus on differences among armed groups—rather than differences among conflicts, cultures, or countries—appear most likely to effectively prevent or control sexual violence.

A key implication of these findings is that armed groups themselves may be best equipped to create policies and institutions to control CRSV. In previous research (Hoover Green 2011), I found suggestive evidence that FMLN cadre, in El Salvador, successfully curbed sexual violence using a combination of strict discipline and political education. Despite a strict disciplinary code, FMLN leaders were troubled by reports of combatants "taking advantage of" civilian women and girls in the early years of the conflict. They soon introduced an education program that specifically addressed gender and sexual violence. Sexual assaults by FMLN cadre, already uncommon, became extremely rare as the conflict continued. Similarly, Wood (2009) attributes the extremely low level of sexual violence by the Tamil Tigers of Sri Lanka to a combination of rather ascetic ideals and extremely efficient monitoring and discipline by high-level officers.

Research on CRSV has also overturned conventional wisdoms about who suffers rape and other forms of sexual violence and who is likely to perpetrate it. Most evidence suggests that women are disproportionately targeted for sexual violence in most conflicts, but they are far from the only victims. Women and non-combatants, as well as male soldiers, perpetrate wartime sexual violence. Clearly, such findings imply that policy makers must craft programs that can accommodate both male and female perpetrators and victims, and that include both combatants and non-combatants.

Finally, it is now clear that CRSV is not necessarily a "weapon of war." Its causes are many. Despite press coverage and other campaigns that frequently portray sexual violence as strategic, efforts focused on increasing the expected cost of ordering sexual violence might better be directed at informing armed group leaders of methods for successfully prohibiting sexual violence. While some leaders undoubtedly continue to order or expressly condone sexual violence, others recognize that sexual violence is illegal, unethical, and—perhaps most important—poisonous to relations with civilian populations. Policy makers can and should engage these armed group leaders, and the combatants serving under them, wherever possible.

10. LOCALIZING PEACE, RECONSTRUCTION, AND THE EFFECTS OF MASS VIOLENCE

Patrick Vinck and Phuong N. Pham

Effective peacebuilding requires an understanding of the nature and impact of violence on civilians, the drivers of this violence, and individuals' priorities for peace and security. Involvement of the population in planning and implementing peacebuilding is especially important to mitigate the risks of future violence and to enable "a democratization of the transition process, securing legitimacy and public accountability for the policies set forth" (World Bank 2011). It also results in programs that better address the needs of the population and are aligned with their culture and values.

Civilians represent a large proportion of war victims, often as a result of deliberate and systematic mass violence against entire populations (Humphreys and Weinstein 2006). This is especially true during internal conflicts, when civilian communities may be targeted because of their alleged support to warring factions (Colaresi and Carey 2008). In conflict-affected settings, many people may have suffered the loss of family or friends, the loss of property, or other forms of trauma. These individuals and communities are central to peacebuilding processes. Their experiences of and views about the conflict can be expected to shape their attitudes toward peacebuilding efforts, influencing whether or not they receive support and unaddressed grievances and inequalities present risks of future violence and relapse into conflict. Those affected by violence may constitute groups actively favoring or opposing societal repair and long-term development, depending on factors such as exposures to violence, harms, trauma, socio-economic status, and identity. Antagonism and fear between communities, and resorting to self-defense or aggression, may also prolong violence or renew conflicts.

Despite the value of participatory approaches for violence-affected communities, the delivery of peace is frequently carried out as a top-down process. Mediation of conflicts is done at the highest level, between governments in the case of interstate conflict and between a government and armed groups in the case of intrastate conflicts, typically with little or no consultation—let alone representation—of affected populations. In particular, states and international actors play key roles in setting a transitional agenda and making and implementing policies to provide security, establish legitimate institutions, revitalize the economy and social service delivery, and promote social cohesion.

Local participatory processes that involve violence-affected communities in identifying and implementing peacebuilding priorities are the exception, rather than the rule. Even when conflict-affected populations are taken into account, their expectations are broadly assumed to be about peace and security, satisfying basic needs for food and shelter, returning to a normal life, and obtaining reparation and justice. The possibility that individuals' social-economic and cultural characteristics and personal experiences of violence influence their support for peace initiatives is underexplored. In recent years, however, perspectives of relevant individuals and communities in locations around the world have been captured efficiently and effectively via an assortment of social science research methods, including surveys, key informant interviews, and focus groups.

Table 10.1 Overview of Studies

Year	Country	Method	Sample Size	Related Products
2005	Northern Uganda	Survey	2,571	Pham et al. (2005)
2006	Northern Uganda	Existing records	25,231	Pham, Vinck, and Stover (2008)
2007	Democratic Republic of the Congo	Survey Survey	3,753 150 human rights organizations	Vinck and Pham (2008); Vinck et al. (2008); Pham, Vinck, and Weinstein (2010)
2007	Northern Uganda	Survey In-depth interviews	2,875 30	Pham et al. (2007); Pham, Vinck, and Stover (2009); Vinck and Pham (2009)
2008	Cambodia	Survey	1,000	Pham et al. (2009)
2009	Central African Republic	Survey In-depth interviews	1,879 150	Vinck and Pham (2010a, 2010b, 2010c)
2010	Northern Uganda	Survey In-depth interviews	2,498 100	Pham and Vinck (2010)
2010	Cambodia	Survey In-depth interviews	1,000 75	Pham et al. (2011)
2010	Liberia	Survey	4,501	Vinck, Pham, and Kreutzer (2011); Vinck and Pham (2013)
2010	Philippines	Survey	2,759	WFP-WBG (2011)

This chapter examines how the insights from such studies can help shape peacebuilding and social reconstruction policy and initiatives, especially at the local level. First, we examine patterns of exposures to violence, to challenge the notion of victims as a homogeneous group. Second, we examine perceptions of the root causes of violence. Third, we build on that information to contextualize priorities and views about the means to sustain peace and improve security. Our discussion is grounded in a novel set of studies we have conducted in multiple countries affected by mass violence. Table 10.1 offers an overview of these studies; the data and products are also featured on the PeacebuildingData website (http://www.peacebuildingdata.org). Further studies remain ongoing in several countries (Cambodia, Côte d'Ivoire, Democratic Republic of the Congo).

Notes on Methodology

Until the last decade, collection of primary data at the individual and community levels to gauge the characteristics and consequences of large-scale violence was limited, outside of select studies with a narrow focus from particular disciplines (e.g., anthropology, public health, law, international justice, political science). Among the actors directly involved in conflict resolution and peacebuilding (e.g., governments, United Nations agencies, rebel groups), relatively few have conducted systematic consultations with local populations. Even civil society organizations—including those in the human rights field—that engage closely with these populations do not necessarily compile detailed information about their experiences, with some exceptions, such as Physicians for Human Rights.

> *Until the last decade, collection of primary data at the individual and community levels to gauge the characteristics and consequences of large-scale violence was limited, outside of select studies with a narrow focus from particular disciplines.*

Early on, we recognized the need to analyze data about violence, its impact, and the prospect for durable solutions (e.g., peace and justice) and reconstruction in a complementary way. Studies on the prevalence of violence existed and sometimes considered long-term effects on health, mental health, or livelihood outcomes, but rarely focused on the association between experiences of violence and attitudes about reconstruction. Furthermore, there was a need for rigorous research methods that provide an adequate basis for scientific estimates of patterns and trends, generating statistical data on the impact of the conflict and social behaviors that were lacking. Also, the studies were initially designed to inform emerging transitional justice mechanisms, including the International Criminal Court and other international tribunals, about the role that such institutions may have in countries affected by mass violence.

To address these needs and objectives, we adopted a mixed-method approach. One component is large population-based surveys with a mixture of close-ended questions yielding highly structured quantitative data and open-ended questions yielding rich qualitative data. Another component is in-depth key informant interviews.

The survey method relies predominantly on a random selection of respondents, typically using multistage cluster sampling procedures. First, administrative units are selected based on population estimates. Next, households are selected using either lists of households, if available, or geolocation methods. Finally, individuals are selected using lists of all eligible individuals in the household. The sampling universe is the entire adult population. Thus, the surveys provide representative data about this group. The rationale for a large population survey is that a narrower focus on specific victim groups or key informants, such as national and local leaders, politicians, or peacebuilders, would not necessarily represent the views of all those who were victimized (Weinstein et al. 2010).

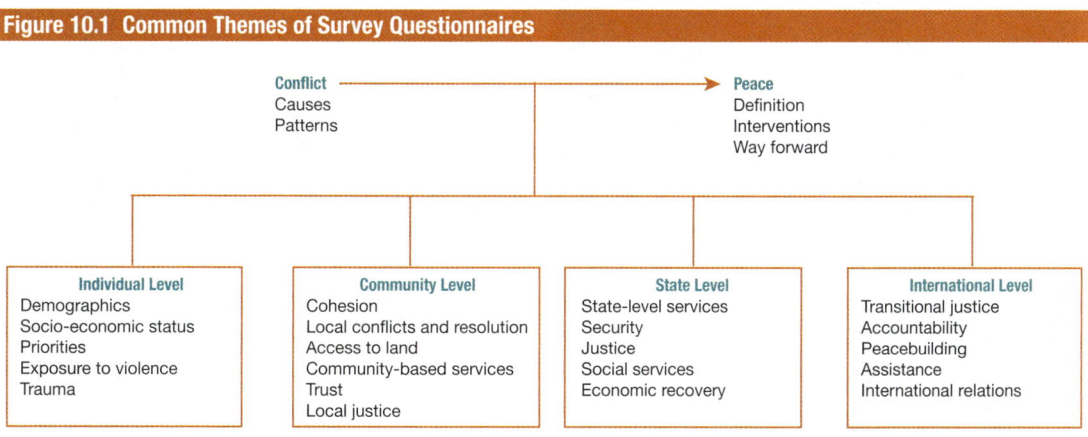

Figure 10.1 Common Themes of Survey Questionnaires

To facilitate cross-national comparison, the basic structure of the survey questionnaires is standardized. Figure 10.1 shows the themes that are covered. Aspects of the questionnaires are tailored for each context, incorporating inputs from local experts. As much as possible, questions use an open-ended format. Response options are never suggested or read to respondents, except when they are asked to answer using Likert scales (e.g., rank access to services from very good to very bad). This technique combines the strength of qualitative methods with quantitative survey design.

The basic objective of the surveys is to understand the relation between conflict and peace and responses at the individual, community, state, and international levels. For each level, the survey explores a number of factors relating to individual perceptions and attitudes. This approach enables multivariate and other advanced statistical analyses, to illuminate individual-level decision making on specific topics such as resettlement and risk factors for local violence, including intimate-partner violence and land conflicts, and broader influences that shape views on peace and justice.

The survey ordinarily takes an hour to administer. Although the interviews are relatively long, the process has proven to be viable across contexts. Most respondents have rarely, if ever, been asked about their views on issues directly affecting them. Various elements of the process are designed to make the respondents feel comfortable to respond to questions openly and honestly. In particular, participation is always voluntary, and information is collected confidentially and generally anonymously. Also, data are collected by trained interviewers who typically match the gender of the respondents.

Figure 10.2 Digital Data Collection as an Innovation in Survey Research

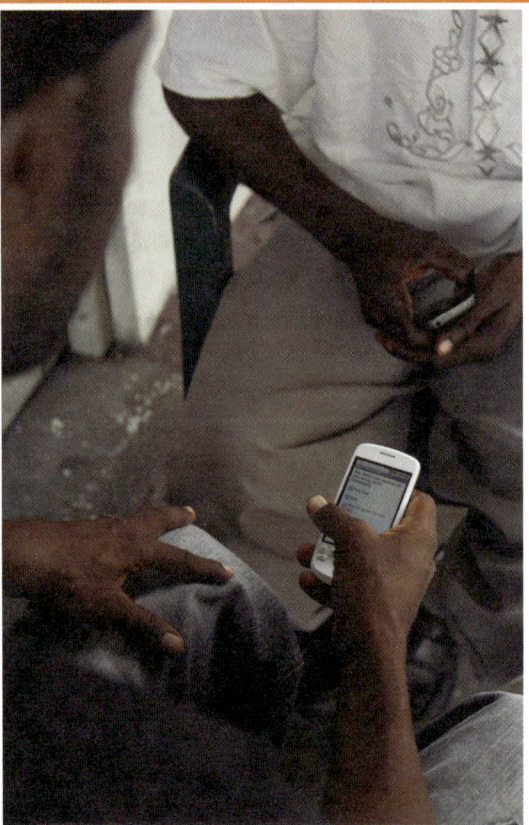

Note: Interviewers using smartphones running KoBoToolbox to record survey responses in Liberia (left) and the Central African Republic (right). Pictures taken by authors during training and mock interviews.

Recognizing the need for rapid processing of the survey answers, in order to provide timely actionable data, the process now relies on digital data collection technology (see Figure 10.2). As a baseline for comparison, an assessment we conducted in Iraq after the fall of Baghdad in 2003 took over a year and a half to produce results because of the time needed for translation, data entry, data cleaning, analysis, and report writing. Digital data collection substantially reduces that time by requiring interviewers to directly encode responses in a digital format, via either a smartphone or tablets running a dedicated software that we created (http://www.kobotoolbox.org). Survey responses are then seamlessly compiled, resulting in a usable database that can be updated daily as data collection progresses. The process can operate with or without telecommunications connectivity (i.e., phone line and/or Internet service) and access to electricity. Information can be downloaded manually or automatically from the data collection device, as warranted. Solar and car chargers provide alternative sources of power. As a further benefit, the technology has built-in verification that reduces the risk of skipping questions or entering erroneous values, resulting in higher quality data compared to paper-based methods. These tools are easily adopted by interviewers with no or little computer literacy.

An essential part of research is dissemination of results, which increasingly relies on technology in addition to in-country outreach. Figure 10.3 shows a snapshot of the PeacebuildingData website, which was developed to provide access to survey data and results, including interactive maps. The mapping capability is especially important to allow the visualization of variation at the sub-national level. Users can thereby conduct their own analysis and arrive at independent conclusions. The website and maps are designed for low bandwidth, to make them more accessible from countries with poor connectivity. In fact, Africa accounts for about 12.5 percent of the traffic on the website. Access to the Internet, however, remains limited, and more active forms of dissemination, which capitalize on media that are more universal, are also used. We have provided results to the community using radio, in some places allowing the listeners to call in questions. In addition, we always organize local dissemination workshops to discuss the results and arrange for one-on-one meetings with key policy makers and implementers.

From Victim to Victims

As mentioned at the outset, a large segment of the population may be exposed to violence and associated effects during a conflict. Individuals may have experienced physical violence, imprisonment, or displacement, had their property seized or destroyed, or lost financial resources. They may also witness such crimes or experience them through a family member. In addition, they may suffer from the consequences of the conflict, such as reduced access to health or educational facilities, whether because of insecurity or because those services are interrupted (Iacopino et al. 2001; de Jong et al. 2001). Yet the extent of victimization due to conflict and its implications for conflict resolution and peacebuilding measures still tend to be poorly assessed.

> *The notion of a victim as an innocent or vulnerable party who deserves recognition and attention, if not repair, is challenged by the diversity of experience and the increasingly blurred distinction between victim, bystander, and perpetrator, especially in contexts where abduction and forced recruitment prevail.*

In this section, we examine how the term "victim" actually covers a large number of individuals with very different experience of conflict, which in turn leads to different needs and expectations. The notion of a victim as an innocent or vulnerable party who deserves

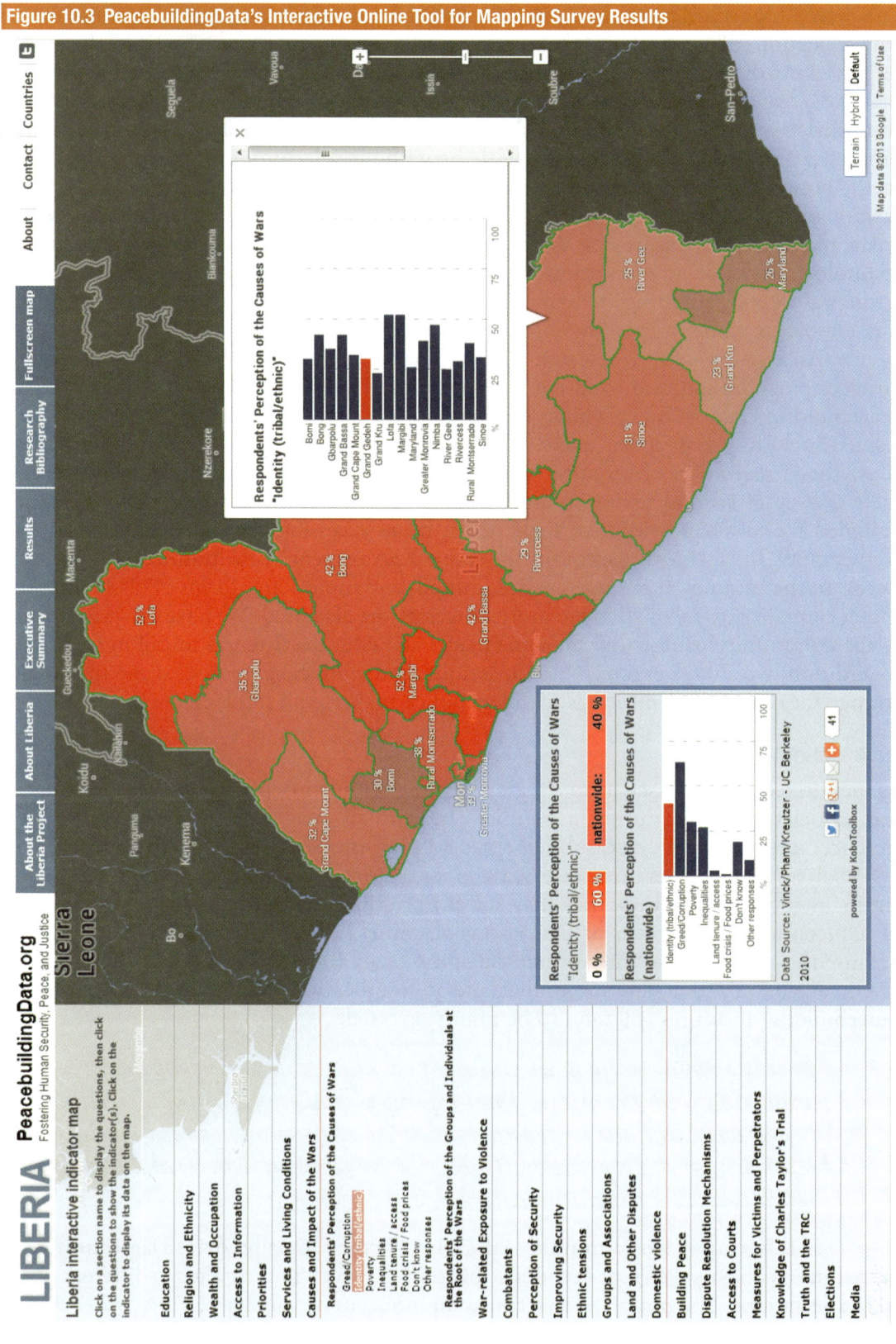

Figure 10.3 PeacebuildingData's Interactive Online Tool for Mapping Survey Results

recognition and attention, if not repair, is challenged by the diversity of experience and the increasingly blurred distinction between victim, bystander, and perpetrator, especially in contexts where abduction and forced recruitment prevail.

Violence against civilians has important, long-term consequences. A large number of adults may have been killed or migrated during the conflict. More generally, high rates of mortality, injuries, and disabilities, including mental trauma, affect the current and future availability of a productive workforce. The education of children may be delayed or hampered. Individuals may no longer invest in the development of livelihood skills and productive assets because they fear losing them. Even years after a conflict, individuals who were exposed to potentially traumatic events continue to be at increased risk of perpetrating intimate-partner physical violence (Vinck and Pham 2013). Witnessing abuses may be associated with violent behavior later in life, as has been documented among male children (APA 1996; Verdú et al. 2008). These experiences are potential risk factors for continued violence or new conflicts. It may, for example, create grievances against individuals or communities, especially where conflicts are fought along ethnic lines, perpetuating a cycle of violence. A range of conflicts may also emerge as displaced individuals return home to find their properties destroyed or used by others.

Despite the evident variety of experiences, a typical approach of peacebuilding is to label all exposed individuals with terms such as "affected communities," "victims," or "survivors." Often at best, there may be some recognition that specific crimes or groups of victims exist. For example, women disproportionately experience sexual violence, coercion, and enslavement at the hand of armed groups (Swiss et al. 1998; Amowitz et al. 2002). Women may also be more likely to suffer from indirect consequences of the conflict (UNICEF 2004). In conjunction, gender-based violence is increasingly given attention in peacebuilding processes. Other groups may be recognized because they are considered the most victimized, or because they hold specific knowledge or positions in the communities (e.g., traditional and religious leaders, civil society representatives).

These approaches, however, fail to recognize the range of exposures to violence among conflict-affected populations. In the process, they may also leave out groups that are less organized or not considered to be as much victims as others. This can have a tangible impact, such as limiting access to services and benefits allocated only to victims.

Our studies consistently show that large majorities of the populations of conflict-affected countries consider themselves to be victims. Even in Cambodia, 30 years after the Khmer Rouge was forced out of power, 80 percent of our survey respondents considered themselves to be victims, including 93 percent who lived under the regime and 51 percent of those who did not. This illustrates the long-term impact of violence and potentially persistent grievances.

There is accumulating evidence that those with differing exposures to violence may have different needs and expectations during and after conflicts (Beber, Roessler, and Scacco 2012; Pham, Weinstein, and Longman 2004; Vinck et al. 2007). The surveys we have conducted allow the exploration of various experiences of violence by capturing self-reported exposure to different types of violations observed during conflicts. The list is specific to each of the situations surveyed, but also includes common events. The results concern situations with various geographies, timelines, and dynamics, which limit comparability between surveys. Nonetheless, some general findings emerge, including the high exposure to violence, reflecting the substantial toll on civilians.

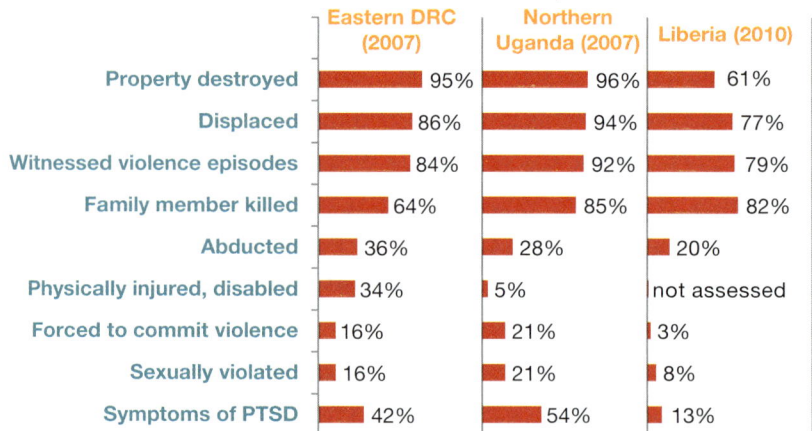

Figure 10.4 Cross-National Comparison of Select Exposures to Conflict

Figure 10.4 presents the prevalence of exposure to various forms of violence in eastern DRC, northern Uganda, and Liberia, which suffered recent mass violence. Nearly everyone in all three places is affected by certain exposures, including displacement, the destruction of property, and witnessing violence. Other types, including direct exposure to violence and sexual violence, and injuries, affect a smaller proportion of individuals. Finally, the shares of individuals affected by coercion vary across countries.

The circumstance of being forced to commit violence, which is strongly associated with abduction, highlights the complexity of the notion of victims. Some individuals' experiences make them as much perpetrators—with at least some complicity, even if not directly implicated in violations—as victims. In northern Uganda alone, where abduction has been a core recruitment tactic for the Lord's Resistance Army, 39 percent of those who were abducted reported having been forced to loot, 20 percent were forced to beat someone, and 9 percent were forced to kill someone. As the length of abduction increased, the proportion of those forced to commit violence increased. Among those abducted for at least a week, those frequencies increased to 59 percent, 33 percent, and 14 percent, respectively. Among those who were abducted by the LRA for at least a year, 90 percent were forced to loot, 74 percent were forced to beat someone, and 50 percent were forced to kill someone (Pham, Vinck, and Stover 2009).

Considering the extent of the violence, the results suggest that nearly everyone can be considered as victimized by the conflict. At the same time, the differences in patterns of exposure tend to result in weighing gravity as a basis for determining victimhood, considering criteria such as the number of exposures, the types, and subjective assessments of their severity. This approach has serious implications, as it leads to ranking individual suffering and, in turn, prioritizes the needs and expectations of some in a context of limited resources. Assistance programs, for example, typically focus on specific groups of victims (e.g., female victims of sexual violence, victims with medical needs), while the rest remain largely unrecognized as deserving this status.

Assistance programs...typically focus on specific groups of victims... while the rest remain largely unrecognized as deserving this status.

From the insights on individuals' experience of the conflict, we can start unpacking the concept of victimhood. Several empirical approaches have been employed in the literature to define categories of victims, based on physiological factors (e.g., injuries), sociological factors (e.g., level of disruption), economic factors (e.g., property loss), total exposure, or measures of psychological impact (e.g., Post-Traumatic Stress Disorder).

Our research introduces another useful way to think about victims, utilizing a latent class analysis (LCA) of the survey data on exposure to violence. LCA is a statistical method for finding subtypes of related cases. Given a number of cases, the method explores a series of variables to determine a small number of groups in which those cases can be classified (Tabachnick and Fidell 2006). Applying the method to survey data from conflict-affected populations suggests four classes with compound exposure to violence:

- Those with *general exposure*, reflecting the most common events that affect nearly everyone, including displacement and the destruction and loss of properties.

- Those who *witnessed violence*, observing atrocities firsthand. In addition, they typically experienced general exposures to violence.

- Those who had a *direct exposure to the conflict*, in the form of physical experiences of violence and/or threats. Most of these individuals also experienced general exposures and were witnesses.

- Those *coerced by armed groups* through abduction and forcible recruitment to loot or commit violence. Most of these individuals experienced general exposures, witnessing, and direct exposures.

Figure 10.5 presents the original LCA using data from the survey we conducted in northern Uganda in 2005 (Vinck et al. 2007). The results illustrate how the patterns of exposure to violence differ in conspicuous ways across the four classes.

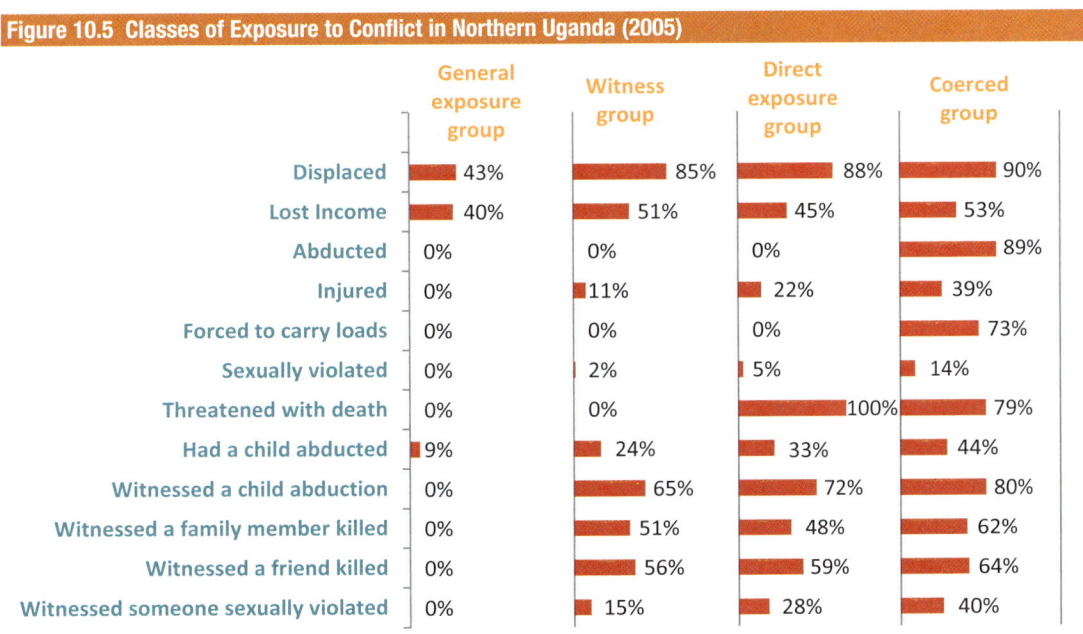

Figure 10.5 Classes of Exposure to Conflict in Northern Uganda (2005)

	General exposure group	Witness group	Direct exposure group	Coerced group
Displaced	43%	85%	88%	90%
Lost Income	40%	51%	45%	53%
Abducted	0%	0%	0%	89%
Injured	0%	11%	22%	39%
Forced to carry loads	0%	0%	0%	73%
Sexually violated	0%	2%	5%	14%
Threatened with death	0%	0%	100%	79%
Had a child abducted	9%	24%	33%	44%
Witnessed a child abduction	0%	65%	72%	80%
Witnessed a family member killed	0%	51%	48%	62%
Witnessed a friend killed	0%	56%	59%	64%
Witnessed someone sexually violated	0%	15%	28%	40%

This analysis allows us to better understand what "affected communities" means in the context of violence against civilians. It shows that there may not be such a thing as "victims," at least not one that is reasonably understood as a single, monolithic category. Instead, there is a collection of individuals with various patterns of experience of conflict. The patterns described here for northern Uganda have proved useful when examining other contexts. The underlying proposition, however, is not that these classes should be considered standard across situations. Understanding distinctive patterns of exposure to violence is necessary to elucidate one of the key underlying factors shaping perception and attitudes toward peace and reconstruction. In Uganda, for example, we found significant differences across the classes of victims in the prevalence of manifestations of trauma like post-traumatic stress disorder. Mental health problems, in turn, were associated with a more negative outlook on peace, and higher support for violent means to end the conflict. These relationships indicate that understanding the characteristics of the people affected by violence is critical when considering options for peacebuilding policies.

Local Drivers of Conflict

Effective peacebuilding requires understanding the drivers of violence. Studies identify numerous risk factors, including exclusion and inequality affecting regional, religious, or ethnic groups (Stewart 2005), poverty, and limited or unequal access to natural resources.

Our surveys highlight the multi-dimensional causes of violence. The factors respondents most often identify—which deviate across countries—are (1) power struggles, the exploitation of natural resources and land, ethnic divisions, and problems of nationality [eastern DRC], (2) power struggles and fighting for independence [Mindanao, the Philippines], (3) greed, ethnic tensions and inequalities, and poverty [Liberia], (4) power struggles, poverty, ethnic divisions, and the exploitation of natural resources [Central African Republic], and (5) regional disparities, power struggles, and ideologies [northern Uganda]. These findings emphasize the importance of security, economic, and political factors, including entrenching principles of good governance, so violence is not seen as a means to gain power. Structural inequalities must also be addressed.

The survey results also highlight important local dynamics. For example, inequalities were seen as major drivers of wars by respondents in the northwestern part of Liberia, but seldom mentioned in the southeast (see Figure 10.6, from PeacebuildingData). Less pronounced sub-national disparities were observed for greed/corruption and tribal/ethnic identity. Views about poverty as a cause of wars were more consistent throughout the country. By comparison, in some areas of Mindanao, the Philippines, respondents identified the fight for self-determination as the root cause of the violence in some areas, whereas in other areas respondents accorded precedence to clans fighting for power.

Local Priorities

A major challenge in countries affected by mass violence is that peacebuilding hinges on a lengthy list of reforms, including establishing security, institutionalizing a legitimate government, and strengthening service delivery (Brinkerhoff and Brinkerhoff 2002). In the early 1990s, post-conflict interventions emphasized economic and social reconstruction (Hänggi 2005). Current approaches suggest that citizen security, justice, and jobs should be prioritized, with most other reforms—including political reform and democratization, decentralization, privatization, and promoting changes in social attitudes—needing to be

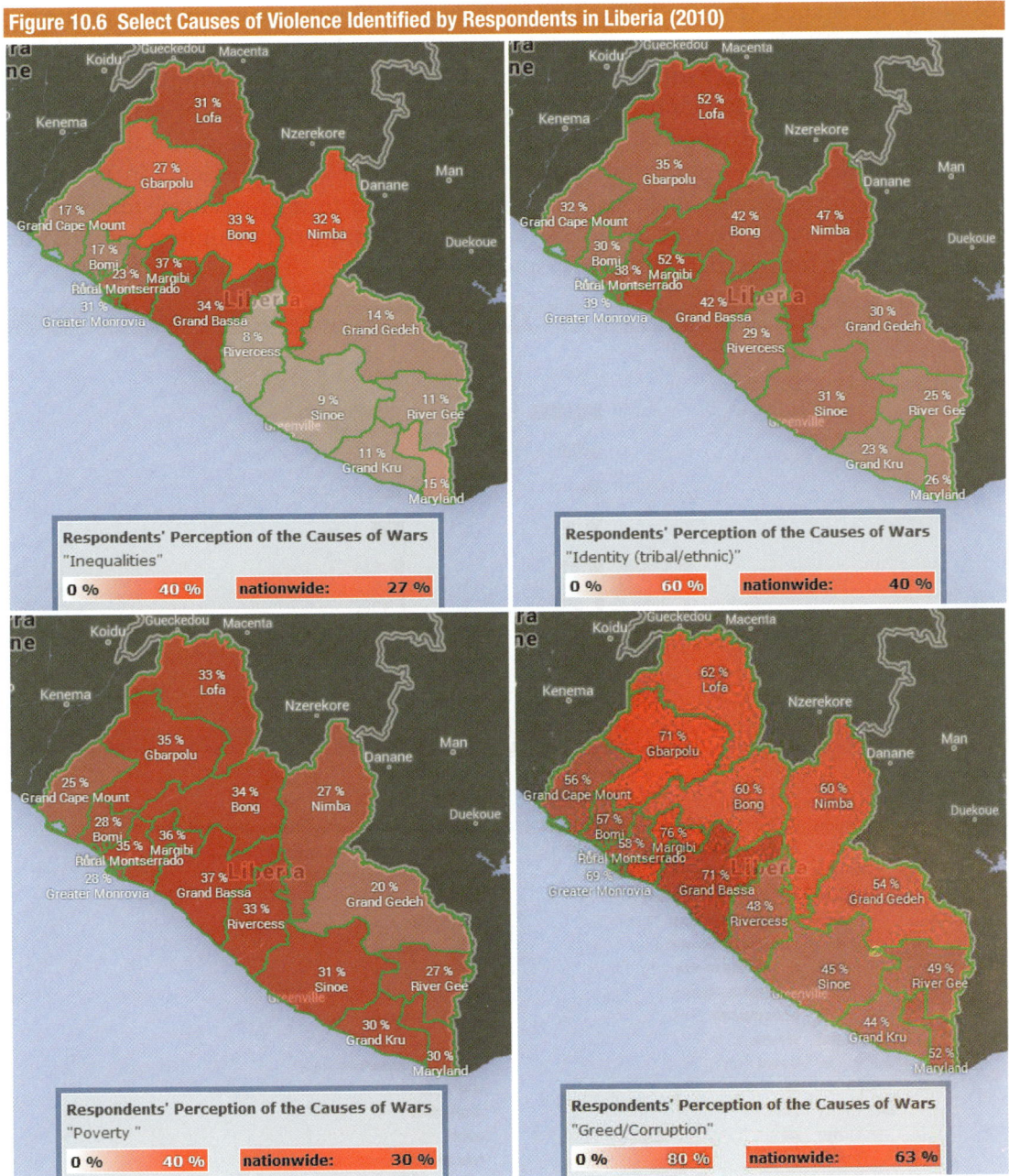

Figure 10.6 Select Causes of Violence Identified by Respondents in Liberia (2010)

sequenced and paced over time (World Bank 2011). Peacebuilding approaches frequently include pillars such as strengthening governance and state presence, economic recovery, and access to social services, which can take decades to be accomplished.

Our research reveals that local priorities differ from this broad agenda and vary over time. Consider, for instance, the example of Uganda. In 2005, when we conducted an initial survey (Pham et al. 2005), there was relative security and ongoing peace talks between the Lord's Resistance Army and the government of Uganda. By 2010, when we conducted a follow-up survey (Pham and Vinck 2010), peace talks had collapsed, but the Lord's Resistance Army had left northern Uganda, allowing people to start returning home. This change in context is reflected in priorities cited by respondents, as displayed in Figure 10.7. In the 2005 survey, we found that respondents' main priorities were food, peace, and social services, including health and education. Also, 59 percent of respondents defined peace as the absence of violence, compared to 18 percent who said freedom and 17 percent who said returning home. Just 5 percent of respondents in the 2010 survey mentioned peace as their main priority, compared to 24 percent of respondents in the previous survey. Meanwhile, access to land and farming opportunities had become important issues for significantly more respondents.

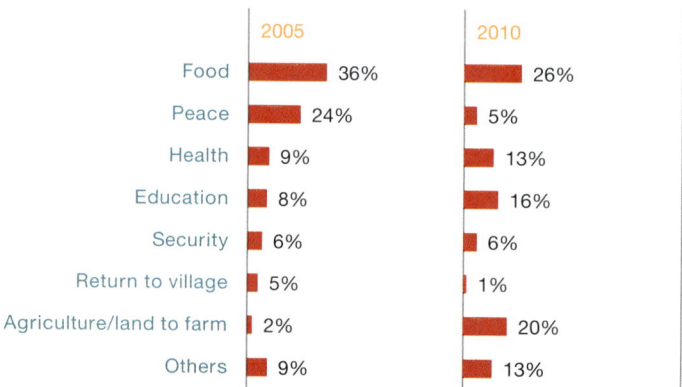

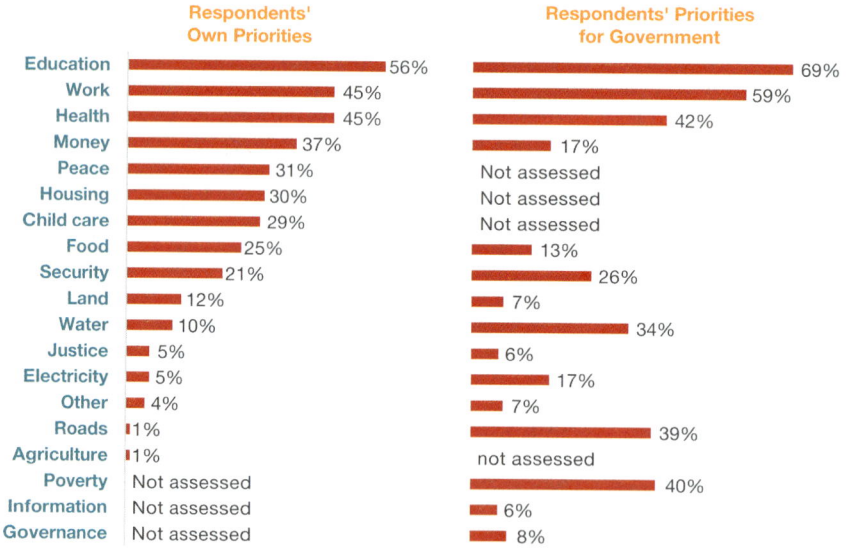

People also make distinctions with respect to the priorities of different actors. In Liberia, for example, respondents were asked to distinguish between their own priorities at the time of the 2010 survey (seven years after the end of the conflict) and what they thought the government should prioritize. As Figure 10.8 shows, there is consistency in some areas, with education, work, and health ranking at the top of both lists, while land and justice ranked near the bottom. Yet noteworthy differences were observed. A miniscule share of respondents mentioned roads among their own priorities, but nearly 40 percent said roads should be a priority of the government. Similarly, a small fraction mentioned water as a personal priority, but more than one-third said water should be a priority of the government. These results suggest that people assign distinctive priorities to the government, with a greater emphasis on infrastructure, reflecting what they may see as the appropriate responsibility of the state. The need for infrastructure was voiced most strongly in Sinoe and Grand Kru Counties, which are located in the remote southeastern part of Liberia. In these two counties, over 70 percent of the population mentioned road improvements as a task that ought to be undertaken by the government, and consultations revealed that accessibility and road construction were viewed as a precondition for all other peacebuilding and development priorities.

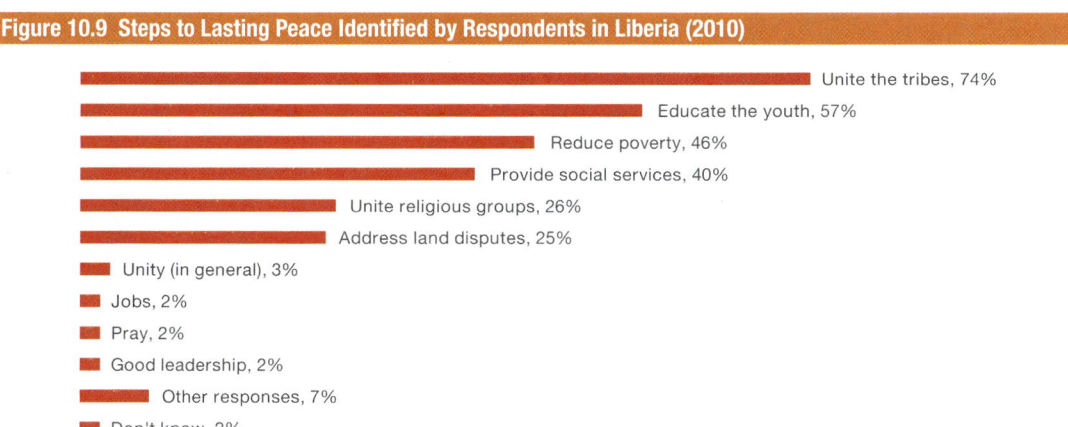

In addition, respondents were asked to specify what they thought should be done to build a lasting peace in Liberia. As Figure 10.9 shows, unity between tribes led the list by a large margin, cited by nearly three-quarters of respondents, while a majority cited education of youth. Poverty reduction and service provision also received substantial attention. Meaningful geographic differences was again observed. For example, over 60 percent of the respondents in the central and northwestern counties of Bong, Grand Bassa, Lofa, Margibi, and Nimba advanced uniting tribes, compared to less than 40 percent in the southeastern counties of Grand Kru, Maryland, and River Gee.

These results show that establishing priorities is complex, and attitudes vary widely across and within countries, as well as over time. The deviations may reflect differences in experiences of the conflict and the local socio-economic context, as well as in perceptions of the root causes of conflicts and current conditions. Left unaddressed, priorities may become frustrations and then grievances that may undermine a peacebuilding process. Rigorous and continuous collection of primary data that is representative of the population and can be disaggregated at sub-national levels is essential to be able to guide peacebuilding and reconstruction efforts that properly address local priorities and needs.

Local Security

The value of disaggregated data to inform peacebuilding efforts is further illustrated when addressing the provision of security. The goal of rebuilding domestic capacity to provide security beyond peacekeeping interventions has become increasingly central over the last two decades. The result is the emergence and promotion of security sector reform (SSR) as an essential set of reforms. The focus of SSR, however, is typically on good governance in the security sector (Ball 2001), working at the macro level to ensure that legal regimes are enforced and police and armed forces are accountable.

At the local level, however, security has a much more concrete and practical connotation. Without sufficient levels of security, the outcomes are things like individuals being unable to go to their fields and access to—or the delivery of—basic health care, education, or other social services is severely hampered. Training and deploying the police or other security actors may be a plausible priority for peacebuilding, but at the local level, what security means, and how to achieve it, may be entirely different.

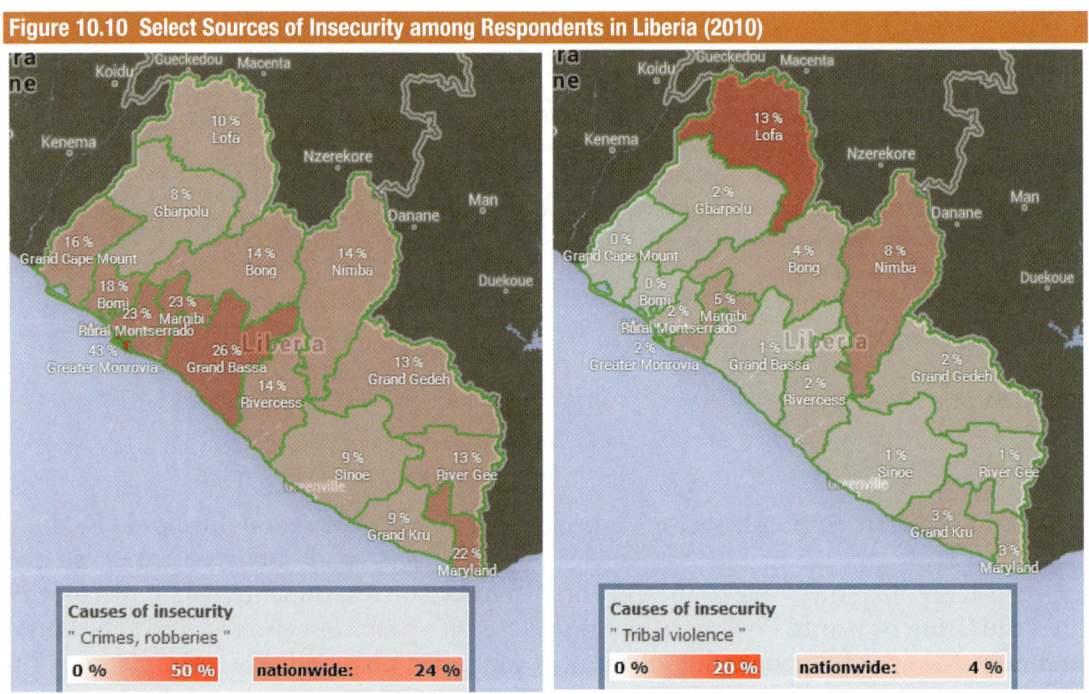

Figure 10.10 Select Sources of Insecurity among Respondents in Liberia (2010)

Returning to Liberia, 55 percent of respondents ranked themselves as being generally safe or very safe from harm at the time of the survey. Yet important geographic differences were observed, with the lowest shares in the capital of Monrovia (37 percent) and neighboring rural parts of Montserrado County (42 percent). Identified sources of insecurity likewise varied geographically, as Figure 10.10 (from PeacebuildingData) shows. Crimes and robberies were the main source cited in Greater Monrovia (43 percent). Ethnic tensions were reported as a source of insecurity nationally by four percent of the population, but in Lofa County, the share was 13 percent. Lofa also exhibited the largest share of respondents who reported experiencing ethnic problems. They attributed the problems to (1) perceived inherent violence of the opposed group, (2) pre-existing hatred from the other group, and (3) perceived unfair treatment by the opposed group. Sources of tension can also be inferred by analyzing responses by ethnic groups. For example, among the Loma respondents, 19 percent reported ethnic problems, the highest proportion in any ethnic group. They associated ethnic problems almost entirely with the

Mandingo (17 percent). The Mandingo respondents had the second highest proportion of reported ethnic problems, but the problems were associated with 11 other groups, including the Loma (7 percent), Gio (4 percent), and Kpelle (4 percent). The Loma and Mandingo are mostly located in Lofa County, where they account for 38 percent and 15 percent of the population, respectively.

Despite the relatively high level of reported security and the priority given to citizen security in peacebuilding, about one-third of respondents indicated that nobody provides security in their community. Across the counties, 15 to 40 percent mentioned the police as providing security. Other actors had regional importance, such as local defense and community watch teams, which were frequent in the northeast, while rubber companies played a significant role in the northwest. Most respondents (86 percent) indicated that disputes are primarily resolved by local village or town leaders, rather than security forces associated with the national government.

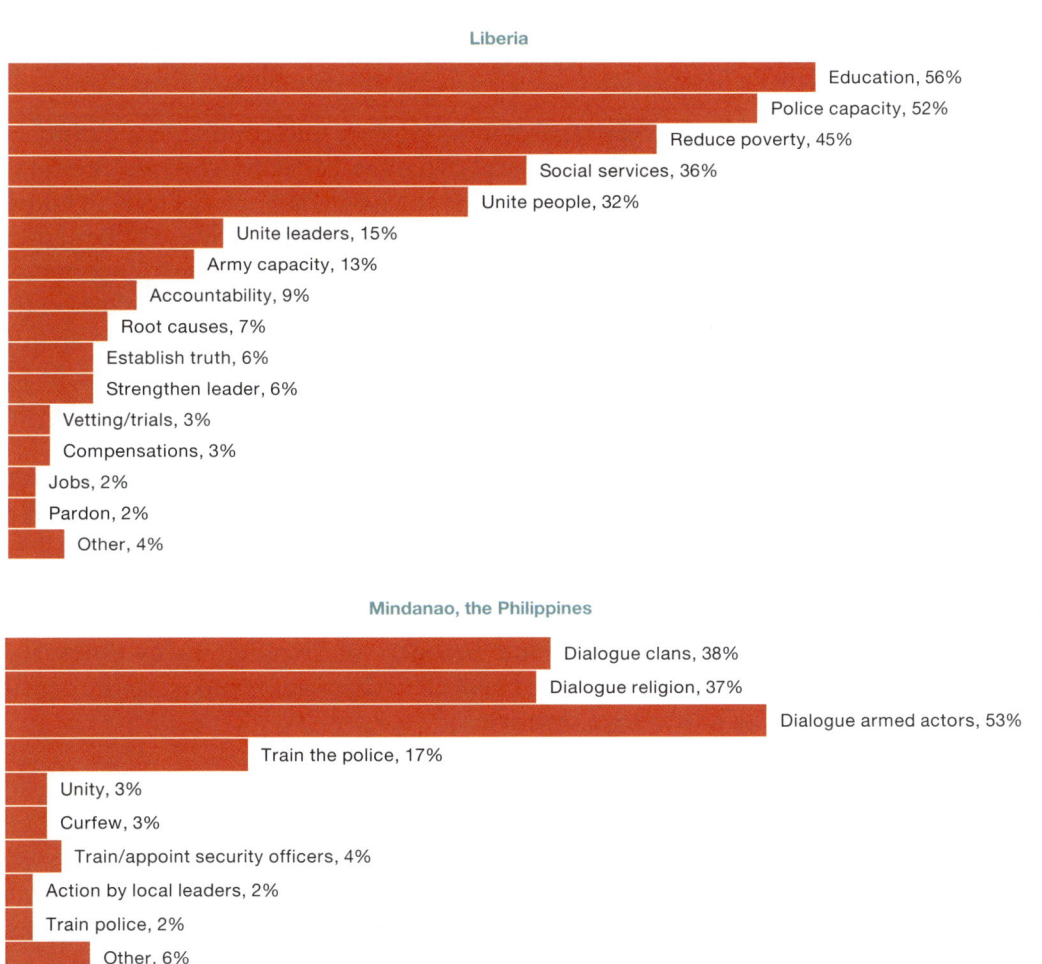

Figure 10.11 Means for Security among Respondents in Liberia (2010) and Mindanao, the Philippines (2010)

Importantly, local considerations on how to improve security may not reflect typical SSR strategies. As Figure 10.11 shows, respondents in Liberia emphasized the need for education, poverty reduction, social services, and social cohesion programs as part of a strategy to improve security. They also mentioned more typical SSR approaches, including improving the capacity of the police and the army, and increasing the accountability of these actors, including via vetting processes.

By contrast, the set of proposed strategies to improve security was vastly different in Mindanao, the Philippines. In particular, dialogue and social cohesion among clans, religious groups, and political and armed groups were emphasized. Training the police was also mentioned, but much less frequently. Within the country, important differences were observed. Of note, the need for dialogue between clans or dialogue between religious groups depended on the local context and heterogeneity of the population.

The results from Liberia and the Philippines illustrate the wide range of options advanced by populations when asked about how to improve security in their communities and, perhaps more important, the significant differences at the sub-national level. This variation highlights the limitations of global or national policy strategy templates that do not take into account local variations in context, experiences of violence, and overall behavior and attitudes among the population.

Conclusion

In this chapter, we examined some key aspects linking peace and conflict as a national or even global issue with peace and conflict as a local dynamic. In the process, we questioned the link between strategies designed and deployed at the national or global level to address circumstances and needs at the local level in conflict-affected settings. We raised questions around the concept of victims, suggesting that it is a complex notion that encompasses individuals with diverse experiences of conflict, which may at times blur the distinction between victims, perpetrators, and bystanders. These experiences contribute to shaping attitudes about peace and multiple aspects of reconstruction, such as resettlement and the reintegration of former combatants, which can compete with or even contradict one another among various victim groups.

We also observed that views on the root causes of the conflict, localized priorities, and perceptions of security needs may differ from what is favored and implemented on a national level, with important regional variation. For example, insecurity in Liberia is primarily understood as resulting from low-level criminality, while ethnic tension is important only in some areas of the country. While SSR is part of the solution, the population generally advanced education and broader social programs as essential to improve security. In the Philippines, dialogue between various actors linked to the conflict was seen as the primary way to improve security.

Views on the root causes of conflict, localized priorities, and perceptions of security needs may differ from what is favored and implemented on a national level, with important regional variation.

These are far from the only insights gained from population-based consultations in conflict-affected settings. Other studies have shown that experiences of violence may be associated with shifting support for warring parties (Lyall, Imai, Blair 2011), greater levels of social engagement (Bellows and Miguel 2009; Blattman 2009), and attitudes toward accountability and justice for perpetrators of the violence (Vinck 2007; Pham, Weinstein, and Longman 2007).

Together, these studies highlight the complexity of building a peace that is inclusive of the civilians who were affected by the conflict. Not only must responses to conflict be mindful of national contexts and culture, they must also take into consideration local dynamics and concerns. Global or national policy strategy templates based on macro analysis of conflicts priorities may not be supported—or even appropriate—at the local level and fail to take into account the local particularities in context, experiences of violence, and overall behavior and attitudes among the population. Furthermore, policy options should be informed not only by what is missing at the macro level (e.g., security sector reform), but also by local resources and individuals' own agency and resilience (e.g., local mechanisms for security and conflict resolution).

Gaining the depth of awareness described in this chapter, about populations' experiences and attitudes, is difficult and not necessarily practical in all conflict or post-conflict settings. Conducting large population surveys may take away scarce resources that are needed to address urgent needs. Our comparative experience shows, however, that this type of research is feasible and can actually be done relatively inexpensively and in a timely fashion by capitalizing on new technologies. Further research and innovations are needed to make consultations more systematic and widespread. In the process, maintaining inclusiveness and not focusing on specific groups of victims is essential.

It is precisely because the policy challenges are enormous and the resources are limited that having reliable information about populations' circumstances and perceptions is crucial. The results that can be gleaned from this primary empirical data help to define an agenda that is mindful of the populations' needs and priorities, as well as to identify the risks of tensions where unpopular reforms must be enacted. In addition, as a fundamental matter, this information contributes to improved two-way communications between the population and key actors in governments and the international community, which is a step toward a more legitimate, democratic, and accountable process of building peace.

11. CROWDSOURCING TO MAP CONFLICT, CRISES, AND HUMANITARIAN RESPONSES

Patrick Meier

In the past five years, mapping of violence and disasters as they unfold, through various technologies, has emerged as a new way to observe and shape crises. Many mapping efforts rely on observations submitted by the "crowd"—a large, loose array of individuals and organizations, often in an online community, acting largely independent of one another to supply information in a distributed fashion. Disaster-affected communities are increasingly the source of Big (Crisis) Data, which they post and share on social media platforms like Twitter. Crowdsourcing the collection of crisis information from this user-generated content has evolved into a powerful and flexible way to detect and document crises in real time and real space. What this means is measurement of the characteristics of crisis situations as events are actually unfolding and at a geographical resolution that facilitates informed, prompt, and targeted decision making. Naturally, the availability of real-time and real-space data has important implications for conceiving, designing, and implementing interventions during crises, which can be more rapid and effective as a consequence.

This chapter enumerates and reflects on lessons learned about tracking and georeferencing user-generated content shared on social media to monitor and respond to humanitarian crises. The chapter also reviews new trends in crowdsourcing crisis information, along with the benefits and difficulties these trends present vis-à-vis research and policy settings. The first section introduces the practicalities of crowdsourcing crisis information, using four case studies: conflicts in Libya (2011) and Syria (2011–present), as well as Typhoon Pablo in the Philippines (2012) and the tornado in Oklahoma (2013). The second section addresses challenges of using social media as a source of big-data information for crisis mapping and humanitarian response. The third section reviews computational and methodological challenges of georeferencing tweets posted during crises. The fourth section concludes with recommendations for research and policy.

Crowdsourcing Crisis Information

Crowdsourcing is the act of outsourcing tasks to the public in the form of an open call. The term "crowdsourcing crisis information" was coined following the use of crowdsourcing to document the violence during and after Kenya's hotly contested national elections in December 2007. Ushahidi ("witness" in Swahili), a non-profit organization based in Nairobi, called on the public to report acts of violence via email and SMS, so that these could be added to a Google map. At the time, the government was downplaying the extent of the violence and had placed restrictions on the media's ability to report on the conflict. In response, Ushahidi sought to crowdsource or distribute the act of witnessing in order to counter the government's narrative and circumvent the media's narrative. In reality, the majority of reports added to Ushahidi's Google map were copied and pasted from various news articles. But this first attempt at crowdsourcing crisis information highlighted the potential power of crowdsourcing to monitor and map crisis in real time and real space.

Ushahidi's crowdsourcing approach was a radical departure from methodologies like those developed by Swisspeace, which relied on networks of in-country field monitors who were paid to fill out structured surveys on a weekly basis using a standard set of peace and conflict indicators. Swisspeace typically had several field monitors in every country they monitored. The Swisspeace model was replicated in a number of regional conflict monitoring and early warning systems such as the Conflict Early Warning and Response Network (CEWARN) in the Horn of Africa. This traditional mode of gathering and reporting crisis information has obvious limitations. For example, field monitors cannot be everywhere at the same time and thus tend to rely on national news, rather than being eyewitnesses themselves. In contrast, crowdsourcing opens up the reporting to the public.

This traditional mode of gathering and reporting crisis information has obvious limitations. For example, field monitors cannot be everywhere at the same time and thus tend to rely on national news, rather than being eyewitnesses themselves. In contrast, crowdsourcing opens up the reporting to the public.

This section presents four case studies that highlight applications of crowdsourcing crisis information. Two cases (Libya and Syria) relate to crisis mapping of conflict zones, often referred to as man-made disasters, while the other two cases (the Philippines and Oklahoma) focus on crisis maps launched in response to natural disasters. Man-made and natural disasters are often viewed as part of the same broad domain of humanitarian practice, because of their similarities—especially in terms of effects and how they can be monitored—and the institutions that have a mandate to address them. Moreover, natural disasters tend to exacerbate vulnerabilities that can lead to conflict. Thus, examining both types of cases together is appropriate.

Each case study outlines the processes used to capture crisis information in real space and close to real time, including the following aspects:

- Who performs this work, including different relationships between local and international actors
- The interdisciplinarity of the work, drawing on models in other fields
- Those who solicit the work
- The nature and timing of deployment
- The topics and content of information that is collected
- The extent of coverage
- The level of precision—i.e., the accuracy and disaggregation of the data
- The volume of information that is analyzed
- Its reliability
- The purpose of the analysis, including utilization and applications
- The audiences for what is produced
- The nature of dissemination and accessibility
- The development of infrastructure that is involved
- Security issues that arise
- The professionalization and institutionalization of the field
- Innovations that have resulted

In these respects, the case studies afford a rich perspective on the recent evolution in the state of the art in crowdsourcing and mapping crisis information.

Libya Crisis Map (2011)[1]

As part of what came to be known as the Arab Spring, opposition protests began in Libya in mid-February 2011. Within days, the conflict escalated into violent clashes between government forces and rebels. In a matter of weeks, Libya was engulfed in full-scale civil war. Attacks, threats, and other punitive measures and antagonistic rhetoric by the government, in particular, raised concerns about a serious humanitarian crisis.

In response, the Standby Task Force (SBTF) launched the Libya Crisis Map in early March 2011 at the request of the United Nations Office for the Coordination of Humanitarian Affairs (OCHA). The SBTF (http://blog.standbytaskforce.com) is an award-winning global network of digital volunteers who support humanitarian organizations by providing free information-based solutions such as live crisis maps. The network is composed of teams that focus on specific information processes such as monitoring, verifying, and geolocating social media reports.[2] For Libya, OCHA requested that the SBTF monitor and map social media traffic related to topics such as movement of people, health, logistics, and security issues. SBTF volunteers, known as "mapsters," manually monitored Twitter, Facebook, Flickr, and YouTube for relevant content.

> *The [Standby Task Force]…is an award-winning global network of digital volunteers who support humanitarian organizations by providing free information-based solutions like live crisis maps. The network is composed of teams that focus on specific information processes such as monitoring, verifying, and geolocating social media reports.*

For security reasons, especially concerns about unwittingly providing the government a means of monitoring those reporting information on the conflict, the resulting detailed, real-time crisis map was not made public. At the request of the UN, however, a public version was later released but placed on a 24-hour delay and restricted to titles of items, omitting all personal identifiers as well as the raw descriptive contents.

More than 300 mapsters on the SBTF Media Monitoring Team contributed to these efforts, mapping 1,430 reports during March 2011. The mapsters monitored around the clock over 100 relevant social media sources. Relevant items were forwarded to the GeoLocation Team. The entire georeferencing process was carried out manually. An initial hurdle was to establish the location of villages, towns, and cities across Libya. For this purpose, the GeoLocation Team used dozens of resources, including Google Maps, Bing Maps, OpenStreetMap, and Lonely Planet, as well as maps shared by humanitarian organizations via the Reliefweb website and information in the mainstream media. Ultimately, the GeoLocation Team compiled a georeferenced gazetteer of place names. Over 60 unique locations were identified as sites of reports forwarded by the Media Monitoring Team. The biggest challenge related to frequent instances of different

---

1 Disclaimer: the author spearheaded the Libya Crisis Map project.

2 In October 2010, the author and several other co-founders launched the SBTF, in order to provide humanitarian organizations with crisis mapping support during major disasters. This work has included partnerships with UNOCHA, UNHCR, WHO, and other international organizations. Today, the SBTF has over 1,000 volunteers in more than 80 different countries and deployed in some 30 operations around the world. The organization is composed of an advisory board (the original co-founders), a core team (executive leadership), team coordinators, and the general membership. All contributors to the SBTF are strictly volunteers and thus unpaid.

spellings of a place name. For example, Tobruk also appears in maps as Tóbruch, Tobruch, Ṭubruq, Tobruck, and Tubru. In addition, some villages and towns share the same names. To address these concerns, mapsters created a set of best practices to disambiguate location names, such as replacing "i" with "ee" and "u" with "q." They also used Wikipedia and Google Translate to identify similar phonetics for place names in Arabic. These strategies enabled them to add a column of alternative spellings in the gazetteer.

Figure 11.1 Snapshot of the UNOCHA/SBTF Crisis Map of the Libyan Conflict

Note: Used under Creative Commons license.

Figure 11.1 displays a snapshot of the homepage of the Libya Crisis Map website (http://libyacrisismap.net), which is now offline. The main feature was the "Big Map," which allowed users to see the locations from which relevant social media items and other reports were posted. As the partial image in Figure 11.1 shows, most of the traffic was concentrated in population centers along the Mediterranean coast. Relatively less traffic came from inland locations, even those that experienced violence, which reflects the lower penetration of technological infrastructure. Additional traffic came from outside the country, some related to Libya but also to ongoing events in neighboring countries—Egypt and Tunisia in particular. The map interface permitted users to filter material by category, to zoom in on specific areas, and to view the set of reports for each location. These reports could also be accessed and downloaded directly. In addition, users could sign up to receive alerts, which made the site a specialized news stream on the unfolding humanitarian crisis. The site also served as a mobilization tool, via which users could volunteer to assist with the project.

During the time it was online, the site received a large volume of hits from a variety of users around the world. In particular, the information was employed heavily within UNOCHA. The compilation and collation of reports, in an accessible and intelligible manner, facilitated studying patterns and trends, which were then inputs in policy making and decisions about programming and the allocation of personnel and resources. The content and resulting statistics were also cited in monitoring reports and used as metrics for assessing the trajectory of the crisis. In a letter to the SBTF, a senior UN official commended the mapsters for their dedication and professionalism, adding: "Your efforts at tackling a difficult problem have definitely reduced the information overload; sorting through the multitude of signals on the crisis is no easy task. The Task Force has given us an output that is manageable and digestible, which in turn contributes to better situational awareness and decision making."[3] Meanwhile, the site was used by others, as indicated by frequent citations by media and in scholarly analyses.

> *The compilation and collation of reports [on the Libya Crisis Map], in accessible and intelligible manner, facilitated studying patterns and trends, which were then inputs in policy making and decisions about programming and the allocation of personnel and resources.*

Several reflections can be offered about this case. One is that the scope and parameters of the data-collection effort were largely dictated by the specific mandate and needs of UNOCHA, which made the original request. Of course, other information about the Libyan crisis could have been compiled (e.g., details about battles and casualties), which would have yielded a different resource, perhaps with more comprehensive compilation and mapping of broader value to a wider range of users wishing to examine more aspects of the conflict. Instead, the Libya Crisis Map was a special purpose, client-driven project, oriented around guiding responses in humanitarian policy and practice. The experience was important in developing an approach to crowdsourcing-based crisis mapping involving a partnership between intergovernmental and non-governmental organizations, capitalizing on a distributed volunteer force. In the process, innovations were made in the protocols for geolocation and security. At the same time, the project was event driven, without an eye toward longer-term archival maintenance of the information for public use, including by researchers.

Syria Tracker (2011–present)[4]

As with Libya and other Arab Spring cases, the conflict in Syria began with demonstrations and protests, which started in January 2011 and subsequently ramped up in frequency and scale from February through April. The repressive, violent responses by Syrian security forces became increasingly more substantial and severe, especially as the country transitioned to full-scale civil war, with reports of an assortment of significant atrocities.

---

3 http://blog.standbytaskforce.com/libya-crisis-map-report.

4 Disclaimer: the author was directly involved in supporting the Syria Tracker efforts.

The Syria Tracker Crisis Map (http://SyriaTracker.crowdmap.com) was launched in early 2011 to document these human rights violations. This is the longest, continually running crisis map to date. The initiative, spearheaded by members of the Syrian diaspora in the United States, involves collecting, verifying, and mapping relevant reports on killings, detainments, and incidents of chemical poisoning, among other violations. The original and still primary purpose is to provide a potential post-Assad criminal tribunal with reliable evidence on atrocities committed in Syria, rather than to inform humanitarian relief, as with the initiative in Libya. At the same time, the data displayed on Syria Tracker is also used by the US Agency for International Development (USAID), the US Office for Foreign Disaster Assistance (OFDA), and other key governmental agencies and intergovernmental and international organizations.

> *The original and still primary purpose [of Syria Tracker] is to provide a potential post-Assad criminal tribunal with reliable evidence on atrocities committed in Syria, rather than to inform humanitarian relief.... At the same time, the data displayed...is also used by the US Agency for International Development (USAID), the US Office for Foreign Disaster Assistance (OFDA) and other key governmental agencies and intergovernmental and international organizations.*

To monitor evidence of human rights violations, Syria Tracker uses data mining to automatically read through some 2,000 English-based news sources that regularly cover the Syrian conflict. Relying on English sources is a practical choice, which avoids challenges such as handling translations from material written in Arabic, French, etc. Due to the limitation, some material may be overlooked, even with the extensive volume of sources, multilingual dissemination by many media outlets, and a degree of natural duplication across sources. Consequently, the results may be biased to an extent. Yet this shortcoming is hopefully minimized and an acceptable, practical trade-off under the circumstances. Also, the sources include pro-Assad news coverage, which mitigates the concern that the information is inevitably skewed towards reporting greater numbers of atrocities and attributing them primarily to the government. In addition to relying on traditional media, Syria Tracker employs information crowdsourced from both social media and email. The team carefully reviews the evidence collected, on average utilizing only about 6 percent of crowdsourced reports. Indeed, the team is meticulous with verification, down to comparing and triangulating the data-mined articles with the crowdsourced items. For example, a specific name for the victim and either a picture or video identifying the victim are required to publish a report of a killing. Syria Tracker has also experimented with adding geotagged information from high-resolution satellite imagery. In conducting the data mining, the team repurposed Harvard's Healthmap platform (http://healthmap.org), which was originally designed for digital disease detection.

The team locates reports of violations on the Syria Tracker Crisis Map using their knowledge of the country's geography and the Geonames gazetteer, which is available online (http://www.geonames.org). Since the outset of its work, the team has mapped over 3,000 unique reports that have occurred in at least 200 locations.

Figure 11.2 Snapshots of the Syria Tracker Crisis Map

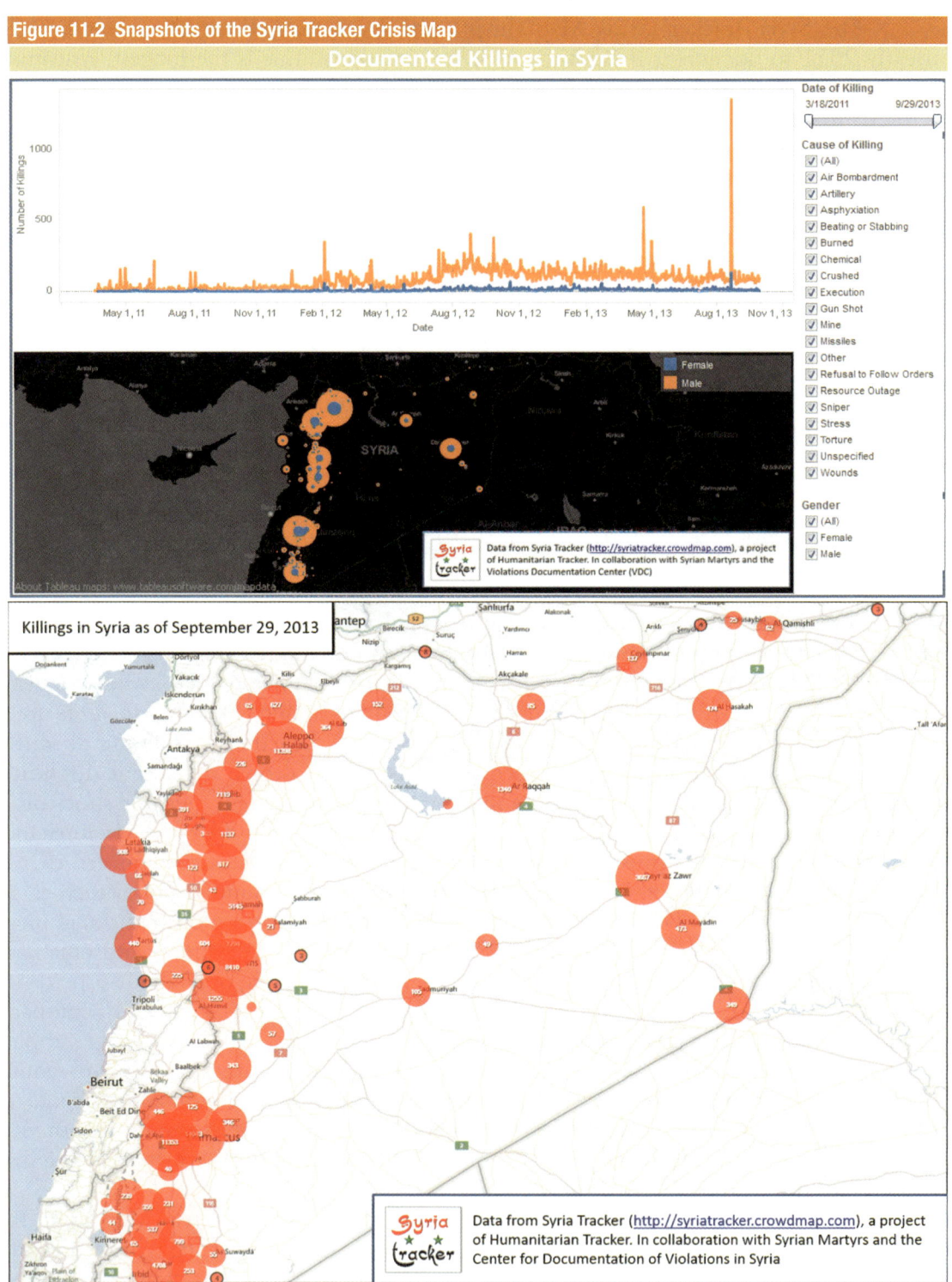

Note: Used under Creative Commons license.

Figure 11.2 displays a pair of snapshots of the results, encompassing reports from March 2011 through September 2013. The basic interface and format of the site resemble the Libya Crisis Map, with the ability to filter and zoom in on reports by type and area. This case highlights how distinctions in the layers of a conflict are pertinent to who does the documentation and for what purpose, which then drives the design of information collection, analysis, and utilization. Because the Syria Tracker team is concerned with accountability for atrocities, they distill different types of information than, for example, the Libya Crisis Map team. The requirements of a prospective legal process also place a premium on verification, as the aim is for the information to be precise at the level of individual reports, rather than sufficiently accurate at a more summary level—enough to guide policy and program decisions. The aspiration of meeting this stricter test has been a catalyst for innovations in techniques and standards of cross-checking among sources.

Man-Made Crises vs. Natural Disasters

The first two case studies concerned man-made crises, namely violent political conflicts that develop and persist over an extended period of time. A similar approach to crisis mapping, using similar technology and data, has also been utilized in response to natural disasters. These fast-moving events are often foreseeable with at least some advance notice, then quickly transition to the aftermath stage of humanitarian response and recovery. As the next two case studies will show, those features greatly accelerate the timeline of mapping efforts, presenting distinct challenges.

> *Real time takes on a different meaning following a natural disaster, when the focus is more strictly about monitoring the current status and providing an assessment of needs to be addressed. When mapping a conflict, by contrast, the unfolding of real time becomes part of the scale on which the severity of the event is measured.*

Real time takes on a different meaning following a natural disaster, when the focus is more strictly about monitoring the current status and providing an assessment of needs to be addressed. When mapping a conflict, by contrast, the unfolding of real time becomes part of the scale on which the severity of the event is measured, yielding knowledge that can be valuable for detecting when things are getting worse (or better) and potentially prompting interventions to mitigate the situation. This aspect is not entirely missing from a disaster aftermath, except the actual damage is relatively static—though additional casualties may still accumulate—and perceived to change mainly in conjunction with the discovery and reporting of its extent. Natural disasters may present fewer security risks and less politicization of information, at least under certain conditions, than do political conflicts. Both types of crises may be affected by communications blackouts, to varying degrees, as the result of intentional suppression of information and damage to infrastructure.

Typhoon Pablo in the Philippines (2012)[5]

In early December 2012, UNOCHA activated the Digital Humanitarian Network (DHN) to carry out a rapid assessment of devastating damage caused by Typhoon Pablo in the Philippines two days after it made landfall. The DHN is a network of volunteer organizations that provides international humanitarian organizations with information

---

[5] Disclaimer: the author co-founded the DHN and spearheaded the digital disaster response efforts in the Philippines.

services during disasters (http://www.DigitalHumanitarians.com). The SBTF, discussed earlier, is a founding member of the DHN. UNOCHA asked the DHN to collect all tweets posted during the first 48 hours after the typhoon made landfall and to identify which ones linked to pictures and/or videos that captured infrastructure damage. This subset of multimedia content would then be georeferenced for purposes of creating a crisis map that would be shared with other UN partners and the Filipino government.

Humanitarian organizations have traditionally taken up to two weeks to carry out "rapid" damage assessments. This is not optimal. Therefore, UNOCHA and others are increasingly turning to alternative methods that leverage real-time information channels, such as social media, to create an early "first draft" damage assessment to accelerate their relief efforts rather than waiting for formal evaluations to be carried out. Shelter damage, for example, provides vital information about the potential number of displaced, injured, and potentially trapped individuals who require emergency medical attention and housing. Unlike in the previous two case studies, which transpired over periods lasting months, this entire effort in the Philippines needed to be completed within 12 hours.

> *Humanitarian organizations have traditionally taken up to two weeks to carry out "rapid" damage assessments. This is not optimal. Therefore, UNOCHA and others are increasingly turning to alternative methods that leverage real-time information channels, such as social media, to create an early "first draft" damage assessment to accelerate their relief efforts rather than waiting for formal evaluations to be carried out.*

Coordinators of DHN invited the SBTF and another volunteer group to carry out the request.[6] The SBTF focused on the second day of tweets. It collaborated with the Qatar Computing Research Institute (QCRI) to automatically collect tweets with links—in total, over 20,000. Next, they partnered with CrowdCrafting, a non-profit organization, to customize a web-based microtasking application to process the tagging of relevant tweets (see Figure 11.3). Microtasking is a methodology that involves breaking down a large task into a set of smaller tasks, each with the same recurring steps. In this instance, tweets with links were displayed on the CrowdCrafting app for volunteers to tag (http://crowdcrafting.org/app/philippinestyphoon/newtask). If a link pointed to an image/video that captured damage, a volunteer would check the appropriate box. If a link provided sufficient geographical information to identify where exactly the image/video was taken, the volunteer would check off the location box. A map would then open up, with the volunteer prompted either to point the cursor to the location in question or to look for the location using the search box. SBTF volunteers used similar strategies to carry out the geotagging as the ones used for the Libya Crisis Map. Just under 100 images/videos from the Philippines were tagged and georeferenced in this way.

An important feature of many microtasking platforms is built-in triangulation. For example, one can request that at least five volunteers tag each tweet. If there is consensus (e.g., all five volunteers tag a tweet as pointing to a picture of damage), then the tag is reliable. Rules can be adopted for circumstances when volunteers' tags differ, such as a threshold level of agreement (e.g., four tags the same) of follow-up by additional volunteers or an expert when the evidence is suggestive, but not conclusive (e.g., two

---

[6] The second organization, Humanity Road, was not involved in the innovative use of microtasking.

Figure 11.3 Snapshot of the CrowdCrafting Microtasking App for Typhoon Pablo

Note: Used under Creative Commons license.

or three tags the same). Similar rules can also apply to geotagging. Such a "vote-based" approach to triangulation enables a crowd of volunteers—if sufficient in number and diligent in their efforts—to generate high-quality data in a short period of time. This approach explains how the DHN was able to complete the required task in less than 12 hours and provide UNOCHA with a database of relevant geotagged multimedia content.

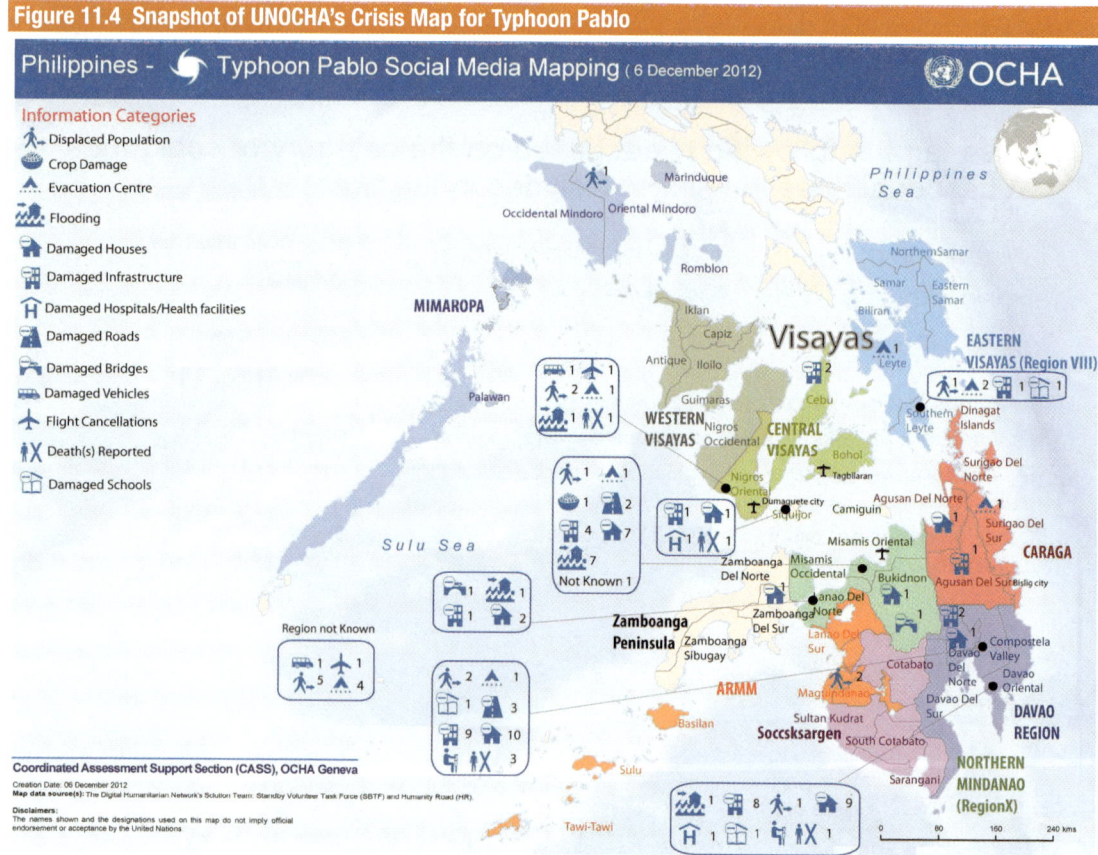

Note: Used under Creative Commons license.

UNOCHA subsequently used the data to create the crisis map displayed in Figure 11.4 (http://reliefweb.int/report/philippines/social-media-mapping-and-analysis-typhoon-bopha-pablo). The map was novel for the organization because it drew entirely from multimedia content shared on Twitter and geotagged by volunteers from around the world using a microtasking platform.

> *The [Philippines typhoon] case also demonstrates the ability to activate and deploy sophisticated monitoring and assessment and generate clear, actionable results, with a combination of speed and coverage that did not exist previously.*

This case study again emphasizes the importance of differences in the mandate and mission, which determine information collection, analysis, reporting, and utilization. Here, the focus was on the physical infrastructure. Select aspects of the human impact were also recorded in the process, but not covered systematically or in depth. The case also demonstrates the ability to activate and deploy sophisticated monitoring and assessment and generate clear, actionable results, with a combination of speed and coverage that did not exist previously. In the past, the typical arrangement is that an expert team would have to be sent out from a hub location, whether inside or outside the country. The only exceptions were instances where the right network of actors, such as local government officials or NGOs, with the right sort of communications infrastructure was already on hand and able and inclined to take on the task. Now, a good amount of rich and reasonably reliable information—a considerable portion of which is supplied in multimedia format—can be obtained from those who happen to be on the scene, including many ordinary citizens, using ICT that is relatively commonplace. This shift in the nature of inputs at the information-gathering stage is transformative. All of society can have agency as active contributors to assessment of the damage from a disaster and remain engaged as monitors of the aftermath, rather than being passive objects. A potential concern is whether such crowdsourced information will be usable and reliable. The case shows, however, that coding and cross-validation procedures can be implemented efficiently, harnessing large teams of volunteers and multiple sources.

Tornado in Oklahoma (2013)[7]

In May 2013, a Category 5 tornado devastated the city of Moore, Oklahoma. Two days later, at the request of the American Red Cross (ARC), QCRI's Crisis Computing Team partnered with The Ohio Center of Excellence in Knowledge-enabled Computing (Kno.e.sis) to collect and analyze tweets posted in the immediate aftermath of the tornado.

Over two million tweets posted during the first 48 hours after the tornado were analyzed. The ARC was specifically interested in needs and requests communicated via Twitter, along with offers of help. With this in mind, QCRI used machine-learning classifiers to automatically identify and extract tweets related to needs and offers of help. About 7 percent of the tweets (~146,000) communicated a need or offer of help. Just over 400 unique, automatically geotagged tweets sought non-monetary donations such as clothing. About 150 unique, geotagged tweets posted during the first 48 hours offered direct assistance. During the first 10 days following the tornado, over 50 percent of all posted tweets had some element of geographic information. This is important because geographic information is necessary to make crowdsourced crisis information actionable. The technicalities behind geotagging tweets are explained later in the chapter.

While only a small fraction of tweets were related to needs and offers of help, these still constitute important—and potentially lifesaving—information requested by the American Red Cross for operational purposes. Consider the following analogy: the vast majority of books in the city library are completely useless to you. After all, you are unlikely to read more than 1 percent of all the books since you have specific interests. Does this mean the library should be leveled and car park built in its place? No, just like Twitter should not be ignored during disasters. The challenge is indeed akin to finding needles in a haystack. The use of machine-learning classifiers means that this information can be easily extracted, within minutes, with very little effort and at no cost to the Red Cross. These classifiers can also extract other types of relevant information such as infrastructure damage, casualties and injuries, eyewitness accounts, etc. The alternative is for Red Cross staff to try and manually

---

[7] Disclaimer: the author directs the Qatar Computing Research Institute's (QCRI) crisis computing and humanitarian technology efforts. He was directly involved in the digital disaster response efforts to the Oklahoma tornado.

read through hundreds of thousands of tweets. Handling this number of phone calls is also far too manually intensive, and the Red Cross does not have enough staff to position one person at the corner of every street in Moore to report on needs and offers of help.[8]

QCRI and Kno.e.sis also analyzed multimedia content (i.e., images/video) shared in the immediate aftermath of the tornado. Over 12,000 images were shared on Twitter during the first 48 hours; the vast majority comprised links to pictures posted on Instagram. In addition, over 5,000 videos, mostly on YouTube, were shared via Twitter. Approximately 40 percent of tweets with links to images had associated geographic information, which meant they could be added to a crisis map.

> *The disaster response to the Oklahoma tornado was the first to leverage advanced computing—that is, artificial intelligence and machine learning. The future of crisis monitoring will necessarily include crisis computing.*

In sum, the disaster response to the Oklahoma tornado was the first to leverage advanced computing—that is, artificial intelligence and machine learning. The future of crisis monitoring will necessarily include crisis computing. To be sure, the volume of user-generated content posted during disasters will only increase in the coming months and years, as the number of Twitter users continues to skyrocket. In 2011, Twitter had 100 million monthly active users; this figure doubled in 2012. Today, users post an average of half-a-billion tweets every month. Obviously, Twitter is not the only available social media platform. Currently, 38 distinct social media platforms exist; more can be expected. Thus, Big "Crisis" Data is here to stay. In that context, humanitarian practitioners and conflict analysis need more sophisticated filters to manage and make sense of the data.

The Challenges of Social Media as an Information Source

The case studies demonstrate the promise inherent in monitoring social media for crisis mapping and humanitarian response, which is already yielding benefits. That said, critics have leveled several concerns about the scale, validity, and reliability of crowdsourced crisis maps. Crowdsourcing and social media certainly present important challenges. The volume, velocity, and variety of information (big data) shared on social media during disasters are often too great for humanitarian and emergency management organizations to manage and make sense of. Thus, there are serious technical and infrastructure challenges with respect to collecting the information in the first place. The unstructured and real-time nature of social media also presents important additional challenges. In addition, the fact that social media information is user-generated raises serious questions with respect to the objectivity and veracity of this information, not to mention the representativeness of the sampled information. This section describes these challenges in more details while also explaining why, despite being correct in many instances about specific claims, critics are mistaken to dismiss the policy value of crowdsourcing maps.

---

[8] Policy also plays an important role here. If emergency responders do not actively or explicitly create demand for relevant and high-quality social media content during crises, then why should supply follow? If the 911 emergency number (999 in the UK) were never advertised, then would anyone call? If 911 were simply a voicemail inbox with no instructions, would callers know what type of actionable information to relay after the beep? Would the volume of 911 calls be as high?

Collecting Big Data from Social Media

In the digital information age, where increasingly large shares of the population around the world have access to ICT tools linked to the Internet, crises generate huge amounts of readily available data. Several examples were described earlier. Another notable recent case is Superstorm Sandy, during which over 20 million tweets and more than 500,000 Instagram pictures were posted. The ability to collect, store, and retrieve this big data requires advanced technical skills, robust infrastructure (cloud computing), and financial capital. Access to the Twitter API is free, but the number of tweets that can be downloaded for analysis is limited to just a few thousand per day. This explains why many technically savvy researchers access the API from dozens of different computers in order to collect many more tweets. Additional technical workarounds exist, but are beyond the scope of this chapter and violate Twitter's terms of service. While the API is free but restricts the number of tweets that can be downloaded, the Twitter "firehose" provides users with access to every single tweet posted during the previous five days (typically). The drawback is that access to the firehose costs around $100,000 per month, depending on the reseller.[9]

A recent study (for more details, see next subsection) that collected and analyzed over a million tweets from Syria found important differences in the sample data derived from the Twitter firehose versus the API. The API is able to capture 90 percent of geotagged tweets available via the firehose.[10] Since accessing the full Twitter firehose is expensive, "only corporate actors and regulators—who possess both the intellectual and financial resources to succeed in this race—can afford to participate."[11] The widening digital divide in the era of big data is very real, prompting the need for public-private partnerships and data philanthropy, which are discussed further in the conclusion of this chapter.

Analyzing Big Data from Social Media

Assuming that humanitarian organizations can access live social media feeds, they face another equally daunting challenge: how to make sense of the gigabytes worth of data shared during major disasters. Consider that over 2,000 tweets were posted per second the day after the 2011 earthquake and tsunami that rocked Japan. This rate translates to over one million tweets—the equivalent of about 10 million words—every 10 minutes. Finding potentially lifesaving information in this information stack is challenging. While digital humanitarian volunteers with the SBTF or DHN can manually monitor thousands of tweets per day in near-real time, this approach does not scale, which explains the use of microtasking and machine learning in the Philippines and Oklahoma case studies.

Gauging the Objectivity and Veracity of Big Data from Social Media

Information shared on social media is frequently wrong and thus unreliable, particularly in conflict zones. When considering the credibility (or lack thereof) of social media, however, it pays to ask: "Credible compared to what?" Mainstream media, perhaps? The *New York Times*, one of the most revered institutions of journalism, acknowledges making over 7,000 errors in 2011.[12] An earlier study of 14 leading newspapers found

---

[9] Twitter's main resellers include DataSift and GNIP.
[10] http://iRevolution.net/2013/05/30/twitter-api-vs-firehose.
[11] https://papers.ssrn.com/sol3/papers.cfm?abstract_id=2206225.
[12] http://www.nytimes.com/2012/02/26/opinion/sunday/the-error-iceberg.html?_r=0.

that 64 percent of their published articles contained at least one error.[13] This comparison indicates that traditional media is hardly immune to issues. Therefore, social media is not unique in this regard, leaving considerable room for improvement.

Of course, the need to verify crisis information is hardly new. Emergency call systems have been around for over 50 years. On average, more than 10 million calls made to 911 in New York City are misdials, falsehoods, or hoaxes.[14] In the UK, only 25 percent of calls made to 999 are actually relevant to that service. Does this misleading traffic and noise in reports mean that national emergency numbers should be abolished? No. Rather, the challenge needs to be managed, with effective strategies designed and implemented to sift out information that is pertinent and valid from that which is not.

Fortunately, social media often acts as a self-correcting mechanism in practice. Several peer-reviewed empirical studies have shown that false or non-credible information posted on Twitter is typically countered and rapidly identified as false by the majority of Twitter users. This response exemplifies the "Wisdom of the Crowds" in action. Advanced computing research has also demonstrated that the credibility of tweets can be predicted without even analyzing their content, since non-credible tweets that propagate across the Twittersphere leave a very distinct signature.[15] Think of a pebble thrown into a pond, causing a ripple effect. In the Twittersphere, those ripples look very different, depending on whether or not a tweet is credible. Twitter users regularly tweet questions about other tweets deemed to be suspect or downright false. Drawing such credibility distinctions can be facilitated by advanced computing, but does not always require this technology, the need for which is determined by the volume of information at hand and the type of verification question being asked. Consider that journalists at the BBC have been monitoring and verifying user-generated content since 2005—a year before Twitter was launched. The BBC's User-Generated Content (UGC) Hub is staffed with investigative journalists who apply their skills to manually sift through a full range of social media.

Even if it is not completely and intentionally false, user-generated content shared on social media is often biased. This is true in terms of what many individual users post. What is more, the content found on social media is often unrepresentative of the overall population. For example, just 3 percent of the world's population is active on Twitter.[16] While those individuals generate over 400 million tweets every day, 50 percent of these are posted by the top 5 percent of users. Twitter users—and in fact social media users more generally—typically constitute a demographic that is younger, more urban, and more affluent than average. These disparities were evident during Superstorm Sandy, when most of the tweets did not come from poorer and more disenfranchised neighborhoods of the city. The digital divide is equally if not more pronounced in developing countries.

While user-generated content may be biased and non-representative, the use of that data for disaster response is not invalid. In these contexts, such information can be the best available data, which is typically better than no data. Big data such as social media still represents "new, large, and arguably unfiltered insights into attitudes and behaviors that were previously difficult to track in the wild."[17] So long as one is conscious and

---

13 http://jmq.sagepub.com/content/82/3/533.abstract.

14 http://iRevolution.net/2013/01/08/disaster-tweets-versus-911-calls.

15 http://iRevolution.net/2012/12/03/predicting-credibility.

16 http://firstmonday.org/ojs/index.php/fm/article/view/4366/3654.

17 http://gigaom.com/2013/05/28/if-youre-disappointed-with-big-data-youre-not-paying-attention.

transparent about the limitations, the information can still be suggestive, with caveats and constraints. Statistical correlations in big data do not imply causation; they simply indicate that something may be worth exploring further. Moreover, there are ways of screening and correcting biases and sub-optimal sampling. In fact, data collected via non-random, non-representative sampling is employed in many fields. For instance, much of the data used for medical research and digital disease detection is the product of convenience sampling. This does not constitute the gold standard of experimental research, as would be required to establish a level of confidence in results to state relationships with certainty, yet can give useful guidance under the right conditions. A practical example is the 911 emergency system, which is essentially a crowdsourcing service. While 911 was set up in 1968, the service and number were not widely known until the 1970s, and many municipalities did not have access until the 1980s. Thus, the system was hardly a representative way to collect emergency information. Does this mean that the millions of calls collected before the system's widespread adoption were all invalid or useless? Not necessarily.[18]

According to a senior UN official involved in the response to Typhoon Pablo in the Philippines, relief operations would have overlooked certain disaster-affected areas had it not been for the social media crisis map produced by DHN.[19] The damage captured by the images and videos taken after Typhoon Pablo was real. Furthermore, it only takes one person to take a picture of a washed-out bridge to reveal the infrastructure damage caused by a typhoon, even if everyone else nearby has never heard of social media.

In addition, the equalizing impact of ICT is encouraging. There has never been a moment when everyone had access to the same communication technology at the same time, which is unlikely to change for quite some time. Nonetheless, the mobile phone is by far the most rapidly distributed and widespread communication technology in history.

Georeferencing Crisis Tweets

Part of what is attractive about the potential of using social media to monitor and respond to crises is the ability to source information directly from witnesses on the ground, offering a rich local perspective whose reach extends to wherever ICT is available. For mapping purposes, however, social media information that does not contain some kind geographical data is useless. Unfortunately, the geography of Twitter is not very well understood. Most studies that focus on Twitter ignore any rigorous analysis of geographic content derivable from Twitter. One exception is Leetaru et al. (2013).[20] This section summarizes the main findings from this study as they relate to georeferencing crisis information.

Part of what is attractive about the potential of using social media to monitor and respond to crises is the ability to source information directly from witnesses on the ground, offering a rich local perspective whose reach extends to wherever ICT is available.

---

[18] It does mean that emergency response unwittingly catered to people who were aware of the 911 service, which represents an unfair allocation of services. The response was also inefficient because of inadequate screening of accuracy, which resulted in considerable false positives and false negatives. When significant resources are involved, and the stakes are life and death, such shortcomings present a concern.

[19] Personal conversation with Daniel Saunders at the UN in NY, May 30, 2013.

[20] http://firstmonday.org/ojs/index.php/fm/article/view/4366/3654. This piece is the source for all quotations and statistics in the rest of the section.

Geographic data can be captured from Twitter in two ways. The first is from the location specified by a user when registering for a Twitter account, which is selected from a drop-down menu of place names. The second is automatically generated from the coordinates of the Twitter user's location when tweeting, which is typically provided via GPS or cellular triangulation. For the latter, users are required to opt in to having their tweets geolocated. According to Leetaru et al. (2013), on a typical day, about 3 percent of tweets can be geotagged either via a user's self-reported location when registering for Twitter or via the opt-in GPS feature.

Of note, Leetaru et al. (2013) have mapped Twitter locations against locations of electric lights based on satellite imagery obtained from NASA. This comparison highlights some notable patterns:

> Iran and China show substantially fewer tweets than their electricity levels would suggest, reflecting their bans on Twitter, while India shows strong clustering of Twitter usage along the coast and its northern border, even as electricity use is far more balanced throughout the country. Russia shows more electricity usage in its eastern half than Twitter usage, while most countries show far more Twitter usage than electricity would suggest.

Overall, however, the Pearson correlation between tweets and lights is 0.79. This indicates that tweets are geographically distributed in a relatively even way, according to the availability of electricity: wherever in the world electricity exists, the chance of there also being Twitter users is very high. The relationship is striking given that Twitter has launched just seven years ago, compared to the light bulb, which was invented in the 1870s. The implication is that Twitter can serve as an important global crisis monitoring tool. Still, just 1 percent of all Twitter users accounted for 66 percent of all georeferenced tweets during the period of study, which means that relying on these tweets alone may provide a skewed view of the Twittersphere, particularly over short stretches. Whether this poses a problem ultimately depends on the research question or task at hand and whether alternative sources of information are even available. The Philippines case study is illustrative. Was the crowdsourced social media information representative? No. Were the underlying images and videos objective? No—they captured the perspective of those taking the pictures. Nonetheless, the damage captured by this data was real damage.

Other means exist of approximating location. The linguistic geography of Twitter is critical: "If English is rarely used outside of the United States, or if English tweets have a fundamentally different geographic profile than other languages outside of the United States, this will significantly skew geocoding results." Leetaru et al. (2013) find that georeferenced tweets with English content comprise 42 percent of all geotagged tweets. Statistical analyses of geotagged English tweets, compared to those in all other languages, suggest that "English offers a spatial proxy for all languages and that a geocoding algorithm which processes only English will still have strong penetration into areas dominated by other languages (though English tweets may discuss different topics or perspectives)." This simply means that geotagged tweets posted in English serve as a robust indicator for the location of non-English tweets. And while the latter may not be easily georeferenced, English tweets are, even when there are very few of them compared to non-English tweets.

Another important source of geographic information is a Twitter user's bio. This public location information was available for 71 percent of all tweets studied by Leetaru et al. (2013). In addition, "approximately 78.4 percent of tweets include the user's time zone in textual format, which offers an approximation of longitude." While certain information that could be used to georeference Twitter traffic is accessible, other factors complicate the task. For example,

> Nearly one-third of all locations on Earth share their name with another location somewhere else on the planet, meaning that a reference to "Urbana" must be disambiguated by a geocoding system to determine which of the 12 cities in the world it might refer to, including 11 cities in the United States with that name.

Therefore, computing experts have created large gazetteers of place names and developed software algorithms to automatically disambiguate and infer correct locations. These computing solutions enable analysts to geocode significantly more tweets even though these do not make direct references to obvious place names. To be sure, "the small volume of georeferenced tweets can be dramatically enhanced by applying geocoding algorithms to the textual content and metadata of each tweet."

Conclusion

Crowdsourcing continues to play a critical role in the collection and geolocation of crisis information during humanitarian emergencies and violence political conflicts. Thanks to the real-time nature of social media, crowdsourced crisis maps can document the evolution of humanitarian crises in close to real time, something that was simply not possible when traditional monitoring mechanisms were developed 10–20 years ago. That said, the increasing volume, velocity, and variety of crisis-related information posted on social media presents a host of new challenges. The case studies presented in this chapter explain how some of these challenges have been addressed over the past three years.

Thanks to the real-time nature of social media, crowdsourced crisis maps can document the evolution of humanitarian crises in close to real time, something that was simply not possible when traditional monitoring mechanisms were developed 10–20 years ago.

The Libya Crisis Map (2011) demonstrated the power of human or "crowd computing" to make sense of social media information by filtering out the noise and mapping the signals on a live, interactive map. This "human filter" required hundreds of volunteers to manually monitor hundreds of social media sources around the clock. This labor-intensive approach explains why the crisis mapping effort could not be continued for more than a few weeks. The Syria Tracker Map (2011–2013) combined the crowdsourcing of crisis information using social media and email with data mining. The project made use of the HealthMap data-mining platform to automatically mine through thousands of English-based sources. This level of automation has been critical to ensuring the sustainability of the efforts over more than a two-year period. The Philippines Disaster Map (2012) was created to rapidly assess the damage caused by Typhoon Pablo. This required a short but intense burst of crowdsourcing and crisis mapping. Digital volunteers used microtasking to accelerate the processing of images and videos linked to on Twitter. Microtasking represents a smarter crowd-filtering approach and one that is highly scalable. Finally, the Oklahoma tornado (2013) promoted the first—and to date only—operational use of artificial intelligence and machine learning for disaster response. The approach only required two volunteers to run the algorithms and share the results with professional responders. This approach is massively scalable.

None of these case studies would have been possible without crowdsourcing and social media. This presents a powerful argument for the continued and expanded use of crowdsourcing to map conflicts, natural disasters, and humanitarian crises. Extreme events are not static; they change rapidly over time and space. Having real-time sensors and feedback loops is imperative for making timely and targeted decisions. Crisis information that is devoid of geographic information is not actionable. This explains why geographic information played an instrumental role in each of these case studies. Methods ranged from manually geotagging crowdsourced crisis information to automated approaches and combinations. Since the vast majority of social media reports are not automatically geotagged, advanced computing solutions have been developed to derive or infer locations. This continues to be an active area of research in the field of computing.

While more sophisticated solutions will be developed in the coming months and years, the use of crowdsourcing and social media for crisis mapping does present major challenges. First, the sheer volume of information shared on social media during crises is often overwhelming and thus paralyzing. Second, social media reports are not immediately verifiable and do not represent an objective picture of an unfolding crisis or conflict. Nevertheless, this chapter explained why these shortcomings are not unique to social media as a crisis communication tool and why the benefits of crowdsourcing and social media outweigh the limitations vis-à-vis crisis monitoring and humanitarian response. That said, some new challenges are presenting themselves—challenges that may alter this cost-benefit calculus.

Social media is like dark matter: plenty exists, but observing is particularly challenging given the various terms of service put in place by leading social media companies. As already discussed, Twitter's API limits the number of accessible tweets to just a few thousand a day. Facebook is even more closed, while Instagram and YouTube limit the amount of metadata (GPS coordinates, etc.) that can be accessed from the service. Besides social media data, Call Record Data (CRDs) and SIM card data are also out of reach of both researchers and humanitarian organizations.

A potential solution is big-data philanthropy, which involves companies sharing proprietary datasets for social good. Companies like Twitter and Facebook (including Instagram) ought to develop data-sharing protocols with established humanitarian organizations to provide full but temporary access to traffic posted during major disasters.

A potential solution is big-data philanthropy, which involves companies sharing proprietary datasets for social good. Companies like Twitter and Facebook (including Instagram) ought to develop data-sharing protocols with established humanitarian organizations to provide full but temporary access to traffic posted during major disasters. Companies that resell social media data, like GNIP, DataSift, and NetBase, should also be invited to support these socially responsible efforts. After all, as argued by the International

Committee of the Red Cross, access to information during disasters is as important as access to food, water, and shelter. Therefore, these companies have a moral duty to share their information for the purposes of saving lives and alleviating suffering during crises. In addition, companies that participate in sharing would benefit from the publicity of supporting such positive and highly visible efforts.

An Emergency Access Initiative could be modeled along the lines of the International Space Charter, whereby certain criteria would need to be met before an activation request could be made to social media companies. These companies would then provide a dedicated account to a consortium such as DHN. Such an account would be available only for 72 hours and monitored by the companies to ensure they are being used strictly for disaster response.

While an Emergency Access Initiative would significantly increase access to relevant social media information during major disasters, the fact of the matter remains that only a small fraction of social media posts includes geographic information. This circumstance is partly because humanitarian organizations and emergency management centers have yet to establish a strong, consistent demand for relevant and geotagged crisis information, let alone institute a norm that such information is the convention. Steps are being taken in this direction, to embrace new technologies and information sources, but further progress is still required. For example, the government of the Philippines did make active use of social media such as Twitter during the 2012 typhoon. Days before the typhoon made landfall, the government created a series of crisis hashtags (e.g., #rescuePH) and widely advocated the use of these hashtags to report crisis information. In the future, governments confronted with disasters should also encourage eyewitnesses to geotag their social media reports, including images and videos.

Promoting such actions necessarily raises important data privacy and protection challenges. Appropriate disclaimers would need to be put in place, along with guidelines and best practices vis-à-vis the reporting of crisis information on social media. Important precedents exist that can be used as models. GSMA recently launched an official code of conduct for the use of SMS in disaster response. In addition, the International Committee of the Red Cross (ICRC) recently published detailed Data Protection Protocols that include a chapter on crowdsourcing and social media use in conflict zones. These alone do not solve all data privacy and protection challenges, but they do raise awareness and increase critical thinking.

12. PROFILES OF ACTIVE ARMED CONFLICTS

Jonathan Wilkenfeld

This chapter describes the origins and evolution of all major and intermediate armed conflicts that were active as of December 31, 2012, reflecting developments since the publication of *Peace and Conflict 2012*. The cases are based on information in the Conflict Database maintained by the Uppsala Conflict Data Program (UCDP) at Uppsala University, Sweden (http://www.pcr.uu.se/research/UCDP/).

Definitions

According to the UCDP, an *armed conflict* is "a contested incompatibility that concerns government and/or territory where the use of armed force between two parties—of which at least one is the government of a state—results in at least 25 battle-related deaths." These conflicts have several key parameters:

- Status: *Terminated* or *active*. Conflicts can terminate for various reasons (e.g., victory, peace accord, ceasefire agreement, low or no activity). This chapter discusses only conflicts that were active—meaning that they resulted in at least 25 battle-related deaths over the calendar year—during 2012, the latest year for which data are currently available from UCDP.

- Intensity: *Minor* (at least 25 battle-related deaths in a given year, but fewer than 1,000 battle-related deaths during the entire conflict), *intermediate* (an accumulated total of at least 1,000 deaths, with at least 25 but fewer than 1,000 battle-related deaths in a given year), and *major* (at least 1,000 battle-related deaths in a given year). This chapter discusses only conflicts classified as major or intermediate, meaning that they have accumulated at least 1,000 battle-related deaths through 2012.

- Protagonists: *Interstate* (between two or more governments), *intrastate* (between a government and a nonstate actor), or *intrastate with foreign involvement* (government and/or nonstate actor(s) are supported with troops from governments of other states). All of the cases discussed in this chapter happen to fall in the last two categories.

Summary

In 2012, UCDP reported 32 active armed conflicts, of which six had not exceeded a total of 1,000 battle-related deaths since 1946 (see Harbom and Sundberg 2013). This chapter describes the remaining 26 armed conflicts that were active in 22 countries as of December 31, 2012. One existing conflict first reached the threshold of 1,000 cumulative battle-related deaths in 2012: Nigeria with Boko Haram. Two dormant conflicts re-emerged in 2012: Azerbaijan with Nagorno-Karabakh and the Democratic Republic of the Congo with M23. The only other new onset of intermediate or major armed conflict since *Peace and Conflict 2012* was published involved the government of Libya, forces loyal to Muammar Gaddafi, and the National Transitional Council in 2011. This reached the 1,000 battle-deaths threshold, but was no longer active in 2012. Four conflicts re-emerged in 2011: Myanmar with KIO, Pakistan with BLA and BRA, Senegal with MFDC, and Syria with FSA and Jabhat al-Nusra li al-Sham. The conflict in Pakistan had been inactive in 2010, while the conflict in Senegal was no longer active in 2012. Seven other conflicts terminated since the publication of *Peace and Conflict 2012*: Chad with UFR (2011), Iran with PJAK (2012), Myanmar with KNU (2012) and RCSS (2012), Peru with Sendero Luminoso (2011), Sri Lanka with LTTE (2010), and Uganda with LRA (2012).

Afghanistan

Intrastate with the Taliban, with Foreign Involvement

Afghanistan has been at war since 1978. Several factors make the country a fertile ground for protracted guerrilla war and transregional insurgencies: the existence of distinct tribal identities, a salient religious element, Afghanistan's geopolitical location as a meeting place of three regions, and the country's landlocked and mountainous geography.

The two main groups at the onset of the insurgency were Jamiat-i-Islami and Hezb-i-Islami, which remain among the central warring parties to the present. Both groups aimed at overthrowing the government and declared a jihad (holy war) against the state in March 1979. The Soviet invasion in December 1979 added the dimension of a national freedom struggle to the religious war. The Soviet troop withdrawal in February 1989 ended the first phase of the Afghan civil war, after approximately one million deaths.

As the Soviet troops withdrew, heavy fighting erupted between the Afghan army and Mujahideen forces. The strategic situation changed in 1992, when parts of the factionalized opposition movement joined forces. The Taliban movement first emerged in 1994, led by Mullah Mohammad Omar. Its stated goal was liberating Afghanistan from the corrupt leadership of warlords and establishing a pure Islamic society. On September 28, 1996, the Taliban forces took control of Kabul, proclaimed the Islamic State of Afghanistan and the enforcement of shari'ah (Islamic rule). Meanwhile, the anti-Taliban opposition formed a political and military front—the Northern Alliance—in June 1996.

The balance of forces changed drastically with the entrance of the United States-led multinational coalition into the conflict in response to the bombings of September 11, 2001. The Northern Alliance, backed by US and UK military force, took control of Kabul. On December 7, the last Taliban stronghold of Kandahar fell. Following intense diplomatic pressure, the parties agreed to the creation of a 29-member interim government headed by Hamid Karzai to lead the country for six months, until a broad-based administration could take over.

The security situation in Afghanistan deteriorated in 2004. In 2005, the armed conflict between remnants of the ousted Taliban regime and the Afghan government escalated further. The Afghan government remains dependent on the United States-led multinational coalition and the NATO-led peacekeeping force to provide security. The Afghan insurgency gained further strength in 2006 with fierce military clashes in the southeastern provinces and a rash of suicide bombings in urban areas. The intensity of the Taliban insurgency reached new heights in 2007. Part of the increase in intensity was due to a concerted Taliban effort to establish stable footholds in the country. In 2009, the United States greatly augmented its troop level in Afghanistan and changed the leadership of its forces in an effort to bring about a decisive victory over the Taliban forces. In 2011 and 2012, the conflict in Afghanistan continued to increase in intensity as the NATO-led forces started handing security control to Afghan forces. In an attempt to undermine the confidence in the local forces' ability to provide security, the insurgents stepped up suicide attacks and other bombings. In late December 2012, the government agreed to set up a political office for the Taliban in Qatar for the purpose of pursuing peace negotiations.

Algeria
Intrastate with GSPC

Algeria gained independence from France in 1962 after a bloody war. Severe economic problems persisted during the following 27 years of socialist one-party rule under the Front de Libération Nationale (FLN).

During the late 1980s, these economic problems prompted violent strikes and riots, leading to the introduction of a multiparty system. The Front Islamique du Salut (FIS) became the most potent opposition force in the country, as its anti-regime stance and Islamic values appealed to the urban poor. After the FIS won the first round of parliamentary elections in 1991, the army cancelled the second round. Amid increasing political violence, FIS was outlawed in 1992. Groups that fought the regime with arms came to dominate the struggle, and the FIS lost the initiative. In response, the party endorsed the armed struggle of the MIA (Mouvement Islamique Armée) in 1993, and its armed wing, Armée Islamique du Salut (AIS). In 1992, a number of small extremist groups set up the Groupe Islamique Armé (GIA). The most prominent splinter group was the Groupe Salafite pour la Prédication et la Combat (GSPC), appearing in 1998. In 1999, Bouteflika won the presidential election after all other candidates withdrew.

In 2000, the AIS agreed to disband. In a referendum on September 29, 2005, 97 percent of Algerians voted in favor of a government proposal for a partial amnesty for former rebels (and for the security forces). The amnesty came into effect in February 2006, but was soon rejected by the GSPC. Clashes continued throughout the year.

In 2007, there was an increase in attacks by GSPC, which in January had changed its name to Al-Qaeda Organization in the Islamic Maghreb (AQIM). Bomb attacks in 2007 led analysts to suspect that the group was about to change its strategy, relying more on high-impact attacks. In 2008 and 2009, AQIM regularly ambushed military, paramilitary, and police units. The next year saw an increased regionalization of AQIM activities, which prompted a regional approach by the affected countries, including the establishment of the Joint Military Staff Committee for Algeria, Mali, Niger, and Mauritania. The conflict in Algeria remained active during 2012. The pattern of violence changed somewhat during the year as the situation in the region was severely affected by an influx of weapons and fighters. This was mostly noticeable in the southern parts of Algeria, where a new group, the Movement for Oneness and Jihad (MUJAO) surfaced, operating in the porous border areas in the Sahel.

In the wake of 9/11, the Algerian government received significant international support, much of it from the United States, for its fight against Muslim extremism. The character of the violence in Algeria has changed dramatically over the years and has expanded to include government officials, representatives of the opposition, foreigners, and journalists. In the mid-1990s, the conflict turned into carnage. GIA, issuing a fatwa that charged the whole Algerian society with apostasy, launched a new strategy, specifically targeting the civilian population. The army's countermeasures became increasingly brutal, resulting in accusations of gross human rights abuses.

Azerbaijan
Intrastate with the Republic of Nagorno-Karabakh

At the beginning of the twentieth century, Nagorno-Karabakh was a part of Armenia, but in the 1920s it was decided that the area was to belong to Azerbaijan. During the Soviet era the underlying conflict in the area was suppressed, but re-emerged with perestroika at the end of the 1980s.

In February 1988, the regional council in Nagorno-Karabakh voted to integrate into Armenia. Moscow responded by imposing direct rule over the territory. As soon as this ended in November 1989, Armenia declared the enclave to be part of a unified Armenian republic. Armenia fought with the USSR over Nagorno Karabakh for two years.

The collapse of the Soviet Union in 1991 did not end the conflict. Rather, the dispute continued within the newly independent Azerbaijan, as Nagorno-Karabakh proclaimed itself a republic. The Azerbaijani leadership responded to Nagorno-Karabakh's proclamation by imposing direct presidential rule over the region. The president of Armenia announced in March 1992 that the status of Nagorno Karabakh was an internal matter of Azerbaijan, and the problem was thus to be solved by Azerbaijan only. Yet Armenia remained involved in the conflict over Nagorno-Karabakh, which resulted in tens of thousands of deaths between 1992 and 1994. After negotiations in Moscow in May 1994 with delegates from the Commonwealth of Independent States, the chair of the National Assembly in Azerbaijan signed a protocol calling for a ceasefire in the war and the deployment of international peacekeeping forces. The agreement was given legal status and extended indefinitely on July 27, 1994, by the defense ministers of Armenia and Azerbaijan and the military leader of Nagorno-Karabakh.

Low-level fighting resumed in 2005. Questions remain regarding the return of refugees, Nagorno-Karabakh's interim status, and the process for determining the region's final status. In 2012, border clashes continued, causing 25 battle-related deaths for the first time since 2005. High-level diplomats repeatedly encouraged talks between the two negotiating parties (Armenia and Azerbaijan), but no agreements were reached.

Colombia
Intrastate with FARC, EPL, and ELN

The Colombian government is involved in a long-term armed conflict with several guerrilla organizations. The conflict, which is active throughout the country, has typically caused the death of thousands of people every year, with the total exceeding 40,000 over the past decade.

The weakness of the Colombian state during the 1970s resulted in the formation of self-defense groups as private armies for rich landowners and drug lords. Subsequently, lucrative drug trafficking and kidnappings made these paramilitary forces increasingly independent. In 1995, the United Self-Defense Forces of Colombia (AUC) was formed as an umbrella organization for several local paramilitary groups.

In 2002, President Uribe stated his determination to fight "outlaws" on both the left and right of the political spectrum. AUC declared a ceasefire in December 2002. In June 2003, the government, AUC, and Catholic Church representatives signed an accord stipulating complete AUC demobilization by December 31, 2005. As of the end of 2005, half of AUC's 20,000 fighters had handed in their arms. Demobilization of the AUC was completed in 2006.

As a result, whereas several groups were fighting the government at the beginning of the 1990s, only the two main left guerrilla groups remained active (the People's Liberation Army, EPL, was also active as late as 2004). One is the Revolutionary Armed Forces of Colombia–the People's Army (FARC–EP), the only peasant-based guerrilla movement. The other is the National Liberation Army (ELN), which was created by a group of students whose objective was to bring down the government. The ELN declared itself to be the military wing of the Communist Party of Colombia Marxist Leninist (PCML). Uribe's hope was that FARC-EP and ELN would follow AUC's example, but this did not come to pass.

The United States has supported Colombia mainly by providing financial support for the government's anti-narcotics policies. The support expanded to counter-terrorism in 2001. FARC, ELN, and AUC are listed on the US Department of State's Current List of Designated Foreign Terrorist Organizations.

Since 2006, the conflict intensity has decreased every year. In both 2007 and 2008, marches, protesting against kidnappings and demanding the liberation of hostages, have been organized nationwide. In 2008, FARC lost its two top commanders: Manuel "Shureshot" Marulanda, who died of a heart attack, and Raul Reyes, who was shot by the army on Ecuadorean territory, causing tense diplomatic relations between the two bordering countries. That same year, FARC released a total of six high-ranking politicians, in two separate instances, that they had held hostage. In 2009 and 2010, the conflict remained active at the same intensity level, but members of ELN and FARC were reported to have been surrendering arms.

Peace negotiations between the government and FARC opened in Oslo in October 2012. Meanwhile, President Santos continued military airstrikes on rebel camps throughout the year and declared that the government would not consider a ceasefire until a final agreement was reached. In November, when peace talks continued in Havana, FARC declared a unilateral ceasefire as a goodwill gesture. As of December 2012, however. the conflict in Colombia was still ongoing.

Democratic Republic of the Congo (Zaire)
Intrastate with M23, with Foreign Involvement

Large-scale conflict began in the Democratic Republic of Congo (DRC) in the mid-1990s. Remnants of the Interhamwe militia responsible for perpetrating the genocide in Rwanda fled to the DRC (then Zaire), where they staged attacks from refugee camps against ethnic Tutsi Banyamulenge.

Following the Interhamwe influx, armed Banyamulenge groups joined forces under the banner of the Alliance des forces démocratiques pour la libération du Congo (AFDL) with other rebels opposed to DRC dictator Mobutu. After toppling Mobutu in 1997, AFDL leader Laurent Kabila seized power, quickly alienating his former supporters. Concerned at Kabila's anti-Banyamulenge stance, armed Banyamulenge, joined by loyal Mobutuists, formed the anti-Kabila rebel group Rassemblement congolais pour la démocratie (RCD).

Several foreign governments were involved with the conflict in the DRC. Initially, the Rwandan, Ugandan, and Angolan governments aided AFDL as a strike against

Mobutu, who allowed rebel groups from all three countries to launch attacks from DRC soil. By the conflict's second phase, alliances had shifted, with Rwanda and Uganda turning on Kabila to support the rebel opposition, and Angola, Chad, Zimbabwe, and Namibia intervening on behalf of Kabila.

Peace accords providing for the disarmament of militias and the deployment of a UN peacekeeping force were signed in mid-1999. Little progress was made in implementing the agreement until the 2001 death of Kabila left his more accommodating son in control. In 2006, Joseph Kabila became the DRC's first democratically elected president in 40 years.

Dissatisfied with the outcome of the conflict, former RDC rebel Laurent Nkunda launched the Congrès National pour la Défense du Peuple (CNDP). In 2007, violence between the government and CNDP escalated.

Negotiations yielded a January 23, 2008, ceasefire agreement that mandated the creation of a UN buffer zone and promised amnesty to militia fighters. Despite this fragile peace agreement, fighting flared up again in August 2008 in North Kivu, amid rumors that CNDP was recruiting and rearming. The violence escalated in October as the combined efforts of the DRC army and UN forces failed to contain major CNDP advances, and tensions continued to mount over Rwandan support for Nkunda. A ceasefire, declared by Nkunda on November 16, 2008, grew increasingly tenuous as talks between CNDP and the government deadlocked in December, prompting CNDP to refuse to recommit to the ceasefire and threaten to advance into the UN buffer zone.

On January 23, 2009, Laurent Nkunda was arrested by the Rwandan government during a Rwandan military operation within DRC borders aimed at hunting down the Hutu rebel group FDLR. In the wake of Nkunda's arrest, this phase of the conflict ended in an agreement on March 23, 2009, in which it CNDP agreed to become a political party in exchange for the release of its imprisoned members. About 6,000 CNDP combatants were subsequently integrated into the Forces Armées de la République Démocratique du Congo (FARDC).

In April 2012, former CNDP soldiers, allegedly sponsored by the government of the neighboring Rwanda, mutinied against the DRC government, which has been supported by the peacekeeping contingent of the United Nations Organization Stabilization Mission in the Democratic Republic of the Congo (MONUSCO). Mutineers formed a rebel group called the March 23 Movement (M23). The primary grievance of M23 was the slow implementation of the 2009 peace agreement.

Active fighting commenced in July 2012, with M23 attacks that led FARDC troops to flee from several towns in North Kivu province. On November 20, 2012, M23 took control of Goma, the provincial capital. By the end of November, the conflict had forced more than 140,000 people to flee their homes, according to UNHCR, on top of those already forcibly displaced by previous conflict in the region. After repelling an ill-organized government counterattack and making some further gains, M23 agreed to withdraw from Goma on its own and left the city in early December.

Ethiopia

Intrastate with OLF

Since the state of Oromiya fell under Ethiopian control in the late 1890s, the Oromo people have lacked political influence and proportionate representation. In response to repressive government policies targeting Oromo cultural, social, and political movements, the Oromo Liberation Front (OLF) was formed in 1974, with the stated goal of realizing "national self-determination for the Oromo people and their liberation from oppression and exploitation in all forms." Over the years, the OLF has experienced internal tension, particularly between its Christian wing, based in the territory's west, and its Muslim and animist backers, active in the region's east and south, but the group remains intact.

The OLF experienced a difficult first decade. To isolate and contain the group, the Dergue regime initiated a series of resettlement, villagization, and collectivization policies during the 1970s that succeeded in limiting the OLF's influence. By the mid-1980s, however, the Oromo population had grown increasingly resentful of these policies, allowing the OLF to rally a larger following. Despite its rising popularity, the OLF remained crippled by the pronounced disparity between its military resources and those of the Ethiopian government. Lacking any outside suppliers, the OLF was forced to build its arsenal of weapons and supplies through surprise raids against government troops, a strategy that proved only marginally successful.

Except for a brief pause in the armed struggle while the OLF attempted to negotiate with the Ethiopian People's Revolutionary Democratic Front (EPRDF) government in the wake of its ouster of the Dergue, the OLF continued its low-level anti-government violence throughout the 1990s. Following failed negotiations with the government in 1997, the more militant wing of the group gained traction. The violence escalated in 1999 when Ethiopia's war with neighboring Eritrea provided the OLF with a window of opportunity. Emboldened by arms shipments from Eritrea, the OLF took advantage of the Ethiopian military's preoccupation by intensifying its attacks.

In late 2004, the OLF, under intense pressure to participate in the 2005 elections, appeared to be on the brink of a major policy shift, publicly stating its willingness to open negotiations. Ultimately, however, the OLF refused to participate in the elections.

The possibility of negotiation completely evaporated when the government brutally put down street protests in Oromiya in late 2005. The next year saw the government launch a large-scale offensive on rebel positions, but due to the extreme drought that hit the region, the offensive lost its momentum. Since then the conflict has continued, albeit at a low level. Fighting still takes place, and the rebels admit to losing between 10 and 20 fighters each month. From 2010 onwards, Ethiopia has cooperated increasingly closely with the Kenyan government, which has clamped down hard on OLF activities and rebels on its soil. Hundreds of OLF fighters are reported to have been arrested and deported. The operation was reportedly helped by the ongoing drought, which flushed the rebels from their hiding to look for water and food.

Ethiopia

Intrastate with ONLF

In 1984, the Ogaden National Liberation Front (ONLF) was established to struggle for self-determination. In January 1996, armed conflict broke out when ONLF declared a holy war against Ethiopia and launched an attack on Ethiopian government troops with the stated aim of liberating Ogaden from the Ethiopian colonial power. ONLF offered the government a negotiated dialogue, but these proposals were turned down.

In June 1996, ONLF signed a military agreement on an alliance with the Oromo Liberation Front (OLF), though the parties still acted separately. On August 15, 1997, ONLF and one faction of Afar Revolutionary Democratic Unity Front (ARDUF) signed a document in which the two organizations agreed to cooperate and coordinate their political, diplomatic, and military efforts.

Around that time, ONLF split into two factions: one that wanted to continue armed operations against the regime in Addis Ababa, the other that saw its fight as occurring within the framework of the Somali regional state (which was now led by one of its officials, Mohamed Maalim). In June 1998, the latter faction merged with the Ethiopian-Somali Democratic League (ESDL) and formed a new party called the Somali Democratic Party, with the intention of establishing a new regional government. The remaining faction of ONLF continued the armed struggle.

The conflict was inactive in 1997, but erupted again the following year and has persisted ever since. ONLF and OLF engaged in joint operations against the government in 2006 and 2007. The low-intensity conflict escalated when an April 24, 2007, attack on a Chinese-run oil field in the remote Ogaden region killed 74 people, including nine Chinese employees. ONLF claimed responsibility. Subsequently, fighting has remained at a high level. ONLF accused the Ethiopian government of punishing civilians for rebel activity in the Ogaden region and even alleged attempted genocide. In April 2009, the government announced that the rebel group was on its last leg, something that was immediately refuted by ONLF. The rebels' declaration of strength gained some credibility when large-scale fighting erupted in mid-November, claiming hundreds of deaths on both sides.

In 2010, divisions within the rebel group surfaced, as a break-away faction under Salahdin Abdulrahman Ma'ow signed a peace agreement with the government in October. In 2012, a process towards the initiation of formal negotiations between the main body of the group and the government was initiated, but it soon ran into trouble, and fighting continued at a low intensity.

India

Intrastate with CPI-M

In the late 1960s, several elements of the Indian communist movement revolted against the prevailing Communist Party of India (CPI-M), accusing it of being counterrevolutionary. This Naxalite movement became a revolutionary party with the establishment of the Communist Party of India (Marxist-Leninist) in 1969. Other groups that formed during this period and later, with differing views on the best strategy for agrarian revolutionary struggle, included the Communist Party of India (Marxist-Leninist), the People's War Group (PWG), and the Maoist Communist Centre (MCC). The PWG and MCC led the Maoist insurgency against the Indian state during the 1990s. The revolutionary aim included the abolition of the feudal order in rural India. The Naxalite organizations have primarily mobilized among the peasantry, particularly among the tribals and landless poor in the jungle districts of Andhra Pradesh, Maharahstra, Madhya Pradesh, and Orissa. The low-intensity conflict between the Indian government and the rebel opposition was only one dimension of the deteriorating security situation in the Naxalite strongholds of Bihar and Andhra Pradesh during the 1990s.

During 2004, the PWG and MCC were extending and consolidating their influence in their communist strongholds, while also further strengthening cross-border links with Nepalese Maoist cadres. The government in Andhra Pradesh declared a unilateral ceasefire with the PWG in June 2004. Peace talks were initiated in October, but ended without any substantial progress. On October 14, 2004, the MCC announced its merger with the PWG to form the Communist Party of India (Maoist) (CPI-M). Negotiations between CPI-M and the Andhra Pradesh state government broke down in mid-January 2005, after the rebels accused authorities of not addressing their demands for a written truce, release of prisoners, and redistribution of land.

CPI-M continued to consolidate its hold on large rural areas in several Indian states (Andhra Pradesh, Bihar, Chattisgarh, Jharkand, etc.). The conflict escalated in 2006–2009, affecting 13 of India's 28 states. In particular, the formation of a state-sponsored militia, the Salwa Judum, in the state of Chattisgarh catalyzed a sharp increase in violence. With each state responsible for its own security, there is no comprehensive, coordinated approach by the various state governments to the Maoist conflict, resulting in an increase in violence. The central government continues to treat the conflict as purely a security issue and opposes negotiating with the CPI-M until it agrees to lay down arms.

The conflict remained active in 2012, though with fewer fatalities than 2011, contributing to a trend of declining intensity that began in 2009. The Maoists continued to prepare landmine and IED ambushes on Indian security forces, including two deadly in January and March that captured national media attention. Meanwhile, security forces continued to conduct raids into Maoist territory.

India

Intrastate with Kashmir Insurgents

The insurgency in Kashmir results from the state's disputed accession to India following partition in 1947. The dispute escalated into full-fledged war with Pakistan in 1948. The UN-mediated ceasefire line agreed to in 1949 divided Kashmir between Indian- and Pakistani-controlled sections.

Anti-government demonstrations, strikes, and violent attacks on government targets launched in 1988 marked the onset of the Kashmir insurgency. By 1990, as many as 40 different militant groups existed. The main division is between the pro-Pakistani elements, which favor accession to Pakistan, and the pro-Azadi elements, which favor Kashmir's complete independence.

The intrastate conflict has become closely entangled with the interstate relations between Pakistan and India. India has repeatedly accused Pakistan of supporting the Kashmir separatists, while Pakistan has denied these allegations and stated that its support to the insurgents is limited to political, cultural, and diplomatic matters.

Positive moves by both parties in mid-2000 and early 2001 raised hope for a political dialogue, but no progress was made. Discussions have been deadlocked by irreconcilable preconditions. The Indian government insists that Kashmir is a purely internal matter and all talks must take place within the framework of the Indian constitution. The insurgents demand that Pakistan participate in the negotiations and that any talks must address the Kashmiris' demand for independence.

Cross-border infiltration has dipped thanks to the building of a new fence along the Line of Control and the cessation of military hostilities between India and Pakistan. Nonetheless, Kashmir insurgents continue to engage the Indian army.

The level of violence in Kashmir dropped in 2006, leading to an increase in tourism and development aid projects in the state. At the same time, disturbing indications continued throughout the year that civilians were increasingly becoming the target for militant violence. In particular, some groups appeared to redirect their energies towards large-scale attacks on soft targets outside of Kashmir, such as the Mumbai train bombings of July 2006, which were reportedly committed by the Kashmiri insurgent group Lashkar-e-Toiba.

After conflict fatalities and attacks on civilians declined sharply in 2007, violence rose in India-controlled Kashmir in 2008. One stimulus was the resumption of protests sparked by a planned land transfer of the site of a Hindu shrine. Also, the involvement of Pakistan-based militants in the November 2008 Mumbai attacks prompted a sharp escalation in tensions.

In 2010, despite a lack of progress in attempts to solve the conflict through dialogue, the intensity of the conflict decreased. There were concerns, however, that some rebel groups were shifting their focus to soft targets, following the Mumbai attack.

The conflict persisted into 2012. Even though fatalities increased slightly from the previous year, the intensity of the conflict remained exceptionally low—at less than half the level of 2010. The violence that did occur often resulted from the attempts of Kashmir insurgents to cross the Line of Control.

Iraq

Intrastate with TQJBR, Al-Mahdi Army, Jaish Ansar Al-Sunna, and ISI

After Iraq was defeated in the interstate conflict against the United States, United Kingdom, and Australia in 2003, forces from a United States-led coalition of countries remained in Iraq to support the new government. The situation remained volatile, with the Shi'a-dominated government unable to control spreading violence among insurgent groups.

The first was Jaish Ansar Al-Sunna (Army of Ansar Al-Sunna) in northern Iraq. This group stated in the fall of 2003 that it wanted to overthrow the Iraqi government.

As the number of casualties increased in the early months of 2004, the "Military Department" of the Zarqawi group stated their intention to overthrow the government, expel the US forces, and establish a Sunni Islamic state with shari'ah law. The group named itself TQJBR (Tanzim Qaidat al-Jihad fi Bilad al-Rafidayn, The Organization of Jihad's Base in the Country of the Two Rivers).

In early 2004, political discontent also grew among the Shi'a population, especially targeting the foreign presence in the country. One of the more outspoken critics was radical Shi'ite cleric Muqtada al-Sadr, who had previously formed a militia, the Al-Mahdi

Army. In April 2004, the Al-Mahdi Army launched coordinated attacks on government positions in southern Iraq, as well as in Baghdad. Subsequently, the militia fought the government intensively during that year. In late August, the main Shi'ite cleric in Iraq, Ayatollah Ali al-Sistani, intervened and negotiated a ceasefire. While some clashes continued, Muqtada al-Sadr focused on preparing for the elections in January 2005, ultimately winning 30 seats in the new parliament.

Meanwhile, activity by TQJBR and the Jaish Ansar al-Sunna escalated in 2005. Incidents included intercommunal violence and attacks on civilians. In addition, Ansar al-Islam was active during 2004–2007 (and again in 2011).

Originally, the security forces cooperated with paramilitary forces of former rebel groups, such as the Kurdish KDP and PUK forces in the north and the Badr Brigades in Baghdad and in southern Iraq. By 2007, these paramilitaries had largely been incorporated into the official Iraqi police and army.

Growing discontent among the traditional tribal leadership with the behavior of several insurgent groups led to the formation of paramilitary tribal militias, which started to attack insurgents locally, particularly in Anbar province. The government encouraged this development and promoted it in other parts of the country as well.

The "surge" by the United States-led coalition in 2007 led to an intensification of the conflict. As the conflict eventually became less intense in Baghdad, the capital, there was an escalation of fighting further north in Iraq. Towards the end of the year, the number of incidents decreased, even though the number of casualties remained very high, as the insurgents started to focus on fewer, larger-scale attacks.

Violence gradually diminished during 2008 and into 2009, as the impact of the US troop surge took hold. Muqtada Sadr announced a six-month extension of his Mahdi Army ceasefire in February 2008. In November 2008, a long-term security pact between US and Iraq was signed, providing for US troop withdrawal by end of 2011.

The next step towards a full withdrawal of US forces was taken on August 31, 2010, when "Operation Iraqi Freedom" was officially ended and succeeded by "Operation New Dawn." This marked an end to the US combat mission in Iraq.

Violence in Iraq has persisted at a high level. To a large extent, the attacks against civilians, especially Shi'ite pilgrims, has continued. Islamic State in Iraq (ISI) mounted large-scale attacks involving suicide bombers and car bombs. In late 2012, it was reported that ISI had gained renewed strength and more than doubled its troops to about 2,500.

Israel

Intrastate with Fatah, Palestinian Islamic Jihad, and Hamas (and Hezbollah 2006)

The roots of the conflict lie in ancient and competing claims for the territory known as Palestine. The UN-mandated partition of Palestine in 1947 led to the establishment of the State of Israel in 1948, which was followed by five interstate wars with Arab countries between 1948 and the present. Two outcomes of the wars fed the Israeli-Palestinian part of the Israeli-Arab conflict: Palestinian refugees from the 1948–1949 war, and Israeli occupation of the West Bank and Gaza—from Jordan and Egypt—in 1967.

In 1959, Yasser Arafat founded Fatah and became an important player in the Palestinian Liberation Organization (PLO), an umbrella organization. Other Palestinian organizations took up arms soon after Fatah. Hezbollah has its origins in the Israeli occupation of southern Lebanon, after its intervention in the Lebanese civil war in 1982.

In the West Bank and Gaza, Islamic groups such as Palestinian Islamic Jihad (PIJ) and Hamas conducted their first attacks during the later half of the 1980s. Local Palestinian leaders in December 1987 initiated violent demonstrations against the Israeli occupation, the so-called Intifada (Uprising).

The Oslo Accord, signed on September 13, 1993, called for the establishment of a Palestinian Interim Self-Government Authority and a preparatory transfer of power and responsibilities from Israel to authorized Palestinians, with a final settlement to be reached within five years. The second Intifada began in 2000 and all but ended any chance that the Oslo Accord would be implemented.

In early 2005, Israel proceeded with the construction of a security wall roughly along the Green Line separating Israel from the West Bank. Israel's pullout from Gaza and the official ceasefire led to a decrease in conflict activity in 2005.

In early 2006, Hamas won legislative elections in the West Bank and Gaza. Violence subsequently escalated between Israelis and Palestinians, while tensions also rose between Hamas and Fatah. The refusal by Hamas to recognize Israel and respect previously signed agreements led to an almost complete blockade from Western countries.

At the peak of Israeli-Palestinian clashes, the conflict with Hezbollah in southern Lebanon reignited in 2006, following the abduction of two Israeli soldiers in July. A fragile UN-brokered ceasefire commenced on August 14. Nonetheless, Israeli-Palestinian tit-for-tat fighting continued in 2007. In June, Hamas-Fatah hostilities resulted in the breakup of the Palestinian territories into a Hamas-controlled Gaza Strip and a Fatah-controlled West Bank.

The first months of 2008 saw a continuation of rocket fire from Gaza towards southern Israel, as well as Israeli targeting of Hamas, with the blockade in force. A six-month ceasefire was reached through Egyptian mediation in June. As the truce ended in December, rocket fire began anew, as did Israeli attacks on rocket-launching crews and activists. On December 27, Israel launched a massive air assault and later ground assault on Hamas throughout the Gaza Strip. An internationally brokered ceasefire took hold on January 18, 2009. Hamas asserted firmer control over the firing of rockets from the Gaza Strip, policing other armed groups in the area so as to not provoke further Israeli attacks.

Fatah/PNA and Hamas signed a reconciliation agreement in May 2011, but no negotiations were held that year between Fatah/PNA and the government of Israel. The conflict continued to be active through 2012. Rocket attacks and airstrikes, perpetrated by both sides, were particularly intense during the second half of November 2012.

Myanmar (Burma)

Intrastate with KIO

The Kachin (or Jinghaw) ethnic group is based in the north of Myanmar, with parts of the population living in the neighboring areas of China's Sichuan and Yunnan provinces and India's Arunachal Pradesh.

The Kachin participated in discussions on Burmese independence, requesting the formation of a Kachin autonomous area with regional self-administration. In the Panglong conference on February 12, 1947, it was decided that "such a state is desirable." Yet few resources were allocated to developing Kachin-dominated areas. This led to a growing sense of discontent among the Kachin population, which manifested through the formation of nationalistic organizations at universities.

After Burma's independence in 1948, its original armed forces were organized along ethnic lines. The government survived mainly because of the ethnic parts of the army. In particular, the 1st Kachin Rifles unit, led by former anti-Japanese guerrilla commander Naw Seng, was notoriously successful in anti-communist campaigns.

When Naw Seng was ordered to attack the growing Karen insurgency in 1949, he instead mutinied and joined the Karen National Union (KNU). Following a series of successful offensives, Naw Seng left the KNU and established the Pawngywng National Defense Force (PNDF) and continued north to fight for an independent Kachin state. After having settled in isolated areas near the Chinese border, PNDF was attacked by government forces. Following talks with the local Chinese authorities, the PNDF crossed into China as refugees on May 5, 1950.

The Kachin Independence Organization (KIO) formed in 1961 and launched an armed struggle. Naw Seng returned to Burma as part of an offensive by the Communist Party of Burma (CPB) into northern Burma in early 1968.

In 1989, the aging leadership of KIO decided to change their goal from independence to self-determination. When the CPB disintegrated in 1989, several ethnically based factions emerged, including several Kachin factions that signed ceasefires with the government. In October 1993, a permanent ceasefire was announced between the government and the KIO, which was given formal authority over territory under the group's control, with the right to create a local civil administration and to develop the region. The ceasefire held for almost two decades, but little integration between the KIO-controlled areas and the rest of Myanmar occurred.

After the new constitution for Myanmar came into force in 2007, the KIO refused to reform its armed force into a army-controlled Border Guard Force, which increased tension between the two sides. The government started referring to KIO as an "insurgent organization," imposed partial boycotts on trade with KIO-controlled areas, and eventually sent forces into the area in 2011 that led to the breakdown of the ceasefire. Clashes continued throughout 2011. While fighting has continued, there were several rounds of Chinese-sponsored talks during 2011 and 2012. In 2012, the fighting escalated between the government and KIA across Kachin State. The fighting also included the involvement of at least four other Burmese rebel organizations in Kachin and northern Shan State. While these groups fought together against the government of Myanmar, they had differing goals from the KIO.

Nigeria

Intrastate with Jama'atu Ahlis Sunna Lidda'awati wal-Jihad (Boko Haram)

Nigeria, Africa's most populous country, is a heterogeneous state comprising numerous ethnicities, languages, and religious groups. On several occasions since independence, Nigeria has experienced different forms of conflict related to divisions between Muslims and Christians.

The Muslim population is mainly concentrated in the north. Since 1999, a number of northern states have adopted shari'ah law. Jama'atu Ahlis Sunna Lidda'awati wal-Jihad, commonly known as Boko Haram, was formed in 2002 or 2003 in Maiduguri of Borno State in northern Nigeria, with a stated goal of toppling the government and setting up fundamentalist Islamic rule. The founders of the group were reportedly inspired by the Taliban of Afghanistan. There have been allegations that local politicians were involved in the establishment of the Boko Haram, with the purpose of orchestrating violence to secure political power, but such claims have not been verified. Followers of the group, drawn from various ethnic groups and social backgrounds, reportedly pray in separate mosques and can be distinguished by their long beards and black or red headscarves. According to their belief, all who do not follow their strict interpretation of Islam should be considered infidels.

Boko Haram has in most reports been translated roughly as meaning "Western education is a sin" in the Hausa language spoken by many in northern Nigeria. In 2010, the group announced that rather than the commonly used Boko Haram, their official name was Jama'atu Ahlis Sunna Lidda'awati wal-Jihad, which means "Group Committed to Propagating the Prophet's Teachings and Jihad."

Until 2009, Jama'atu Ahlis Sunna Lidda'awati wal-Jihad was relatively unknown. In late July of that year, it launched an attack against a police station, marking the beginning of an armed conflict with the government. The violence culminated as the security forces lay siege to the group's base in Maiduguri, and the rebel leader Mohammed Yussuf was captured and killed. Although the government reported that most of the group's members had been killed or captured, some managed to escape and later made threats of renewed violence.

After Yussuf's death, the leadership and cohesion of the group became unclear. Many believe the main faction of the group has since been led by Abubakar Shekau, who was Yussuf's deputy leader. On August 14, 2009, however, a statement signed by a purported acting leader, Mallam Sanni Umaru, stated that the armed struggle would continue and warned that attacks would soon be launched all over Nigeria.

Following a period of relative calm, the group began to resurface in late 2010. Attacks on government targets became increasingly sophisticated and deadly in 2011. Activity increased in 2012, with the group responsible for over 700 deaths.

Pakistan (Baluchistan)

Intrastate with the BLA, BRA, and BLF

The armed conflict over the status of the territory known as Baluchistan, a sparsely populated but resource-rich province of Pakistan, began in 1974, when the national government disbanded a provincial government supporting Baluch grievances. An armed insurgency by the Baluch Liberation Front (BLF), under the leadership of Jumma Khan Marri, was subsequently launched and raged from 1974–1977.

The current conflict arose from local opposition to government development projects initiated in the region following Pervez Musharraf's ascent to power in 1999. Natural gas pipelines, new railroad and road networks, an international airport, and a deep-sea port were planned, along with the construction of new military bases to provide security for this new infrastructure. The infrastructure projects and heightened military presence soon earned the resentment of local ethnic Baluch, who accused the government of acquiring ancestral land without adequate compensation, displacing thousands from their homes, and failing to provide employment for the local population.

In September 2003, the Baluchistan Provincial Assembly unanimously passed a resolution against planned military cantonments in several cities. That same month, several nationalist Baluch political groups formed Baluch Ittehad (Baluch Unity), whose stated objective was to resist "anti-Baluchistan projects." By the end of 2003, small bombings and incidences of sabotage targeting new infrastructure were frequent.

The government responded by increasing its military presence, drawing vehement criticism from the Baluch. By the end of 2005 Baluch Ittehad had declared an autonomous Baluchistan, and large-scale fighting was under way.

Following government offensives against Baluch Ittehad and the eventual death of leader Nawab Akbar Bugti in August 2006, Bugti's successor announced that the struggle against the government would thereafter be directed by the Baluchistan Liberation Army (BLA). Operational since a June 2004 attack against a paramilitary checkpoint, the BLA was officially listed as a terrorist group by the Pakistani government in 2006. Joining forces with the remnants of Baluch Ittehad, the BLA carried out ambushes and rocket attacks on government infrastructure. Baluch activists claimed that heavy fighting, including government attacks against civilians in the region, persisted in 2007. In November 2007, the BLA stepped up its attacks against government forces amid rumors of internal discord.

On September 1, 2008, the insurgents suddenly announced an unconditional and unilateral ceasefire. On October 26, 2008, the Pakistani government unveiled a road map for the resolution of the conflict, one that emphasized constitutional changes, the rebuilding of institutions, and the redistribution of natural resource revenues. Yet no visible progress was subsequently observed toward settling the conflict. In early January 2009, both the BLA and the BRA (Baluchistan Republican Army) announced that their armed activities would resume.

The conflict ramped up significantly in 2012. Clashes occurred between BLA and the Pakistani government for the second year in a row. BRA and BLF returned to action after being dormant for 2 and 34 years, respectively. As it was the case with previous years, the responsibility for the majority of ambushes and attacks remained unclear.

The Pakistani government has accused India of backing Baluch groups, and suspects US and British intelligence agencies of aiding the Baluch in an attempt to counter Chinese influence in the region. Both India and the Baluch have denied any such involvement, along with claims that Afghan warlords are among the BLA rebels fighting in Baluchistan. The United States has been cooperating with the Pakistani army in the "War on Terror" in northern Baluchistan, but there have been no indications of overt American involvement in this conflict.

Pakistan
Intrastate with TTP

Following partition in 1947, many Urdu-speaking refugees (referred to as Mohajir) crossed the border from India and settled mainly around Karachi and other urban areas in the Sindh province of Pakistan. During the 1980s, the Mohajir Quami Movement (MQM), or Mohajir People's Movement, started promoting an agenda of political reform. In 1986, MQM leader Altaf Hussain encouraged Mohajir youth to begin an armed struggle. MQM demanded recognition of the Mohajir as a distinct ethnic group, increased political rights, and a territorial dimension. Street violence followed.

Late in 1990, following a coup, MQM participated in elections. The period from 1991 to 1994 was marked by subsequent factionalization of MQM, internecine clashes within the Mohajir community, and a series of harsh government crackdowns. In early

1996, MQM started to restrict its armed campaign and focused on demonstrating its commitment to a peaceful solution.

Meanwhile, the government faced criticism, mainly related to its overall legitimacy and the operation of the legal system in particular. Groups pressing for greater influence of Islamic traditions became increasingly prominent and militant, especially in the areas along the Afghani border such as the North-West Frontier Province and the Federally Administered Tribal Areas.

One such organization was Tehreek-e-Nifaz-e-shari'aht-e-Mohammadi (TNSM), or the Movement for the Enforcement of Islamic Laws, which was formed in 1989 with the stated objective of promoting the imposition of shari'ah-based laws in the Malakand region of the North-West Frontier Province. Following an unsuccessful attempt to fight alongside the Taliban government in the Afghanistan conflict in 2001, the practical leadership of the organization passed to Maulana Fazlullah, who started making increasingly militant statements against the Pakistani political system and against the government. In 2007, Fazlullah encouraged his followers to start attacking government forces. During the subsequent months, TNSM expanded its control over areas in the Swat valley, as police and government forces withdrew.

Fazlullah and his militant faction eventually joined an alliance of commanders against the government, Tehrik-i-Taleban Pakistan (TTP). This alliance was formed by commanders who were critical of the government's policy concerning the Federally Administered Tribal Areas and the North-West Frontier Province and who wanted political change in Pakistan, including the legislation of shari'ah law in the country. Intense fighting between TTP commanders and the government took place throughout 2008 and 2009. In late February 2009, a ceasefire was agreed to in the Swat valley, but large-scale fighting erupted in April. In response, the government launched offensives in the North-West Frontier Province and the Federally Administered Tribal Areas that continued throughout the year. These attacks led to high-intensity fighting, which dislodged TTP from territory that it controlled in most regions. TTP responded by increasing bomb attacks in population centers in the south of the country.

The camps of TTP commanders often coincided with al-Qaeda hideouts. As a result, US aerial attacks on al-Qaeda, which continued in 2009, also had an effect on the Pakistani conflict. The attempted car bomb attack in New York City's Times Square on May 1, 2010, revealed TTP's far-reaching aspirations beyond the destabilization of the Pakistani government.

Fighting between the Pakistani government and the TTP has continued at high intensity since 2010. Government security forces have launched military offensives against militant strongholds. Meanwhile, TTP has targeted security forces and pro-government tribal elders and peace committees. In addition, the conflict continued to be intertwined with other conflicts in the region.

Philippines
Intrastate with CPP

Increasing criticism of US involvement in Filipino affairs led to the formation of several protest groups during the early 1960s. Inspired by the successful revolutions in China, Cuba, and Vietnam, younger members of the Partido Komunista ng Pilipinas (PKP) were eager for the party to resume the type of armed activity that had characterized the party immediately after World War II.

In 1968, the Huk established the Communist Party of the Philippines (CPP), which favored the Maoist idea of an agrarian revolution and developed plans for a military struggle. CPP's military wing, the New People's Army (NPA), was established in 1969. Over the following years, the NPA kept expanding. In 1972, President Marcos declared nationwide martial law to suppress the "state of rebellion" caused by the Communists, as well as the increasing communal conflicts between Moros and Christians in Mindanao.

Fighting between the CPP and the government decreased in the early 1990s, due to several factors. The military was preoccupied with internal struggles. Changes also occurred within the CPP, including internal divisions on what tactics to pursue and as the result of diminishing international political support. Consequently, several factions left the CPP to pursue urban guerrilla warfare.

Conflict activity decreased as formal peace negotiations were held in the mid-1990s. Under President Estrada, peace negotiations stalled in 1998. The economic crisis of 1998–1999 also led to widespread criticism of the government. In addition, the different factions of CPP seemed to unite, followed by the conflict escalating in 1999–2002.

The CPP's main tactics were to connect with rural support and establish strongholds in the two largest islands, Luzon and Mindanao. As a result, it has been able to control substantial territory at times. The conflict continued unabated in 2005 and 2006, with NPA active in 69 of the country's 79 provinces.

In 2006, President Arroyo announced a policy of all-out war against the rebels. The rebels responded by calling for an intensification of the struggle. The violence persisted in 2007. Like previous years, Arroyo ordered the military to "crush" the CPP/NPA, calling them the number one threat to national security. By the end of the decade, the NPA was weakened, but still active, and continued to inflict losses on country's armed forces, as well as on civilians, often in joint attacks with Muslim rebel groups active in the southern part of the island of Mindnao.

Negotiations between the government and CPP broke down in 2011 and did not resume until more than a year later. Meanwhile, violence continued unabated. After unofficial talks in Oslo in June 2012, formal negotiations started in The Hague in late December, coinciding with the announcement of a new Christmas ceasefire.

Philippines

Intrastate with the MILF and Abu Sayyef Group

The government of the Philippines has long been involved in fighting communist and Moro insurgencies in Mindanao. The term "Moro" is more specific than the universal "Muslim," since it denotes the political identity of the local Muslims.

During the 1970s, the Moro National Liberation Front (MNLF) and its military wing engaged in armed struggle against the central government, leading to as many as 120,000 deaths. Under pressure from the Organization of the Islamic Conference, the MNLF dropped its demands for independence and settled for autonomy in 1976. The agreement provided for the granting of autonomy to 13 of the 23 provinces in Mindanao, Sulu, and the Palewan Islands. When the MNLF dropped its demand for independence, breakaway factions emerged, including the Moro Islamic Liberation Front (MILF). Hostilities resumed and continued into the early 1980s. In the early 1990s, increased international attention was directed towards Mindanao, resulting from several high-profile kidnappings. The Abu Sayyaf Group (ASG) was responsible for several attacks on civilians.

In 1996, the Final Peace Agreement was signed. Fighting decreased over the subsequent years. After formal negotiations had resumed, however, the government launched an "all-out war" policy against the Moro groups in 2000, leading to an escalation in conflict and the breakdown of peace talks. In 2003, the conflict between the government and MILF escalated again. During the second half of 2003, several attempts to start peace talks were made. The ceasefire lasted for much of 2004 as well, though sporadic clashes continued in 2004 and 2005 amid fresh peace talks. In 2006, negotiations continued between MILF and the government.

ASG continued to carry out attacks and bombings. In August 2006, the Philippine government launched a major offensive against the rebels on Jolo. In 2007, the MILF became active again as a negotiation deadlock between the warring parties persisted. Also, a new dyad became active in 2007 when a MNLF faction under Habier Malik declared jihad on the government. Around this time, ASG exhibited a tendency toward greater tactical and logistical cooperation with other armed Moro groups, carrying out several attacks separately with MILF, mainstream MNLF, and the new MNLF faction. Clashes in Mindanao between government troops and both MILF and ASG continued throughout 2008, amid sporadic but unsuccessful attempts at negotiation.

In July 2009, MILF signed a unilateral ceasefire and shortly thereafter started negotiating with the government. Yet fighting between government forces and ASG continued, and during the fall of 2009, violent encounters took place in the Sulu province and on the island of Basilan. In 2010, violence decreased substantially as MILF negotiated with the government and ASG was the only group active in the conflict.

In spite of several rounds of peace talks and a stated willingness to conclude a peace deal, violence between the government and MILF escalated in October 2011. Meanwhile, fighting between the government forces and ASG continued unabated.

The government of the Philippines and MILF met for numerous rounds of peace talks during 2012. In October, the parties signed the "Framework Agreement on Bangsamoro." A splinter group from MILF, Bangsamoro Islamic Freedom Movement, renounced the peace agreement and clashed with the government on several occasions. Fighting between the government forces and ASG continued unabated in 2012.

Russia

Intrastate with Forces of the Caucasus Emirate

The fall of the Soviet Union gave rise to separatist movements in the Caucasus, leading to armed conflict over the territory of Chechnya. As the conflict continued into the 2000s, Islamist tendencies within the Chechen pro-independence movement became stronger. Simultaneously, the conflict spread to large parts of the North Caucasus.

This dual development culminated on October 7, 2007, with the abolition of the Chechen Republic of Ichkeria (ChRI), marking the movement's final departure from Chechen nationalism. Doku Umarov, the former ChRI president, declared himself Emir (leader) Abu Usman of the newly instituted Caucasus Emirate. According to Umarov, the Russian Republics of Dagestan, Chechnya, Ingushetia, Ossetia, Karachay-Cherkessia, and Kabardino-Balkaria were provinces of the Caucasus Emirate.

These steps were endorsed by the Jamaats (Islamic communities), which were responsible for a large share of the violence in the North Caucasus. As a result, Chechens no longer constituted a majority among the resistance ranks in the North Caucasus. Although the Jamaats formally acted under the leadership of Umarov, they continued to operate autonomously and at least partly responded to specific local grievances. Starting in the autumn of 2008, they proceeded to launch attacks on a larger scale, conducting simultaneous attacks in different locations. Also, they increasingly used suicide bombings both inside and outside of the North Caucasus region. Examples of the most devastating bombings include attacks on a Moscow-St. Petersburg train in November 2009, the parliament building in Grozny, Chechnya, in October 2010, Moscow metro stations in March 2010, and the Domodedovo Airport in January 2011. The latter two killed dozens of civilians.

Meanwhile, the level of violence across the Caucasus Emirate increased substantially during 2008 and again in 2009, then remained at the level of several hundred deaths in the following years. The conflict displayed geographical variation in intensity. Dagestan replaced Chechnya in 2009 as the hotbed of rebel activity, becoming the Russian republic with the highest level of conflict-related violence. Kabardino-Balkaria, a formerly peaceful region, reached similar levels of violence to Chechnya throughout 2011 and 2012, while North Ossetia exhibited less activity than in previous years.

In 2012, a string of near-daily incidents, including bomb attacks as well as skirmishes and other low-level fighting, claimed over 500 lives. As in the past, most of the incidents took place in Chechnya, Dagestan, Ingushetia, and Kabardino-Balkaria. Also, regions previously untargeted by rebels, such as Tartarstan and the traditionally stable and wealthy Stavropol Territory and Karachay-Cherkessia, became targets of rebel activity. As before, military operations performed by the Russian government had varying degrees of success. Throughout the year, government security forces made claims of killing a number of regional heads of various sections of the Caucasus Emirate. The most senior confirmed kill was Ibragimkhalil Daudov, the Emir of the Dagestani shari'aht Jaamat, the largest of the Jaamats of the Caucasus Emirates.

Rwanda

Intrastate with FDLR

In the nineteenth century, what was to become the states of Rwanda and Burundi fell under the colonial control of first Germany and then Belgium. Although the people who populated these areas were linguistically and culturally homogenous, they were differentiated into three groups: the Hutu, the Tutsi, and the Twa. Belgian rule cultivated a dominant place in society for Tutsis and racial and ideological myths of Tutsi superiority and Hutu inferiority. These circumstances precipitated clashes between the two groups. A notable incident occurred in 1959, while Hutu and Tutsi political parties struggled to gain a place in the emerging democratic institutions of the country. Conflict escalated as the Belgian administration began to replace the Tutsi elite with Hutu representatives in preparation for majority rule.

Rwanda became an independent state in 1962. The independent Rwanda in turn became a state dominated by the Hutu, who violently repressed the Tutsis, killing many civilians, further exacerbating the ethnic divide.

Beginning in the 1960s, small groups of exiled Tutsis began attacking the Hutu-dominated government to regain power. It was not until 1990, however, that a more potent threat to the government of Rwanda appeared in the form of the Rwandan Patriotic Front (RPF), which invaded the country from Uganda, commencing the first phase of the intrastate conflict.

The RPF's struggle against the government was linked to the genocide of 1994, which was set in motion following the assassination of the presidents of both Rwanda and Burundi. Between April and July of that year, the government, the Armed Forces of Rwanda (FAR) and the Interahamwe militia perpetrated mass killings of Tutsis and moderate Hutus throughout Rwanda. At least 500,000 people died as a result of this and surrounding violence, including reprisals by the RPF government, targeting Hutus, after it seized power. The conflict continued, with the RPF government attacking the remnants of the Hutu government and the FAR as they launched an armed struggle from the eastern regions of the Democratic Republic of Congo (DRC), crossing the border into Rwanda. The armed struggle began in an organized manner in 1997, initially under the Peuple en Armes Pour la Liberation du Rwanda (PALIR). In 2000, this group merged with the Forces Democratiques de Liberation du Rwanda (FDLR), which largely supplanted PALIR in the lead role the next year. These two groups were involved in the First and Second Congo Wars, fighting against forces aligned with the governments of Rwanda and Uganda, with the conflict occurring in eastern Democratic Republic of the Congo (DRC), as well as in Rwanda.

In 2010, the conflict between the government of Rwanda and FDLR deescalated, after Rwanda withdrew all of its troops from the DRC in February 2009. A new operation Leo was conducted against FDLR by the DRC, with support from the UN peacekeeping force in the Nord and Sud Kivu Provinces.

Conflict between the government of Rwanda and the FDLR broke out again on Congolese territory in early 2012. Rwanda was also accused of supporting the M23 opposition group in DRC.

Somalia

Intrastate with SICS, with Foreign Involvement

Since the 1991 ouster of dictator Siad Barre, armed factions have been struggling over control of Somalia. Between 1997 and 2000, no effective government existed in Somalia, as fighting raged between rival clan-based militias.

In 2000, a Transitional National Government (TNG) was elected by clan elders at a peace conference boycotted by many opposition parties. Armed conflict continued in 2001, between the TNG and an umbrella organization of armed resistance groups calling itself the Somali Reconciliation and Restoration Council (SRRC).

A ceasefire agreement brokered by the InterGovernmental Authority on Development (IGAD) led to the 2004 creation of an Interim Charter, which outlined a five-year transition for Somalia from factionalized near-anarchy to a federation. In 2005, the new Transitional Federal Government (TFG) suffered a temporary geographic split between factions in Mogadishu and the safer city of Jowhar. By early 2006, the government factions had agreed on a compromise seat of power in Baidoa.

By this time, the Mogadishu faction of the TFG had been forced out of the city by a growing network of local Islamic courts. Having gained control of Mogadishu, the courts' militia declared itself the Supreme Islamic Council of Somalia (SICS) and proceeded to consolidate its power in southern Somalia.

The Ethiopian government, fearing the rise of a nationalist Islamic state on its border, sent troops in late 2006 to help prop up the TFG. SICS was pushed back to Mogadishu, which the group subsequently abandoned, dissolving its administrative wing and retreating to the south, where fighting continued. In January 2007, the United States launched airstrikes targeting al-Qaeda operatives reportedly fighting alongside SICS. Throughout 2007, SICS and affiliated clan militias waged a guerilla-style war in the streets of Mogadishu against government targets and Ethiopian troops. In late 2007, SICS was absorbed by the Alliance for the Re-Liberation of Somalia (ARS), a newly formed, anti-TFG, anti-Ethiopian umbrella group.

Despite the August 2008 signing by the TFG and ARS of the UN-brokered Djibouti Agreement, violence continued through the end of 2008. Disputes over the implementation of the agreement continue, and the peace process has been rejected by hardline camps within both the TFG and ARS, as well as extremist Islamic groups outside the ARS umbrella. As of December 2008, Islamist militias controlled almost all of south-central Somalia's major towns, with the exception of Mogadishu and Baidoa, where the almost-defunct TFG was holding onto tenuous control.

In January 2009, the resignation of TFG president Yusuf, coupled with the withdrawal of Ethiopian troops, fueled fears of government collapse and increasing violence. Despite the formation of a new, more inclusive unity government in early 2009, the conflict pitting the government against Islamist insurgents raged on in 2010. Spearheaded by Al-Shabaab, insurgents took control of most of southern and central Somalia. In Mogadishu, the capital, battles between insurgents and government forces supported by an AU peacekeeping force (AMISOM) have led to hundreds of civilian deaths.

In 2012, the mandate of the TFG ended and a new, ostensibly permanent government was put in place. Al-Shabaab continued its fight against the new government and was also responsible for a number of attacks inside neighboring Kenya, one of the countries providing troops to AMISOM.

Sudan

Intrastate with SLM/A and JEM

In early 2003, while the government and Sudan People's Liberation Movement/Army (SPLM/A) were negotiating a settlement of the conflict in southern Sudan, another conflict broke out in the Darfur region of western Sudan. The Sudan Liberation Movement/Army (SLM/A) declared that it would fight the government to change the political system in Sudan. It demanded a united democratic Sudan based on equality, the separation of religion and the state, complete restructuring and devolution of power, more even development, and cultural and political pluralism. Subsequently, another opposition group, the Justice and Equality Movement (JEM), also launched an armed struggle against the government. Its ambitions were to institute a federal system with autonomy for all states, a rotating presidency, and an equal distribution of natural resources.

SLM/A and JEM have cooperated both militarily and politically, despite internal disagreements and fighting between them. Chad, Eritrea, and Libya have supported SLM/A and JEM. Besides the fighting between the two rebel groups and the army, a government-aligned militia called Janjaweed has been burning villages, looting, and killing. An estimated 180,000 to 300,000 people have died in Darfur since the civil conflict erupted in 2003, with some 2.6 million civilians left homeless. The situation in Darfur also heavily influenced the situation in other parts of Sudan and in neighboring Chad.

Negotiations between the government of Sudan and SLM/A and JEM were held jointly and separately throughout the 2003–2005 period. They stalled over issues about power-sharing and security arrangements. Meanwhile, armed conflict continued in Darfur during 2005, albeit at a significantly lower level of intensity. The decline was due to the presence of African Union Mission in Sudan (AMIS) forces, the flight of most of the population to internally displaced person and refugee camps, pressure by the international community, and consolidation of areas of control by the warring parties.

Violence increased in 2006, accompanied by a deteriorating humanitarian situation and fragmentation among the rebel groups. Most of the fighting took place between the government and the National Redemption Front (NRF), an alliance formed in the beginning of July. Fragmentation among the rebels continued into 2007. Another umbrella movement, called the United Resistance Front (URF), was ultimately formed, unifying some of the SLM/A commanders. In 2008, serious clashes between government and rebel forces continued, despite the signing of a Status of Forces Agreement in February, which removed major barriers to deployment of hybrid peacekeeping force, leading to the arrival of UN Mission in Darfur and African Union troops.

In March 2009, the International Criminal Court (ICC) issued an arrest warrant, charging Sudanese President Bashir with crimes against humanity and war crimes. Following an appeal by the prosecution, the ICC issued a second arrest warrant, including a count of genocide, in July 2010.

In January 2011, South Sudan voted overwhelmingly in a referendum to move toward independence from Sudan. Ahead of the referendum, the Sudanese government, fearing a potential war with South Sudan, wanted to crush as much of the Darfurian rebel resistance as possible, to avoid being caught in a challenging two-front war. As a result, the violence during 2010 was the most intense since 2006. Most of the fighting was between the government and JEM, but significant clashes with SLM/A caused many battle-related deaths. In 2011, the Sudan Revolutionary Front (SRF) was formed, comprised of the SLM/A and JEM, as well as other rebel groups in Darfur and the South Kordofan and Blue Nile regions. All of these areas are severely marginalized, relative to Khartoum, which dominates the political and economic life of Sudan. Heavy fighting on these fronts continued into 2012. The fighting has a clear international dimension, as it is part of the Sudan-South Sudan proxy war.

Syria

Intrastate with FSA and Japhat al-Nusra li al-Sham

Syria was recognized as an independent state in 1946, after having no previous history of independent statehood. Its territory had long been part of the Ottoman Empire, which collapsed following its defeat in World War I, after which the territory of modern-day Syria became a French mandate. At the time of independence, a number of identities competed for dominance in Syria, along tribal, religious, nationalist, and pan-Arab lines.

A key organization in this respect was the Baath party, one of many radical parties that grew out of opposition to the Syrian system of governance that vested power in the landholders. Between 1966 and 1970, Hafiz al-Assad, a member of the Baath military clique, consolidated power in his own hands. Assad enforced his "corrective movement" (sometimes referred to as neo-Baathism) from 1970 onwards, not tolerating political dissent and controlling politics mainly through coercion and repression.

The party's ideology combined Pan-Arabism (the belief that all Arabs formed one nation that had been divided by imperialism), secularism that would include non-Muslims in the community, and socialism that would rid Syria of its "feudal" societal order. As a result of the party's dominance, these aspects of identity were embraced by the bulk of the country's Sunni Muslim majority (approximately 70 percent of the population; an additional 12 percent is Alawite, and 14 percent is Christian Arab). The traits of the ruling Baath party stood in stark contrast to the pious Sunni Islam that also persisted in Syria. This separate Muslim religious identity was institutionalized most overtly in the form of the Muslim Brotherhood.

Large-scale armed conflict erupted in 1979, as the Muslim Brotherhood initiated an armed struggle to try to bring down the autocratic government of Hafez Assad. This rebellion was crushed in 1982 by a bloody assault on the Muslim Brotherhood's stronghold of Hama.

The outbreak of the Arab Spring in 2011 saw protests in Syria against the government of Bashar al-Assad, who came to power following the death of his father in 2000. These protests were met harshly, with mass arrests, torture of detainees, the use of snipers against the crowds, and the deprivation of medical treatments for wounded protestors.

On July 29, 2011, Colonel Riyad al-Asaad, a defector from the military, announced the creation of the Free Syrian Army (FSA). Subsequently, he succeeded in building up an organized rebel group. During the fall of 2011, the FSA posed a considerable challenge to the government. The FSA employed a strategy of holding on to a series of strongholds and using a guerilla-style hit-and-run tactics against military convoys. The government lost control of parts of the territory—mainly the northwest of the country along the Turkish border, as well as Homs and Hama provinces. By the end of December 2011, the FSA even managed to capture some suburbs of Damascus.

The conflict in Syria continued unabated during 2012. It intensified as the year progressed, with high-profile events such as the shelling of Homs in February and the massacre in Houla in May, which killed hundreds of civilians. The regime primarily fought against the FSA, but during the year several other groups emerged, simultaneously fighting the Syrian regime. Both Kofi Annan and Lakhdar Brahimi have acted as mediators, so far without any lasting success.

Thailand

Intrastate with Patani Insurgents

Thailand, and its precursor the Kingdom of Siam, has effectively controlled the territory of former Patani Darussalam (Kingdom of Patani) since the late eighteenth century, exercising direct rule since 1902. In modern times, part of the former Patani belongs to Malaysia, and the rest has become the Thai provinces of Narathiwat, Patani, Yala, and Satun. In the first three of these provinces, located along the border to Malaysia on the eastern coast of Thailand, more than 75 percent of the population is Muslim, and the majority speaks Malay as their first language. Several initiatives have been launched to impose Thai language and customs, but these have often been met with resentment in the region.

Several different insurgent organizations have been active in Patani, but most have pursued distinctly different political objectives, which has caused substantial infighting. The numbers of attacks and casualties increased during 2003, but the government mainly blamed the violence on criminals. Following a large, well-coordinated attack on an army camp on January 4, 2004, the government started boosting its troop strength in the provinces.

This is consistent with a pattern where the government's main response has been to employ military force, even while offering to allocate development funds to the region and to build sport facilities in affected areas. The Thai authorities have been criticized for alleged use of torture in interrogation and extrajudicial killings of civilians, which has increased the tension between the population and the armed forces in the region. The Patani insurgents have also deliberately targeted civilians, especially teachers, who are viewed as representatives of the state.

Following the overthrow of the Thai government by the military on September 19, 2006, there were attempts to initiate negotiations and to promote development in the region. Emergency rule in the region was not removed, however, and the conflict continued unabated.

In 2010, the violence in southern Thailand abated, with fatalities at the lowest since 2003. The conflict escalated, however, in 2011, which registered as the most violent year since 2007. Nonetheless, several reports indicated that secret negotiations took place between representatives from the Southern Border Provinces Administration Centre and Pulo, one of the insurgent groups involved in the fighting.

The intensity of the conflict in 2012 remained roughly equivalent to that of 2011. Patani insurgents continued to use drive-by shootings and remotely detonated, homemade bombs to target soldiers and other individuals connected to the Thai government. At the same time, officials of the Thai government met with members of the insurgency for the first time.

Turkey
Intrastate with PKK

Abdullah Öcalan founded the Kurdistan Workers' Party (PKK) in 1974 as a Marxist-Leninist group. Unlike many other Kurdish organizations, such as KDPI in Iran and KDP and PUK in Iraq, the PKK originally demanded an independent, democratic Kurdish state, instead of Kurdish autonomy.

In August 1984, PKK forces began ambushing Turkish troops on Kurdish territory, initiating what would become a long campaign of violence. Greece, Iran, and Syria have provided the PKK with shelter, training grounds, and/or financial support. Northern Iraq has also been a safe-haven for PKK fighters.

After Öcalan was arrested and tried in 1999, he gave up the idea of a Kurdish state and convinced the PKK's Presidential Council to drop the word "Kurdistan" from the names of PKK's political and military wings (ERNK and ARGK). The PKK retained its sizeable "Public-defense Force."

In April 2002, the PKK changed its name, announcing that it had fulfilled its historical mission and was now dissolved. At the same time, the Congress for Freedom and Democracy in Kurdistan (KADEK) announced its establishment to continue PKK's struggle for the liberation of the Kurds through dialogue and democracy rather than violence. KADEK was dissolved after the summer of 2003, and a new Kurdish group, the People's Congress of Kurdistan (KONGRA-GEL), was formed with the goal of attracting broader support. The group reverted to the name PKK in 2005. That same year, a sharp increase in clashes with the government was reported.

On August 19, 2005, the PKK unilaterally declared a ceasefire after Prime Minister Erdogan announced that his government wanted more reforms for the Kurds. Attacks decreased but nevertheless continued, indicating that neither side fully adhered to the ceasefire. This measure appeared to be an effort by PKK to get their case heard during sensitive negotiations leading up to the October 3, 2005, date for the start of Turkey's entry talks with the European Union.

On three subsequent occasions—in September-October 2006, June 2007, and November 2010—the PKK declared unilateral ceasefires, reflecting its desire to find a peaceful negotiated solution to the conflict. Again, the ceasefires were not adhered to by either side. Instead, armed clashes, as well as the planting of bombs and landmines by the PKK, persisted. The bulk of the fighting took place in the PKK stronghold areas of southeastern Turkey and northern Iraq. In late 2007, the Turkish government had stepped up its military action against the PKK, with Parliament authorizing operations against PKK headquarters in northern Iraq. Cross-border air strikes, as well as ground incursions, continued in 2008. Fighting intensified in 2010, after a constitutional referendum.

Ahead of the June 2011 general elections, the government expressed, via informal channels, some willingness to engage with PKK, acknowledging PKK's ceasefire. This ceasefire ended, however, in the spring of 2011. Violence accompanied the election campaign, including an attack on a rally of Prime Minister Erdogan in early May. When Kurdish candidates were banned from standing for election, PKK intensified the violence in June and July. The Turkish government reacted by launching two intense military campaigns, including bombardments of PKK positions in northern Iraq, during the late summer and the fall.

The violence continued to escalate in 2012, particularly during the second half of the year. At the same time, there were reports of new talks between the Turkish government and the imprisoned PKK leader Öcalan in December. The main focus was the question of PKK's disarmament.

United States

Intrastate with al-Qaeda, with Foreign Involvement

The conflict between the United States and al-Qaeda is an untraditional case, with most of the activity taking place outside of the United States and armed forces from over 20 countries involved.

Al-Qaeda was formed in 1988 by volunteer forces that were fighting alongside the rebels in the Afghanistan conflict, as was discussed earlier. Encouraged by the 1989 withdrawal of Soviet troops that had supported the Afghan government in that conflict, al-Qaeda declared its intent to continue the jihad in defense of Islamic movements. Al-Qaeda's founder, Osama bin Laden, became increasingly critical of the United States and its presence in the Islamic world. A particular target was US airbases in Saudi Arabia.

On September 11, 2001, al-Qaeda launched attacks on civilian targets in New York City, as well as the Pentagon in Washington, DC. A stated goal was to force the United States to abandon its involvement overseas, and specifically in the Middle East.

Following these attacks, US president Bush declared a "war on terror" and al-Qaeda. Several other countries quickly committed their support. US demands that the Taliban extradite the al-Qaeda leaders were rejected. Beginning in October-November 2001, troops were deployed from Australia, Canada, France, Germany, Italy, Poland, Turkey, and the United Kingdom as part of the United States–led "Operation Enduring Freedom," while other countries offered assistance. By March 2002, more than 17,000 military personnel from 17 countries had been deployed alongside US forces as the so-called "coalition of the willing." Suspected al-Qaeda bases in Afghanistan were targeted, as was the Taliban regime itself for harboring and enabling al-Qaeda.

With the defeat of the Taliban government, the US attacks on al-Qaeda intensified. Most surviving al-Qaeda operatives fled across the border into Pakistan in 2002–2003, while others regrouped in Saudi Arabia.

The conflict resumed in 2004, with almost all of the activity taking place in the Pakistani tribal areas of South Waziristan and in Saudi Arabia. Between 2005 and 2007, the conflict activity was concentrated in the border region between Afghanistan and Pakistan. Civilian casualties caused by international forces prompted significant anger among the local population. In March 2006, the Pakistani army also launched a heavy military offensive in the border areas.

At the beginning of the Obama administration in 2009, the United States dramatically increased its troop levels in Afghanistan. This surge of troops was intended to create decisive victories over the Taliban and allow for the gradual withdrawal of US troops beginning in summer 2011. By 2011, the bulk of conflict activity was located in the border areas between Afghanistan and Pakistan, as well as the tribal districts of Pakistan. The campaign continued with CIA-operated drones targeting al-Qaeda and other terrorist networks in Pakistan's tribal area. A cross-border operation into Pakistan resulted in the killing of bin Laden by American special forces, increasing the tensions between the governments in Washington and Islamabad.

Yemen

Intrastate with AQAP

In 1948, the ruling Imam Yahya was ousted in a coup, which was followed by a short intrastate conflict. The following decades were characterized by turbulence in the government, intrastate conflict in 1962–1970, and a border war with South Yemen in 1972 and 1979. An intrastate conflict over government also took place in 1979–1982 between the leftist National Democratic Front (NDF) and the North Yemeni government. In 1990, North Yemen and South Yemen merged into the Republic of Yemen.

The first recorded al-Qaeda attack in Yemen took place in Aden, in southern Yemen, in 1992. Throughout the 1990s and the beginning of the 2000s, al-Qaeda carried out attacks on a low level.

In May 2003, al-Qaeda cells in Saudi Arabia carried out simultaneous suicide attacks on three Western housing compounds, leaving 29 people dead. Saudi security forces eventually managed to kill large parts of the al-Qaeda leadership in Saudi Arabia.

Meanwhile, al-Qaeda in Yemen was considerably strengthened in February 2006, when 23 al-Qaeda members escaped from Sanaa prison. The group recruited new members and set up new bases in Yemen. In September 2008, al-Qaeda cells were linked to a serious attack on the US embassy in Sanaa.

On January 23, 2009, the local al-Qaeda branches in Yemen and Saudi Arabia announced the formation of al-Qaeda in the Arabian Peninsula (AQAP). The group claimed that they had come together in order to launch a holy war in the Arabian Peninsula and establish an Islamic state. Yemen was described as the group's new base. Muslims from around the world were encouraged to travel to Yemen and join AQAP. In a later statement, the group called upon tribal leaders in Yemen to fight against the Yemeni government and support al-Qaeda members living in their areas. The first time al-Qaeda cells in Yemen directed their threats and attacks against the Yemeni government was in 2009. Throughout the year, there were numerous reports of arrests and clashes involving suspected al-Qaeda members. The Yemeni government stated that it would continue a military campaign against AQAP and vowed not to let Yemen become a refuge for terrorists.

In December 2009, the United States launched a missile strike against AQAP strongholds in Yemen. A few days after a failed December 25, 2009, attack on a transatlantic flight to the United States, AQAP claimed responsibility, stating that it was a response to the earlier attack, for which it blamed the US.

In 2010, the conflict between the government of Yemen and AQAP escalated significantly. Several clashes took place in southern Yemen, and a large number of suspected AQAP members were arrested throughout the year. In addition, parcels containing explosives sent from Yemen by AQAP were discovered on two cargo airliners bound for the United States on the October 29, 2010.

In 2011–2012, the conflict escalated further. In May 2012, the Yemeni military launched a large-scale offensive to regain control of the areas captured by AQAP in 2011. The army, heavily supported by local tribes, pushed AQAP on the defensive and ousted the group from the captured areas, including the important port city Zinjibar. Following the intense fighting, AQAP made a strategic shift and focused more on high-profile assassinations and hit-and-run attacks.

REFERENCES

Chapter 2

Collier, Paul, V. L. Elliot, Håvard Hegre, Anke Hoeffler, Marta Reynal-Querol, and Nicholas Sambanis. 2003. "Breaking the Conflict Trap: Civil War and Development Policy." *World Bank Policy Research Report*. Oxford, UK: Oxford University Press.

Collier, Paul, and Anke Hoeffler. 2004. "Greed and Grievance in Civil War." *Oxford Economic Papers* 56(4): 563–595.

Esty, Daniel C., Jack Goldstone, Ted R. Gurr, Barbara Harff, Marc Levy, Geoffrey D. Dabelko, Pamela T. Surko, and Alan N. Unger. 1999. The State Failure Task Force Report: Phase II Findings. McLean, VA: Science Applications International Corporation (SAIC).

Fearon, James D., and David Laitin. 2003. "Ethnicity, Insurgency, and Civil War." *American Political Science Review* 97(1): 75–90.

Gates, Scott, Håvard Hegre, Mark P. Jones, and Håvard Strand. 2006. "Institutional Inconsistency and Political Instability: Polity Duration, 1800–2000." *American Journal of Political Science* 50: 893–908.

Goldstone, Jack A., Ted R. Gurr, Barbara Harff, Marc A. Levy, Monty G. Marshall, Robert H. Bates, David L. Epstein, Colin H. Kahl, Pamela T. Surko, John Ulfelder, and Alan N. Unger. 2000. The State Failure Task Force Report: Phase III Findings. McLean, VA: Science Applications International Corporation.

Goldstone, Jack A., Robert H. Bates, Ted R. Gurr, Michael Lustik, Monty G. Marshall, Jay Ulfelder, and Mark Woodward. 2005. "A Global Forecasting Model of Political Instability." Paper presented at the Annual Meeting of the American Political Science Association, Washington, DC, September 1–4.

Gurr, Ted R.. "Persistence and Change in Political Systems, 1800–1971." *American Political Science Review* 68(4): 1482–1504.

Hegre, Håvard, and Nicholas Sambanis. 2006. "Sensitivity Analysis of Empirical Results on Civil War Onset." *Journal of Conflict Resolution* 50(4): 508–535.

Hegre, Håvard, Tanja Ellingsen, Scott Gates, and Nils Petter Gleditsch. 2001. "Toward a Democratic Civil Peace? Democracy, Political Change, and Civil War, 1816–1992." *American Political Science Review* 95(1): 33–48.

Hegre, Håvard, Ranveig Gissinger, and Nils Petter Gleditsch. 2003. "Globalization and Internal Conflict." In Gerald Schneider, Katherine Barbieri, and Nils Petter Gleditsch (eds.). *Globalization and Armed Conflict*. Lanham, MD: Rowman and Littlefield Publishers.

Hewitt, J. Joseph. 2008. "The Peace and Conflict Instability Ledger: Ranking States on Future Risk." In J. Joseph Hewitt, Jonathan Wilkenfeld, and Ted R. Gurr (eds.). *Peace and Conflict 2010*. Boulder, CO: Paradigm Publishers.

Hewitt, J. Joseph. 2010. "The Peace and Conflict Instability Ledger: Ranking States on Future Risk." In J. Joseph Hewitt, Jonathan Wilkenfeld, and Ted R. Gurr (eds.). *Peace and Conflict 2010*. Boulder, CO: Paradigm Publishers.

Hewitt, J. Joseph. 2012. "The Peace and Conflict Instability Ledger: Ranking States on Future Risk." In J. Joseph Hewitt, Jonathan Wilkenfeld, and Ted R. Gurr (eds.). *Peace and Conflict 2012*. Boulder, CO: Paradigm Publishers.

King, Gary, and Langche Zeng. 2001. "Improving Forecasts of State Failure." *World Politics* 53(4): 623–658.

Pate, Amy. 2008. "Trends in Democratization: A Focus on Instability in Anocracies." In J. Joseph Hewitt, Jonathan Wilkenfeld, and Ted R. Gurr (eds.). *Peace and Conflict 2008*. Boulder, CO: Paradigm Publishers.

Sambanis, Nicholas. 2001. "Do Ethnic and Non-Ethnic Civil Wars Have the Same Causes? A Theoretical and Empirical Inquiry (Part 1)." *Journal of Conflict Resolution* 45(3): 259–282.

———. 2002. "A Review of Recent Advances and Future Directions in the Quantitative Literature on Civil Wars." *Defense and Peace Economics* 13(3): 215–243.

———. 2004. "What Is a Civil War? Conceptual and Empirical Complexities of an Operational Definition." *Journal of Conflict Resolution* 48(6): 814–858.

United States Agency for International Development. 2005. "Measuring Fragility: Indicators and Methods for Rating State Performance." Washington, DC: United States Agency for International Development.

Chapter 3

Gleditsch, Kristian S. 2002. "Expanded Trade and GDP Data." *Journal of Conflict Resolution* 46(5): 712–724.

Chapter 4

Banks, Arthur S. 2001. Cross-National Time Series Data Archive, available at: http://www.databanks.sitehosting.net/Default.htm.

Geddes, Barbara. 1999. "What Do We Know about Democratization After Twenty Years?" *Annual Review of Political Science* 2: 115–144.

Goemans, Henk E., Kristian Skrede Gleditsch, and Giacomo Chiozza. 2009a. "Introducing Archigos: A Dataset of Political Leaders." *Journal of Peace Research* 46(2): 269–283.

Goemans, Henk E., Kristian Skrede Gleditsch, and Giacomo Chiozza. 2009b. "Archigos: A Data Set on Leaders, 1875–2004 (Version 2.9)." http://www.rochester.edu/college/faculty/hgoemans/Archigos.2.9-August.pdf.

Polity IV Project. 2011. "Polity Regime Characteristics and Transitions, 1800–2011." Polity IV Project website, http://www.systemicpeace.org/polity/polity4.htm.

Polity IV Project. 2010. "Polity Regime Characteristics and Transitions, 1800–2010: Dataset Users' Manual." Polity IV Project website, http://www.systemicpeace.org/inscr/p4manualv2010.pdf.

Chapter 5

Carr, David. 2012. "Using War as Cover to Target Journalists." *New York Times*, November 25.

Enders, Walter, Todd Sandler, and Khusrav Gaibulloev. 2011. "Domestic Versus Transnational Terrorism: Data, Decomposition and Dynamics." *Journal of Peace Research* 48(3): 319–337.

LaFree, Gary, and Laura Dugan. 2007. "Introducing the Global Terrorism Database." *Political Violence and Terrorism* 19:181–204.

LaFree, Gary, and Laura Dugan. 2009. "Research on Terrorism and Countering Terrorism." In M. Tonry (ed.). *Crime and Justice: A Review of Research*. Chicago: University of Chicago Press.

LaFree, Gary, Laura Dugan, and Kim Cragin. 2010. "Trends in Terrorism, 1970–2007." In J. Joseph Hewitt, Jonathan Wilkenfeld, Ted R. Gurr (eds.). *Peace and Conflict 2010*. Boulder, Colorado: Paradigm Publishers.

LaFree, Gary, Laura Dugan, and Susan Fahey. 2008. "Global Terrorism and Failed States." In J. Joseph Hewitt, Jonathan Wilkenfeld, Ted R. Gurr (eds.). *Peace and Conflict 2008*. Boulder, CO: Paradigm Publishers.

LaFree, Gary, Sue-Ming Yang, and Martha Crenshaw. 2009. "Trajectories of Terrorism: Attack Patterns of Foreign Groups That Have Targeted the United States, 1970–2004." *Criminology and Public Policy* 8(3): 445–473.

Chapter 6

Annan, Jeannie, Christopher Blattman, Dyan Mazurana, and Khristopher Carlson. 2011. "Civil War, Reintegration, and Gender in Northern Uganda." *Journal of Conflict Resolution* 55(6): 877–908.

Azam, Jean-Paul. 2002. "Looking at Conflict between Ethnoregional Groups: Lessons for State Formation in Africa." *Journal of Conflict Resolution* 46(1): 131–153.

Badiuzzaman, Mohammad, John Cameron, and Syed M. Murshed. 2011. "Household Decision Making under Threat of Violence: A Micro-Level Study in the Chittagong Hill Tracts of Bangladesh." Working paper.

Bakke, Kristin M., Kathleen G. Cunningham and Lee J. M. Seymour. 2012. "A Plague of Initials: Fragmentation, Cohesion, and Infighting in Civil Wars." *Perspectives on Politics* 10(2): 265–283.

Balcells, Laia. 2010. "Rivalry and Revenge: Violence against Civilians in Conventional Civil Wars." *International Studies Quarterly* 54(2): 291–313.

Balcells, Laia. 2011. "Continuation of Policy by Two Means: Direct and Indirect Violence in Civil War." *Journal of Conflict Resolution* 55(3): 397–422.

Barron, Patrick, Kai Kaiser, and Menno Pradhan. 2004. "Local Conflict in Indonesia: Measuring Incidents and Identifying Patterns." *World Bank Policy Research Working Paper #3384.*

Bhavnani, Ravi, and David Backer. 2000. "Localized Ethnic Conflict and Genocide: Accounting for Differences in Rwanda and Burundi." *Journal of Conflict Resolution* 44(3): 283–306.

Bhavnani, Ravi. 2006. "Ethnic Norms and Interethnic Violence: Accounting for Mass Participation in the Rwandan Genocide." *Journal of Conflict Resolution* 43(6): 651–669.

Bhavnani, Ravi, Dan Miodownik, and Hyun Jin Choi. 2011. "Three Two Tango: Territorial Control and Selective Violence in Israel, the West Bank, and Gaza." *Journal of Conflict Resolution* 55(1): 133–158.

Bhavnani, Ravi, and Karsten Donnay. 2012. "Here's Looking at You: The Arab Spring and Violence in Gaza, Israel and the West Bank." *Swiss Political Science Review* 18(1): 124–131.

Bhavnani, Ravi, Karsten Donnay, Dan Miodownik, Maayan Mor, and Dirk Helbing. 2013. "Group Segregation and Urban Violence." *American Journal of Political Science*. doi: 10.1111/ajps.12045.

Blair, Robert, Christopher Blattman, and Alexandra Hartman. 2012. "Predicting Local-Level Violence." Unpublished paper.

Bohlken, Anjali T., and Ernest J. Sergenti. 2010. "Economic Growth and Ethnic Violence: An Empirical Investigation of Hindu-Muslim Riots in India." *Journal of Peace Research* 47(5): 589–600.

Bosi, Lorenzo, and Donattella Della Porta. 2012. "Micro-Mobilization into Armed Groups: Ideological, Instrumental and Solidaristic Paths." *Qualitative Sociology* 35(4): 361–383.

Bozzoli, Carlos, and Tilman Brück. 2009. "Agriculture, Poverty, and Postwar Reconstruction: Micro-Level Evidence from Northern Mozambique." *Journal of Peace Research* 46(3): 377–397.

Braithwaite, Alex, and Shane D. Johnson. 2012. "Space-Time Modeling of Insurgency and Counterinsurgency in Iraq." *Journal of Quantitative Criminology* 28(1): 31–48.

Buhaug, Halvard, and Jan K. Rød. 2006. "Local Determinants of African Civil Wars 1970–2001." *Political Geography* 25(3): 315–335.

Buhaug, Halvard, Scott Gates, and Päivi Lujala. 2009. "Geography, Rebel Capability, and the Duration of Civil Conflict." *Journal of Conflict Resolution* 53(4): 544–569.

Buhaug, Halvard, Kristian S. Gleditsch, Helge Holtermann, Gudrun Østby, and Andreas F. Tollefsen. 2011. "It's the Local Economy, Stupid! Geographic Wealth Dispersion and Conflict Outbreak Location." *Journal of Conflict Resolution* 55(5): 814–840.

Butler, Christopher K., and Scott Gates. 2012. "African Range Wars: Climate, Conflict, and Property Rights." *Journal of Peace Research* 49(1): 23–34.

Cederman, Lars-Erik, and Kristian S. Gleditsch. 2009. "Introduction to Special Issue on 'Disaggregating Civil War'." *Journal of Conflict Resolution* 53(4): 487–495.

Cederman, Lars-Erik, Nils B. Weidmann, and Kristian S. Gleditsch. 2011. "Horizontal Inequalities and Ethnonationalist Civil War: A Global Comparison." *American Political Science Review* 105(3): 478–495.

Chojnacki, Sven, Christian Ickler, Michael Spies, and John Wiesel. 2012. "Event Data on Armed Conflict and Security: New Perspectives, Old Challenges, and Some Solutions." *International Interactions* 38(4): 382–401.

Collier, Paul, and Anke Hoeffler. 1998. "On the Economic Causes of Civil War." *Oxford Economic Papers* 50(4): 563–573.

Condra, Luke N., and Jacob N. Shapiro. 2012. "Who Takes the Blame? The Strategic Effects of Collateral Damage." *American Journal of Political Science* 56(1): 167–187.

Czaika, Mathias, and Krisztina Kis-Katos. 2009. "Civil Conflict and Displacement: Village-Level Determinants of Forced Migration in Aceh." *Journal of Peace Research* 46(3): 399–418.

Dabalen, Andrew L., Ephraim Kebede, and Saumik Paul. 2012. "Causes of Civil War: Micro Level Evidence from Côte d'Ivoire." *Households in Conflict Working Paper* No. 118.

Davenport, Christian, and Patrick Ball. 2002. "Views to a Kill: Exploring the Implications of Source Selection in the Case of Guatemalan State Terror, 1977–1995." *Journal of Conflict Resolution* 64(3): 427–450.

Do, Quy-Toan, and Lakshmi Iyer. 2010. "Geography, Poverty and Conflict in Nepal." *Journal of Conflict Resolution* 47(6): 735–748.

Eck, Kristine. 2012. "In Data We Trust? A Comparison of UCDP GED and ACLED Conflict Events Datasets." *Cooperation and Conflict* 47(1): 124–141.

Fearon, James. D., and David Laitin. 2003. "Ethnicity, Insurgency, and Civil War." *American Political Science Review* 97(1): 75–90.

Field, Erica, Matthew Levinson, Rohini Pande, and Sujata Visaria. 2008. "Segregation, Rent Control, and Riots: The Economics of Religious Conflict in an Indian City." *American Economic Review* 98(2): 505–510.

Florez-Morris, Mauricio. 2010. "Why Some Colombian Guerrilla Members Stayed in the Movement until Demobilization: A Micro-Sociological Case Study of Factors That Influenced Members' Commitment to Three Former Rebel Organizations: M-19, EPL, and CRS." *Terrorism and Political Violence* 22(2): 216–241.

Gubler, Joshua, and Joel S. Selway. 2012. "Horizontal Inequality, Crosscutting Cleavages, and Civil War." *Journal of Conflict Resolution* 56(2): 206–232.

Haushofer, Johannes, Anat Biletzki, and Nancy Kanwisher. 2010. "Both Sides Retaliate in the Israeli-Palestinian Conflict." *Proceedings of the National Academy of Sciences of the United States of America* 107:17927–17932.

Hegre, Håvard, Gudrun Østby, and Clionadh Raleigh. 2009. "Poverty and Civil War Events: A Disaggregated Study of Liberia." *Journal of Conflict Resolution* 53(4): 598–623.

Herreros, Francisco, and Henar Criado. 2009. "Pre-emptive or Arbitrary: Two Forms of Lethal Violence in Civil War." *Journal of Conflict Resolutions* 53(3): 419–445.

Hug, Simon. 2003. "Selection Bias in Comparative Research: The Case of Incomplete Data Sets." *Political Analysis* 11(3): 255–274.

Humphreys, Macartan, and Jeremy M. Weinstein. 2006. "Handling and Manhandling Civilians in Civil War." *American Political Science Review* 100(3): 429–447.

Humphreys, Macartan, and Jeremy M. Weinstein. 2008. "Who Fights? The Determinants of Participation in Civil War." *American Journal of Political Science* 52(2): 436–455.

Humphreys, Macartan, and Jeremy M. Weinstein. 2009. "Field Experiments and the Political Economy of Development." *Annual Review of Political Science* 12(1): 367–378.

Ibáñez, Ana María, and Andrea Velásquez. 2009. "Identifying Victims of Civil Conflicts: An Evaluation of Forced Displaced Households in Colombia." *Journal of Peace Research* 46(3): 431–451.

Jaeger, David A., and M. Daniele Passerman. 2006. "Israel, the Palestinian factions, and the Cycle of Violence." *American Economic Review* 96: 45–49.

Jaeger, David A., and M. Daniele Passerman. 2008. "The Cycle of Violence? An Empirical Analysis of Fatalities in the Palestinian-Israeli Conflict." *American Economic Review* 98(4): 1591–1604.

Justino, Patricia. 2009. "Poverty and Violent Conflict: A Micro-level Perspective on the Causes and Duration of Warfare." *Journal of Peace Research* 46(3): 315–333.

Justino, Patricia, Tilman Brück, and Philip Verwimp. 2013. "Micro-level Dynamics of Conflict, Violence and Development: A New Analytical Framework." Working paper.

Justino, Patricia, and Philip Verwimp. 2013. "Poverty Dynamics, Violent Conflict, and Convergence in Rwanda." *The Review of Income and Wealth* 59(1): 66–90.

K'Akumu, Owiti A., and Washington A. Olima. 2007. "The Dynamics and Implications of Residential Segregation in Nairobi." *Habitat International* 31(1): 87–99.

Kalyvas, Stathis N. 2006. *The Logic of Violence in Civil War*. Cambridge: Cambridge University Press.

Kalyvas, Stathis N. 2008. "Promises and Pitfalls of an Emerging Research Program: The Microdynamics of Civil War." In Stathis N. Kalyvas, Ian Shapiro, and Tarek Masoud (eds.). *Order, Conflict, and Violence*. New York: Cambridge University Press.

Kalyvas, Stathis N. 2012. "Micro-level Studies of Violence in Civil War: Refining and Extending the Control-Collaboration Model." *Terrorism and Political Violence* 24(4): 658–668.

Kasara, Kimuli. 2013. "Separate and Suspicious: Local Social and Political Context and Ethnic Tolerance in Kenya." *Journal of Politics* 75(4): 921–936.

Kingoriah, George K. 1980. "Policy Impacts on Urban Land Use Patterns in Nairobi, Kenya 1899–1979." PhD thesis, Indiana State University.

Leetaru, Kalev, and Philip A. Schrodt. 2013. "GDELT: Global Data on Events, Location and Tone, 1979–2012." Paper presented at the Annual Meeting of the International Studies Association, San Francisco, CA, April 2013.

Linke, Andrew, Frank Wittmer, and John O'Loughlin. 2012. "Space-Time Granger Analysis of the War in Iraq: A Study of Coalition and Insurgent Action and Reaction." *International Interactions* 38(4): 402–425.

Lujala, Päivi. 2010. "The Spoils of Nature: Armed Civil Conflict and Rebel Access to Natural Resources." *Journal of Peace Research* 47(1): 15–28.

Lyall, Jason. 2009. "Does Indiscriminate Violence Incite Insurgent Attacks? Evidence from Chechnya." *Journal of Conflict Resolution* 53(3): 331–362.

Lyall, Jason. 2010. "Are Coethnics More Effective Counterinsurgents? Evidence from the Second Chechen War." *American Political Science Review* 104(1): 1–20.

Lyall, Jason. 2013. "Dynamic Coercion in Civil War: Evidence from Air Operations in Afghanistan." Working paper.

Lyall, Jason, and Isaiah Wilson. 2009. "Rage Against the Machines: Explaining Outcomes in Counterinsurgency Wars." *International Organization* 63(1): 67–106.

McCauley, John F. 2013. "Economic Development Strategies and Communal Violence in Africa: The Cases of Côte d'Ivoire and Ghana." *Comparative Politics Studies* 46(2): 182–211.

Muldoon, Orla T., Katrina McLaughlin, Nathalie Rougier, and Karent Trew. 2008. "Adolescents' Explanations for Paramilitary Involvement." *Journal of Peace Research* 45(5): 681–695.

Nepal, Mani, Alok K. Bohara, and Kishore Gawande. 2011. "More Inequality, More Killings: The Maoist Insurgency in Nepal." *American Journal of Political Science* 55(4): 886–906.

Openshaw, S., and P. J. Taylor. 1979. "A Million or So Correlated Coefficients: Three Experiments on the Modifiable Areal Unit Problem." In N. Wrigley (ed.), *Statistical Applications in the Spatial Sciences*. London: Pion.

Østby Gudrun, Ragnhild Nordås, and Jan K. Rød. 2009. "Regional Inequalities and Civil Conflict in Sub-Saharan Africa." *International Studies Quarterly* 53(2): 301–324.

Pappas, Takis S. 2008. "Political Leadership and the Emergence of Radical Mass Movements in Democracy." *Comparative Political Studies* 41(8): 1117–1140.

Raleigh, Clionadh, and Håvard Hegre. 2009. "Population Size, Concentration, and Civil War. A Geographically Disaggregated Analysis." *Political Geography* 28(4): 224–238.

Raleigh, Clionadh, Andrew Linke, Håvard Hegre, and Joackim Karlsen. 2010. "Introducing ACLED: An Armed Conflict Location and Event Dataset." *Journal of Peace Research* 47(5): 1–10.

Salehyan, Idean, Kristian. S. Gleditsch, and David E. Cunningham. 2011. "Explaining External Support for Insurgent Groups." *International Organization* 65(4): 709–744.

Schutte, Sebastian, and Nils B. Weidmann. 2011. "Diffusion Patterns of Violence in Civil War." *Political Geography* 30(3): 143–152.

Sekulic, Dusko, Garth Massey, and Randy Hodson. 2006. "Ethnic Intolerance and Ethnic Conflict in the Dissolution of Yugoslavia." *Ethnic and Racial Studies* 29(5): 797–827.

Shellman, Stephen M., Clare Hatfield, and Maggie J. Mills. 2010. Disaggregating Actors in Intranational Conflict." *Journal of Peace Research* 47(1): 83–90.

Staniland, Paul. 2012. "Between a Rock and a Hard Place: Insurgent Fratricide, Ethnic Defection, and the Rise of Pro-State Paramilitaries." *Journal of Conflict Resolution* 56(1): 16–40.

Steele, Abbey. 2009. "Seeking Safety: Avoiding Displacement and Choosing Destinations in Civil Wars." *Journal of Peace Research* 46(3): 419–429.

Strauss, Scott. 2007. "What Is the Relationship between Hate Radio and Violence? Rethinking Rwanda's 'Radio Machete'." *Politics and Society* 35(4): 609–637.

Sundberg, Ralf, Methilda Lindgren, and Ausra Padskocimaite. 2010. UCDP GED Codebook (Version 1.5–2011). http://www.ucdp.uu.se/ged/.

Taydas, Zeynep, and Dursun Peksen. 2012. "Can States Buy Peace? Social Welfare Spending and Civil Conflicts." *Journal of Peace Research* 49(2): 273–287.

Verwimp, Philip. 2005. "An Economic Profile of Peasant Perpetrators of Genocide: Micro-level Evidence from Rwanda." *Journal of Development Economics* 77(2): 297–323.

Verwimp, Philip. 2006. "Machetes and Firearms: The Organization of Massacres in Rwanda." *Journal of Peace Research* 43(1): 5–22.

Voors, Marten J., and Erwin H. Bulte. 2008. "Unbundling Institutions at the Local Level: Conflict, Institutions and Income in Burundi." Working paper.

Voors, Marten J., Eleonora E.M. Nillesen, Philip Verwimp, Erwin H. Bulte, Robert Lensink, and Daan P. Van Soest. 2012. "Violent Conflict and Behavior: A Field Experiment in Burundi." *American Economic Review* 102(2): 941–964.

Weidmann, Nils B., and Idean Salehyan. 2013. "Violence and Ethnic Segregation: A Computational Model Applied to Baghdad." *International Studies Quarterly* 57(1): 52–64.

Weidmann, Nils B. 2013. "The Higher the Better? The Limits of Analytical Resolution in Conflict Event Datasets." *Cooperation and Conflict* 48(4): 567–576.

Weinstein, Jeremy M., and Macartan Humphreys. 2006. "Handling and Manhandling Civilians in Civil War." *American Political Science Review* 100(3): 429–447.

Williams, Nathalie, Dirgha J. Ghimire, William G. Axinn, Elyse Jennings, and Meeta Pradhan. 2012. "A Micro-level Event-Centered Approach to Investigating Armed Conflict and Population Responses." *Demography* 49(4): 1521–1546.

Zeitzoff, Thomas. 2011. "Using Social Media to Measure Conflict Dynamics: An Application to the 2008–2009 Gaza Conflict." *Journal of Conflict Resolution* 55(6): 938–969.

Chapter 7

Ackerson, Christine, Emily Adams, John Arnold, Sarah Fiorenza, Hoor Jangda, Amy Knop-Narbutis, and Vera Magero. 2013. "Climate Change and Development in Africa." Austin, TX: Strauss Center for International Security and Law.

Alix-Garcia, Jennifer, Anne Bartlett, and David Saah. 2012. "Displaced Populations, Humanitarian Assistance and Hosts: A Framework for Analyzing Impacts on Semi-urban Households." *World Development* 40(2): 373–386.

Berenter, Jared. 2012a. "'Ground Truthing' Vulnerability in Africa." Austin, TX: Strauss Center for International Security and Law.

———. 2012b. "'Ground Truthing' Vulnerability and Adaptation in Africa." Austin, TX: Strauss Center for International Security and Law.

Bolaji, M. H. A. 2010. "Shari'ah in Northern Nigeria in the Light of Asymmetrical Federalism." *Publius: The Journal of Federalism* 40(1): 114–135.

Bratton, Michael. 2008. "Vote Buying and Violence in Nigerian Election Campaigns." *Electoral Studies* 27(4): 621–632.

Bratton, Michael, and Nicholas van de Walle. 1997. *Democratic Experiments in Africa: Regime Transitions in Comparative Perspective.* Cambridge: Cambridge University Press.

Busby, Joshua W., Kerry H. Cook, Edward K. Vizy, Todd G. Smith, and Mesfin Bekalo. 2013. "Identifying Hot Spots of Security Vulnerability Associated with Climate Change in Africa." Unpublished manuscript.

Busby, Joshua W., Jay Gulledge, Todd G. Smith, and Kaiba White. 2012. "Of Climate Change and Crystal Balls: The Future Consequences of Climate Change in Africa." *Air & Space Power Journal Africa and Francophonie* 3: 4–44.

Busby, Joshua W., and Jennifer Hazen. 2011. "Mapping and Modeling Climate Security Vulnerability: Workshop Report." Austin, TX: Strauss Center for International Security and Law.

Busby, Joshua W., Jennifer Hazen, Todd G. Smith, Nisha Krishnan, and Mesfin Bekalo. 2013. "Hot Spots: Climate Change and Africa's Strategic Significance to the United States." Paper presented at the Annual Meeting of the International Studies Association. San Francisco, CA.

Busby, Joshua W., Todd G. Smith, Nisha Krishnan, and Mesfin Bekalo. 2013a. "Climate Security Vulnerability in Africa Mapping 3.0." Paper presented at the Annual Meeting of the International Studies Association. San Francisco, CA.

———. 2013b. "Advances in Mapping Climate Security Vulnerability in Africa." Austin, TX: Strauss Center for International Security and Law.

Busby, Joshua W., Todd G. Smith, and Kaiba White. 2011. "Locating Climate Insecurity: Where Are the Most Vulnerable Places in Africa." Austin, TX: Strauss Center for International Security and Law.

———. 2012. "Climate Security and East Africa: A GIS-Based Analysis of Vulnerability." In Gebre Hiwot Mulugeta and Jean-Bosco Butera (eds.). *Climate Change, Pastoral Traditional Coping Mechanisms and Conflict in the Horn of Africa.* Addis Ababa: UPEACE.

Busby, Joshua W., Todd G. Smith, Kaiba White, and Shawn M. Strange. 2010. "Locating Climate Insecurity: Where Are the Most Vulnerable Places in Africa?" Austin, TX: Strauss Center for International Security and Law.

———. 2012. "Locating Climate Insecurity: Where Are the Most Vulnerable Places in Africa?" In Jurgen Scheffran, Michael Brzoska, Hans Günter Brauch, Peter Michael Link, and Janpeter Schilling (eds.). *Climate Change, Human Security and Violent Conflict.* New York: Springer.

———. 2013. "Climate Change and Insecurity: Mapping Vulnerability in Africa." *International Security* 37(4): 132–172.

Busby, Joshua W., Kaiba White, and Todd G. Smith. 2010. "Mapping Climate Change and Security in North Africa." German Marshall Fund of the United States.

Checchi, Francesco, and W. Courtland Robinson. 2013. "Mortality among Populations of Southern and Central Somalia Affected by Severe Food Insecurity and Famine During 2010–2012." FAO and FEWS NET.

Choi, Hyun Jin, and Clionadh Raleigh. 2013. "Dominant Forms of Conflict in Changing Political Systems." Unpublished manuscript.

Cook, Kerry H., and Edward K. Vizy. 2012. "Impact of Climate Change on Mid-Twenty-First Century Growing Seasons in Africa." *Climate Dynamics* 39(12): 2937–2955.

Centre For Research on the Epidemiology of Disasters. 2011. "EM-DAT: The OFDA/CRED International Disaster Database." http://www.emdat.net.

Daxecker, Ursula E. 2012. "The Cost of Exposing Cheating: International Election Monitoring, Fraud, and Post-election Violence in Africa." *Journal of Peace Research* 49(4): 503–516.

Dowd, Caitriona. 2013. "Tracking Islamist Militia and Rebel Groups." Austin, TX: Strauss Center for International Security and Law.

Dowd, Caitriona, and Clionadh Raleigh. 2013a. "Sahel State Political Violence." *Stability: International Journal of Security & Development* 2(2): 1–11.

———. 2013b. "The Myth of Global Islamic Terrorism and Local Conflict in Mali and the Sahel." *African Affairs* 112(448): 498–509.

Eifert, Benn, Edward Miguel, and Daniel N. Posner. 2010. "Political Competition and Ethnic Identification in Africa." *American Journal of Political Science* 54(2): 494–510.

Gleditsch, Nils Petter, Peter Wallensteen, Mikael Eriksson, Margareta Sollenberg, and Håvard Strand. 2002. "Armed Conflict 1946–2001: A New Dataset." *Journal of Peace Research* 39(5): 615–637.

Hegre, Håvard, Gudrun Østby, and Clionadh Raleigh. 2009. "Poverty and Civil War Events: A Disaggregated Study of Liberia." *Journal of Conflict Resolution* 53(4): 598–623.

Hendrix, Cullen S. 2013. "Climate Change, Global Food Markets, and Urban Unrest." Austin, TX: Strauss Center for International Security and Law.

Hendrix, Cullen S., and Idean Salehyan. 2012. "Climate Change, Rainfall, and Social Conflict in Africa." *Journal of Peace Research* 49(1): 35–50.

Ikelegbe, Austine. 2005. "State, Ethnic Militias, and Conflict in Nigeria." *Canadian Journal of African Studies / Revue Canadienne Des Études Africaines* 39(3): 490–516.

Krause, Jana. 2011. "A Deadly Cycle: Ethno-Religious Conflict in Jos, Plateau State, Nigeria." Geneva Declaration Secretariat, Small Arms Survey.

Macias, Lee. 2013. "Complex Emergencies." Austin, TX: Strauss Center for International Security and Law.

Maplecroft. 2012. "Cities of Dhaka, Manila, Bangkok, Yangon and Jakarta Face Highest Climate Change Risks." November 15.

Maystadt, Jean-Francois, Olivier Ecker, and Athur Mabiso, 2013. "Extreme Weather and Civil War in Somalia: Does Drought Fuel Conflict through Livestock Price Shocks?" *LICOS Discussion Papers* #32613, LICOS—Centre for Institutions and Economic Performance, KU Leuven.

McGowan, Patrick J. 2003. "African Military Coups D'état, 1956–2001: Frequency, Trends and Distribution." *Journal of Modern African Studies* 41(3): 339–370.

Meier, Patrick, Doug Bond, and Joe Bond. 2007. "Environmental Influences on Pastoral Conflict in the Horn of Africa." *Political Geography* 26(6): 716–735.

O'Loughlin, John, Frank D. W. Witmer, Andrew M. Linke, Arlene Laing, Andrew Gettelman, and Jimy Dudhia. 2012. "Climate Variability and Conflict Risk in East Africa, 1990–2009." Proceedings of the National Academy of Sciences.

Obioha, Emeka E. 2008. "Climate Change, Population Drift and Violent Conflict Over Land Resources in Northeastern Nigeria." *Journal of Human Ecology* 23(4): 311–324.

Oyefusi, Aderoju. 2008. "Oil and the Probability of Rebel Participation among Youths in the Niger Delta of Nigeria." *Journal of Peace Research* 45(4): 539–555.

Raleigh, Clionadh. 2010. "Political Marginalization, Climate Change, and Conflict in African Sahel States." *International Studies Review* 12(1): 69–86.

———. 2011. "The Search for Safety: The Effects of Conflict, Poverty and Ecological Influences on Migration in the Developing World." *Global Environmental Change* 21(S1): S82–S93.

———. 2012. "Violence against Civilians: A Disaggregated Analysis." *International Interactions* 38(4): 462–481.

———. 2013a. "Conflict Landscapes." Unpublished manuscript.

———. 2013b. "Militias as the New Agents of Political Violence Across Africa." Unpublished manuscript.

———. 2013c. "Urban Vulnerability and Conflict Across Africa." Unpublished manuscript.

Raleigh, Clionadh, and Caitriona Dowd. 2013. "Governance and Conflict in the Sahel's 'Ungoverned Space'." *Stability: International Journal of Security & Development* 2(2): 32:1–17.

Raleigh, Clionadh, and Håvard Hegre. 2009. "Population Size, Concentration, and Civil War. A Geographically Disaggregated Analysis." *Political Geography* 28(4): 224–238.

Raleigh, Clionadh, and Dominic Kniveton. 2012. "Come Rain or Shine: An Analysis of Conflict and Climate Variability in East Africa." *Journal of Peace Research* 49(1): 51–64.

Raleigh, Clionadh, Andrew M. Linke, and Caitriona Dowd. 2012. Armed Conflict Location and Event Dataset (ACLED) Codebook (Version 2). Trinity College Dublin.

Raleigh, Clionadh, Andrew Linke, Håvard Hegre, and J. Karlsen. 2010. "Introducing ACLED: An Armed Conflict Location and Event Dataset: Special Data Feature." *Journal of Peace Research* 47(5): 651–660.

Salehyan, Idean. 2013. "Elections and Social Conflict in Africa." Austin, TX: Strauss Center for International Security and Law.

Scarritt, James R., and Susan McMillan. 1995. "Protest and Rebellion in Africa: Explaining Conflicts between Ethnic Minorities and the State in the 1980s." *Comparative Political Studies* 28(3): 323–349.

Scheffran, Jurgen, P. Michael Link, and Jan Peter Schilling. 2012. "Theories and Models of the Climate Security Link." University of Hamburg: Research Group Climate Change and Security, Working paper #CLISEC–3.

Smith, Todd G. 2013. "Food Price Spikes and Social Unrest in Africa." Austin, TX: Strauss Center for International Security and Law.

Smith, Todd G., Joshua Busby, and Anustubh Agnihotri. 2013. "Sub–national African Education and Infrastructure Access Data." Austin, TX: Strauss Center for International Security and Law.

Theisen, Ole Magnus. 2011. "The Implications of Modeling Choices for Geographically Disaggregated Designs." Memo for Workshop on Mapping and Modeling Climate Security Vulnerability. Austin, TX: Strauss Center for International Security and Law.

Theisen, Ole Magnus, Helge Holtermann, and Halvard Buhaug. 2012. "Climate Wars? Assessing the Claim That Drought Breeds Conflict." *International Security* 36(3): 79–106.

Ukiwo, Ukoha. 2003. "Politics, Ethno-Religious Conflicts and Democratic Consolidation in Nigeria." *Journal of Modern African Studies* 41(1): 115–138.

Vizy, Edward K., and Kerry H. Cook. 2012. "Mid-Twenty-First Century Changes in Extreme Events over Northern and Tropical Africa." *Journal of Climate* 25(17): 5748–5767.

Weaver, Catherine, and Christian Peratsakis. 2011. "Tracking Adaptation Aid." Austin, TX: Strauss Center for International Security and Law.

Weidmann, Nils B., and Michael Callen. 2013. "Violence and Election Fraud: Evidence from Afghanistan." *British Journal of Political Science* 43(1): 53–75.

Wheeler, David. 2011. "Quantifying Vulnerability to Climate Change: Implications for Adaptation Assistance." Center for Global Development.

Chapter 8

Birnir, Jóhanna, Jonathan Wilkenfeld, James Fearon, David Laitin, Ted R. Gurr, Dawn Brancati, Stephen Saideman, Amy Pate. n.d. "The Reason We Don't Yet Know 'Why Groups Rebel': Lessons Learned in the Development of the (All) Minorities at Risk Data." University of Maryland, CIDCM working paper.

Bormann, Nils-Christian, Lars-Erik Cederman, and Manuel Vogt. 2013. "Ethnonationalist Cleavages in Civil Wars: Allah's Wrath or Babel's Legacy?" Paper prepared for presentation at the Annual Meeting of the European Political Science Association, Barcelona, June 20–22.

Bruk, Solomon I., and V. S. Apenchenko (eds.). 1964. *Atlas Narodov Mira*. Moscow: Glavnoe upravlenie geodezii i kartografii gosudarstvennogo geologicheskogo komiteta SSSR and Institut etnografii im. H. H. Miklukho-Maklaia, Akademiia nauk SSSR.

Cederman, Lars-Erik. 2013. "Nationalism and Ethnicity." In Walter Carlsnaes, Thomas Risse, and Beth Simmons (eds.). *The Handbook of International Relations* (2nd edition). London: Sage.

Cederman, Lars-Erik, and Luc Girardin. 2007. "Beyond Fractionalization: Mapping Ethnicity onto Nationalist Insurgencies." *American Political Science Review* 101(1): 173–185.

Cederman, Lars-Erik, Kristian Skrede Gleditsch, and Halvard Buhaug. 2013. *Inequality, Grievances, and Civil War*. Cambridge: Cambridge University Press.

Cederman, Lars-Erik, Kristian Skrede Gleditsch, and Simon Hug. 2013. "Elections and Ethnic Civil War." *Comparative Political Studies* 46(3): 387–417

Cederman, Lars-Erik, Kristian Skrede Gleditsch, Idean Salehyan, and Julian Wucherpfennig. 2013. "Transborder Ethnic Kin and Civil War." *International Organization* 67(2): 389–410.

Cederman, Lars-Erik, Nils B. Weidmann, and Kristian Skrede Gleditsch. 2011. "Horizontal Inequalities and Ethno-Nationalist Civil War: A Global Comparison." *American Political Science Review* 105(3): 478–495.

Cederman, Lars-Erik, Andreas Wimmer, and Brian Min. 2010. "Why Do Ethnic Groups Rebel? New Data and Analysis." *World Politics* 62(1): 87–119.

Collier, Paul, and Anke Hoeffler. 2004. "Greed and Grievance in Civil Wars." *Oxford Economic Papers* 56: 563–595.

Cunningham, David E., Kristian Skrede Gleditsch, and Idean Salehyan. 2009. "It Takes Two: A Dyadic Analysis of Civil War Duration and Outcome." *Journal of Conflict Resolution* 53(4): 570–597.

Fearon, James D. 2004. "Why Do Some Civil Wars Last So Much Longer Than Others?" *Journal of Peace Research* 41(3): 275–301.

Fearon, James D., and David D. Laitin. 2000. "Violence and the Social Construction of Ethnic Identity." *International Organization* 54(4): 845–877.

Fjelde, Hanne, and Lisa Hultman. 2013. "Weakening the Enemy: A Disaggregated Study of Violence against Civilians in Africa." *Journal of Conflict Resolution*. doi: 10.1177/0022002713492648.

Gleditsch, Nils Petter, Peter Wallensteen, Mikael Eriksson, Margareta Sollenberg, and Håvard Strand. 2002. "Armed Conflict 1946–2001: A New Dataset." *Journal of Peace Research* 39(5): 615–637.

Gurr, Ted R.. 1993a. *Minorities at Risk: A Global View of Ethnopolitical Conflicts*. Washington, DC: United States Institute of Peace Press.

Gurr, Ted R.. 1993b. "Why Minorities Rebel: A Global Analysis of Communal Mobilization and Conflict since 1945." *International Political Science Review* 14(2): 161–201.

Gurr, Ted R.. 2000. *Peoples Versus States: Minorities at Risk in the New Century*. Washington, DC: United States Institute of Peace Press.

Hug, Simon. 2013. "Use and Misuse of MAR." *Annual Review of Political Science* 16: 191–208.

Hunziker, Philipp. 2011. GROW^{up} Research Front End Documentation (Release 1.0). http://www.icr.ethz.ch/data/growup/RFE_ Documentation. pdf.

Min, Brian, Lars-Erik Cederman, and Andreas Wimmer. 2012. "Ethnic Exclusion, State Power, and Economic Growth." Unpublished paper.

Nordhaus, William D. 2006. "Geography and Macroeconomics: New Data and New Findings." *Proceedings of the National Academy of Sciences* 103(10): 3510–3517.

Stewart, Frances. 2008. "Horizontal Inequalities and Conflict: An Introduction and Some Hypotheses." In Frances Stewart (ed.). *Horizontal Inequalities and Conflict: Understanding Group Violence in Multiethnic Societies*. Houndmills: Palgrave Macmillan.

Roessler, Philip G. 2011. "The Enemy Within: Personal Rule, Coups, and Civil Wars in Africa." *World Politics* 53(2): 300–346.

Rüegger, Seraina. 2013. "Refugee Movements, Transnational Ethnic Linkages and Conflict Diffusion." Unpublished paper.

Saideman, Stephen M., and Erin K. Jenne. 2009. "The International Relations of Ethnic Conflict." In Manus I. Midlarsky (ed.). *Handbook of War Studies III: The Intrastate Dimension*. Ann Arbor, MI: University of Michigan Press.

Weidmann, Nils B., Jan Ketil Rød, and Lars-Erik Cederman. 2010. "Representing Ethnic Groups in Space: A New Dataset." *Journal of Peace Research* 47(4): 87–119.

Weiner, Myron. 1978. *Sons of the Soil*. Princeton, NJ: Princeton University Press.

Wucherpfennig, Julian. 2011. "Fighting for Change: Onset, Duration, and Recurrence of Ethnic Conflict." PhD dissertation, ETH Zürich.

Wucherpfennig, Julian, Nils W. Metternich, Lars-Erik Cederman, and Kristian Skrede Gleditsch. 2012. "Ethnicity, the State, and the Duration of Civil War." *World Politics* 64(1): 79–115.

Wucherpfennig, Julian, Nils B. Weidmann, Luc Girardin, Lars-Erik Cederman, and Andreas Wimmer. 2011. "Politically Relevant Ethnic Groups Across Space and Time: Introducing the GeoEPR Dataset." *Conflict Management and Peace Science* 28: 423–437.

Chapter 9

Adhikari, Prakash. 2012. "The Plight of the Forgotten Ones: Civil War and Forced Migration." *International Studies Quarterly* 56(3): 590–606.

Albertus, Michael, and Oliver Kaplan. 2013. "Land Reform as a Counterinsurgency Policy: Evidence from Colombia." *Journal of Conflict Resolution* 57(2): 198–231.

Alison, Miranda. 2007. "Wartime Sexual Violence: Women's Human Rights and Questions of Masculinity." *Review of International Studies* 33(1): 75–90.

Allen, Beverly. 1996. *Rape Warfare: The Hidden Genocide in Bosnia-Herzegovina and Croatia*. Minneapolis, MN: University of Minnesota Press.

Amnesty International. 2013. "Tackling Rape as a Weapon of War." http://www2.amnesty.org.uk/blogs/campaigns/tackling-rape-weapon-war.

Amowitz, Lynn L., Chen Reis, Kristina Hare Lyons, Beth Vann, Binta Mansaray, Adyinka M. Akinsulure-Smith, Louise Taylor, and Vincent Iacopino. 2002. "Prevalence of War-Related Sexual Violence and Other Human Rights Abuses among Internally Displaced Persons in Sierra Leone." *JAMA: Journal of the American Medical Association* 287(4): 513–521.

Amowitz, Lynn L., Glen Kim, Chen Reis, Jana L. Asher, and Vincent Iacopino. 2004. "Human Rights Abuses and Concerns about Women's Health and Human Rights in Southern Iraq." *JAMA: Journal of the American Medical Association* 291(12): 1471–1479.

Ball, Patrick, Jana Asher, David Sulmont, and Daniel Manrique. 2003. "How Many Peruvians Have Died? An Estimate of the Total Number of Victims Killed or Disappeared in the Armed Internal Conflict between 1980 and 2000." Report of the Benetech Human Rights Program. https://hrdag.org/wp–content/uploads/2013/02/aaas_peru_5.pdf.

Benard, Cheryl. 1994. "Rape as Terror: The Case of Bosnia." *Terrorism and Political Violence* 6(1): 29–43.

Card, Claudia. 1996. "Rape as a Weapon of War." *Hypatia* 11(4): 5–18.

Cohen, Dara Kay. 2013. "Explaining Rape during War: Cross-National Evidence (1980–2009)." *American Political Science Review* 107(3): 461–477.

Cohen, Dara Kay, and Amelia Hoover Green. 2012. "Dueling Incentives: Sexual Violence in Liberia and the Politics of Human Rights Advocacy." *Journal of Peace Research* 49(3): 445–458.

Cohen, Dara Kay, Amelia Hoover Green, and Elisabeth Jean Wood. 2013. Wartime Sexual Violence: Misconceptions, Implications, and Ways Forward. *United States Institute of Peace Special Report* #323. http://www.usip.org/files/resources/SR323.pdf.

Comisión de la Verdad y Reconciliación de Perú. 2003. *Informe Final*. Lima, Peru: Comisión de la Verdad y Reconciliación. http://www.cverdad.org.pe/ifinal/index.php.

Davenport, Christian, and Patrick Ball. 2002. "Views to a Kill: Exploring the Implications of Source Selection in the Case of Guatemalan State Terror, 1977–1995." *Journal of Conflict Resolution* 46(3): 427–450.

Diken, Bülent, and Carsten Bagge Laustsen. 2005. "Becoming Abject: Rape as a Weapon of War." *Body & Society* 11(1): 111–128.

Fisher, Bonnie S. 2009. "The Effects of Survey Question Wording on Rape Estimates: Evidence from a Quasi-Experimental Design." *Violence against Women* 15(2): 133–147.

Fisher, Siobhan K. 1996. "Occupation of the Womb: Forced Impregnation as Genocide." *Duke Law Journal* 46(1): 91.

Freedom House. *Freedom in the World 2013*. http://www.freedomhouse.org/report/freedom-world/freedom-world-2013.

Sanín, Francisco Gutiérrez. 2008. "Telling the Difference: Guerrillas and Paramilitaries in the Colombian War." *Politics & Society* 36(1): 3–34.

Henry, Nicola. 2011. *War and Rape: Law, Memory, and Justice*. London: Routledge.

Hoover Green, Amelia. 2011. "Repertoires of Violence against Noncombatants: The Role of Armed Group Institutions and Ideologies." PhD dissertation, Yale University.

Hoover Green, Amelia, Dara Kay Cohen, and Elisabeth Jean Wood. 2012. "Is Wartime Rape Declining on a Global Scale? We Don't Know—And It Doesn't Matter." *Political Violence at a Glance*. http://politicalviolenceataglance.org/2012/11/01/is-wartime-rape-declining-on-a-global-scale-we-dont-know-and-it-doesnt-matter/.

Human Security Report Project. 2012. *Human Security Report 2012*. http://hsrgroup.org/docs/Publications/HSR2012/2012HumanSecurityReport-FullText.pdf.

Johnson, Kirsten, Jana Asher, Stephanie Rosborough, Amisha Raja, Rajesh Panjabi, Charles Beadling, and Lynn Lawry. 2008. "Association of Combatant Status and Sexual Violence with Health and Mental Health Outcomes in Postconflict Liberia." *JAMA: Journal of the American Medical Association* 300(6): 676–690.

Johnson Kirsten, and Jennifer Scott. 2010. "Association of Sexual Violence and Human Rights Violations with Physical and Mental Health in Territories of the Eastern Democratic Republic of the Congo." *JAMA: Journal of the American Medical Association* 304(5): 553–562.

Kalyvas, Stathis N. *The Logic of Violence in Civil War*. Cambridge: Cambridge University Press, 2006.

Leiby, Michele. 2009a. "Wartime Sexual Violence in Guatemala and Peru." *International Studies Quarterly* 53(2): 445–468.

———. 2009b. "Digging in the Archives: The Promise and Perils of Primary Documents." *Politics & Society* 37(1): 75–99.

MacKinnon, Catharine A. 1994. "Rape, Genocide, and Women's Human Rights." *Harvard Women's Law Journal* 17: 5.

Marshall, Monty G., Keith Jaggers, and Ted R. Gurr. 2002. "Polity IV Dataset." Center for International Development and Conflict Management at the University of Maryland College Park.

Marshall, Monty G., and Keith Jaggers. 2002. "Polity IV Project: Political Regime Characteristics and Transitions, 1800–2002." http://www.citeulike.org/group/582/article/369537.

Mukengere Mukwege, Denis, and Cathy Nangini. 2009. "Rape with Extreme Violence: The New Pathology in South Kivu, Democratic Republic of Congo." *PLoS Med* 6(12): e1000204.

National Statistics Directorate of Timor-Leste, Ministry of Finance of Timor-Leste, and ICF Macro. 2010. Timor-Leste Demographic and Health Survey 2009–10. Dili, Timor-Leste: National Statistics Directorate and ICF Macro.

Nordas, Ragnhild, and Dara Kay Cohen. 2012. "Sexual Violence in African Conflicts: What the Data Show." Oslo, Norway: Peace Research Institute Oslo. http://file.prio.no/publication_files/cscw/Nordas-Cohen-Sexual-Violence-in-African-Conflicts-1989-2009-CSCW-Policy-Brief-02-2012.pdf.

Ojeda, Gabriel, Myriam Ordoñez, and Luis Hernando Ochoa. 2010. *Encuesta Nacional de Demografía y Salud 2010*. Bogota, Colombia: Asociación Probienestar de la Familia Colombiana.

Onsrud, Mathias, Solbjørg Sjøveian, Roger Luhiriri, and Dennis Mukwege. 2008. "Sexual Violence-related Fistulas in the Democratic Republic of Congo." *International Journal of Gynecology & Obstetrics* 103(3): 265–269.

Oosterhoff, Pauline, Prisca Zwanikken, and Evert Ketting. 2004. "Sexual Torture of Men in Croatia and Other Conflict Situations: An Open Secret." *Reproductive Health Matters* 12(23): 68–77.

Oxfam/Casa de la Mujer. 2010. "Violencia Sexual en Contra de las Mujeres in el Contexto del Conflict Armado Colombiano, 2001–2009." Bogotá: Oxfam/Casa de la Mujer.

Peterman, Amber, Tia Palermo, and Caryn Bredenkamp. 2011. "Estimates and Determinants of Sexual Violence against Women in the Democratic Republic of Congo." *American Journal of Public Health* 101(6): 1060–1067.

Pierskalla, Jan H., and Florian M. Hollenbach. 2013. "Technology and Collective Action: The Effect of Cell Phone Coverage on Political Violence in Africa." *American Political Science Review* 107(2): 207–224.

Ron, James. 1997. "Varying Methods of State Violence." *International Organization* 51(2): 275–300.

Ron, James. 2000. "Boundaries and Violence: Repertoires of State Action along the Bosnia/Yugoslavia Divide." *Theory and Society* 29(5): 609–649.

Roth, Francoise, Tamy Guberek, and Amelia Hoover Green. 2011. "Using Quantitative Data to Assess Conflict-Related Sexual Violence in Colombia: Challenges and Opportunities." Bogotá, Colombia: Corporación Punto de Vista & Benetech Human Rights Program. https://hrdag.org/wp-content/uploads/2013/02/SV-report_2011-04-26.pdf.

Sharlach, Lisa. 1999. "Gender and Genocide in Rwanda: Women as Agents and Objects of Genocide." *Journal of Genocide Research* 1(3): 387–399.

Sivakumaran, Sandesh. 2007. "Sexual Violence against Men in Armed Conflict." *European Journal of International Law* 18(2): 253–276.

Skjelsbaek, Inger. 2001. "Sexual Violence and War: Mapping Out a Complex Relationship." *European Journal of International Relations* 7(2): 211–237.

Snyder, Cindy S., Wesley J. Gabbard, J. Dean May, and Nihada Zulcic. 2006. "On the Battleground of Women's Bodies: Mass Rape in Bosnia-Herzegovina." *Affilia* 21(2): 184–195.

Stark, Lindsay, and Alastair Ager. 2011. "A Systematic Review of Prevalence Studies of Gender-Based Violence in Complex Emergencies." *Trauma, Violence, & Abuse* 12(3): 127–134.

Stark, Lindsay, Les Roberts, Wendy Wheaton, Anne Acham, Neil Boothby, and Alastair Ager. 2010. "Measuring Violence against Women amidst War and Displacement in Northern Uganda Using the 'Neighborhood Method." *Journal of Epidemiology and Community Health* 64(12): 1056–61.

Stiglmayer, Alexandra (ed.). 1994. *Mass Rape: The War against Women in Bosnia-Herzegovina*. Lincoln, NE: University of Nebraska Press.

Swiss, Shana, and Peggy J. Jennings. 2006. "Documenting the Impact of Conflict on Women Living in Internally Displaced Persons Camps in Sri Lanka: Some Ethical Considerations." Albuquerque, NM: Women's Rights International. http://womens-rights.org/Publications/Ethics_IDPSurvey.pdf.

Swiss, Shana, Peggy J. Jennings, Gladys V. Aryee, Grace H. Brown, Ruth M. Jappah-Samukai, Mary S. Kamara, Rosana DH Schaack, and Rojatu S. Turay-Kanneh. 1998. "Violence against Women during the Liberian Civil Conflict." *JAMA: Journal of the American Medical Association* 279(8): 625–629.

Uganda Bureau of Statistics and Macro International Inc. 2007. Uganda Demographic and Health Survey 2006. Calverton, MD: Uganda Bureau of Statistics and Macro International Inc.

United Nations Office of the High Commissioner for Human Rights. 2008. "Rape: Weapon of War." http://www.ohchr.org/en/newsevents/pages/rapeweaponwar.aspx.

United Nations Security Council. 20098. Resolution 1889 on Women, Peace and Security. Document S/RES/1889. http://www.un.org/ga/search/view_doc.asp?symbol=S/RES/1889.

Utas, Mats. 2005. "Victimcy, Girlfriending, Soldiering: Tactic Agency in a Young Woman's Social Navigation of the Liberian War Zone." *Anthropological Quarterly* 78(2): 403–430.

Vinck, Patrick, Phuong N. Pham, Suliman Baldo, and Rachel Shigekane. 2008. "Living with Fear: A Population-Based Survey on Attitudes about Peace, Justice, and Social Reconstruction in Eastern Democratic Republic of the Congo." Human Rights Center, University of California, Berkeley.

Vinck, Patrick, Phuong N. Pham, Eric Stover, and Harvey Weinstein. 2007. "Exposure to War Crimes and Implications for Peace Building in Northern Uganda." *JAMA: Journal of the American Medical Association* 298(5): 543–554.

Wakabi, Wairagala. 2008. "Sexual Violence Increasing in Democratic Republic of Congo." *Lancet* 371(9606): 15–16.

Wood, Elisabeth Jean. 2006. "Variation in Sexual Violence During War." *Politics & Society* 34(3): 307–342.

_____. 2008. "The Social Processes of Civil War: The Wartime Transformation of Social Networks." *Annual Review of Political Science* 11(1): 539–561.

_____. 2009. "Armed Groups and Sexual Violence: When Is Wartime Rape Rare?" *Politics & Society* 37(1): 131–161.

Wood, Reed M., and Mark Gibney. 2010. "The Political Terror Scale (PTS): A Re-introduction and a Comparison to CIRI." *Human Rights Quarterly* 32(2): 367–400.

Chapter 10

American Psychological Association. 1996. "Violence and the Family: Report of the American Psychological Association Presidential Task Force on Violence and the Family." Washington, DC: American Psychological Association.

Amowitz, Lynn L., Chen Reis, Kristina Hare Lyons, Beth Vann, Binta Mansaray, Adyinka M. Akinsulure-Smith, Louise Taylor, and Vincent Iacopino. 2002. "Prevalence of War-Related Sexual Violence and Other Human Rights Abuses among Internally Displaced Persons in Sierra Leone." *JAMA: Journal of the American Medical Association* 287(4): 513–521.

Ball, Nicole. 2001. "The Challenge of Rebuilding War-Torn Societies." In Chester A. Crocker, Fen Osler Hampson, and Pamela R. Aall (eds.). *Turbulent Peace: The Challenges of Managing International Conflict*. Washington, DC: United States Institute of Peace Press.

Beber, Bernd, Philip Roessler, and Alexandra Scacco. 2012. "Who Supports Partition? Violence and Political Attitudes in a Dividing Sudan." Working paper.

Bellows, John, and Edward Miguel. 2009. "War and Local Collective Action in Sierra Leone." *Journal of Public Economics* 93(11): 1144–1157.

Blattman, Christopher. 2009. "From Violence to Voting: War and Political Participation in Uganda." *American Political Science Review* 103(2): 231–247.

Brinkerhoff, Derick W., and Jennifer M. Brinkerhoff. 2002. "Governance Reforms and Failed States: Challenges and Implications." *International Review of Administrative Sciences* 68(4): 511–531.

Colaresi, Michael, and Sabine C. Carey. 2008. "To Kill or to Protect Security Forces, Domestic Institutions, and Genocide." *Journal of Conflict Resolution* 52(1): 39–67.

De Jong, Joop TVM, Ivan H. Komproe, Mark Van Ommeren, Mustafa El Masri, Mesfin Araya, Noureddine Khaled, Willem van de Put, and Daya Somasundaram. 2001. "Lifetime Events and Posttraumatic Stress Disorder in 4 Postconflict Settings." *JAMA: Journal of the American Medical Association* 286(5): 555–562.

Hänggi, Heiner. 2005. "Approaching Peacebuilding from a Security Governance Perspective." In Alan Bryden and Heiner Hänggi (eds.). *Security Governance in Post-Conflict Peacebuilding*. Geneva: Geneva Centre for the Democratic Control of Armed Forces.

Humphreys, Macartan, and Jeremy M. Weinstein. 2006. "Handling and Manhandling Civilians in Civil War." *American Political Science Review* 100(3): 429–447.

Iacopino, Vincent, Martina W. Frank, Heidi M. Bauer, Allen S. Keller, Sheri L. Fink, Doug Ford, Daniel J. Pallin, and Ronald Waldman. 2001. "A Population-Based Assessment of Human Rights Abuses Committed against Ethnic Albanian Refugees from Kosovo." *American Journal of Public Health* 91(12): 2013–2018.

Lyall, Jason, Kosuke Imai, and Graeme Blair. 2011. "Explaining Support for Combatants during Wartime: A Survey Experiment in Afghanistan." *Simons Papers in Security and Development*, technical report.

Pham, Phuong N., and Patrick Vinck. 2010. "Transitioning to Peace: A Population-Based Survey on Attitudes about Social Reconstruction and Justice in Northern Uganda." Human Rights Center, University of California, Berkeley.

Pham, Phuong N., Patrick Vinck, Mychelle Balthazard, and Sokhom Hean. 2011. "After the First Trial: A Population-Based Survey on Knowledge and Perceptions of Justice and the Extraordinary Chambers in the Courts of Cambodia." Human Rights Center, University of California, Berkeley.

Pham, Phuong N., Patrick Vinck, Mychelle Balthazard, Sokhom Hean, and Eric Stover. 2009. "So We Will Never Forget: A Population-Based Survey on Attitudes about Social Reconstruction and the Extraordinary Chambers in the Courts of Cambodia." Human Rights Center, University of California, Berkeley.

Pham Phuong N., Patrick Vinck, and Eric Stover. 2008. "The Lord's Resistance Army and Forced Conscription in Northern Uganda." *Human Rights Quarterly* 30(2): 404–411.

Pham, Phuong N., Patrick Vinck, and Eric Stover. 2009. "Returning Home: Forced Conscription, Reintegration, and Mental Health Status of Former Abductees of the Lord's Resistance Army in Northern Uganda." *BMC Psychiatry* 9(1): 23.

Pham, Phuong N., Patrick Vinck, Eric Stover, Andrew Moss, and Marieke Wierda. 2007. "When the War Ends. A Population-Based Survey on Attitudes about Peace, Justice and Social Reconstruction in Northern Uganda." Human Rights Center, University of California, Berkeley; Payson Center for International Development, Tulane University; International Center for Transitional Justice, New York.

Pham, Phuong N., Patrick Vinck, and Harvey Weinstein. 2010. "Sense of Cohesion and Its Association with Exposure to Traumatic Events, Post-Traumatic Stress Disorder, and Depression in Eastern Democratic Republic of the Congo." *Journal of Traumatic Stress* 23(3): 313–321.

Pham, Phuong N., Patrick Vinck, Marieke Wierda, Eric Stover, and Adrian di Giovanni. 2005. "Forgotten Voices: A Population-Based Survey of Attitudes about Peace and Justice in Northern Uganda." International Center for Transitional Justice and Human Rights Center, University of California, Berkeley.

Pham, Phuong N., Harvey M. Weinstein, and Timothy Longman. 2004. "Trauma and PTSD Symptoms in Rwanda." *JAMA: Journal of the American Medical Association* 292(5): 602–612.

Stewart, Frances. 2005. "Horizontal Inequalities: A Neglected Dimension of Development." In United Nations University-World Institute for Development Economics Research (ed.). *Wider Perspectives on Global Development*. Helsinki: United Nations University-World Institute for Development Economics Research.

Swiss, Shana, Peggy J. Jennings, Gladys V. Aryee, Grace H. Brown, Ruth M. Jappah-Samukai, Mary S. Kamara, Rosana DH Schaack, and Rojatu S. Turay-Kanneh. 1998. "Violence against Women during the Liberian Civil Conflict." *JAMA: Journal of the American Medical Association* 279(8): 625–629.

Tabachnick, Barbara G., and Linda S. Fidell. 2006. *Using Multivariate Statistics*. New York: Allyn & Bacon.

UNICEF. 2004. *The Situation of Women and Girls: Facts and Figures*. New York: UNICEF. http://www.unicef.org/gender/index_factsandfigures.html.

Verdú, Rodrigo G., Wendy Cunningham, Linda McGinnis, Cornelia Tesliuc, and Dorte Verner. 2008. *Youth at Risk in Latin America and the Caribbean. Understanding the Causes, Realizing the Potential*. Washington, DC: World Bank.

Vinck, Patrick, and Phuong N. Pham. 2008. "Ownership and Participation in Transitional Justice Mechanisms: A Sustainable Human Development Perspective from Eastern Democratic Republic of Congo." *International Journal of Transitional Justice* 2(3): 398–411.

_____. 2009. "Peace-Building and Displacement in Northern Uganda: A Cross-Sectional Study of Intentions to Move and Attitudes towards Former Combatants." *Refugee Survey Quarterly* 28(1): 59–77.

_____. 2010a. "Association of Exposure to Violence and Potential Traumatic Events with Self-Reported Physical and Mental Health Status in the Central African Republic," *JAMA: Journal of the American Medical Association* 304(5): 544–552.

_____. 2010b. "Building Peace, Seeking Justice: A Population-Based Survey on Attitudes about Accountability and Social Reconstruction in the Central African Republic." Human Rights Center, University of California, Berkeley.

_____. 2010c. "Outreach Evaluation: The International Criminal Court in the Central African Republic." *International Journal of Transitional Justice* 4(3): 421–442.

_____. 2013. "Association of Exposure to Intimate-Partner Physical Violence and Potentially Traumatic War-Related Events with Mental Health in Liberia." *Social Science and Medicine* 77: 41–49.

Vinck, Patrick, Phuong N. Pham, Suliman Baldo, and Rachel Shigekane. 2008. "Living with Fear: A Population-Based Survey on Attitudes about Peace, Justice and Social Reconstruction in Eastern Congo." Human Rights Center, University of California, Berkeley; Payson Center for International Development, Tulane University; International Center for Transitional Justice, New York.

Vinck, Patrick, Phuong N. Pham, and Tino Kreutzer. 2011. "Talking Peace: A Population-Based Survey on Attitudes about Security, Dispute Resolution, and Post-Conflict Reconstruction in Liberia." Human Rights Center, University of California, Berkeley.

Vinck, Patrick, Phuong N. Pham, Eric Stover, and Harvey M. Weinstein. 2007. "Exposure to War Crimes and Implications for Peacebuilding in Northern Uganda." *JAMA: Journal of the American Medical Association* 298(5): 543–554.

Weinstein, Harvey M., Laurel E. Fletcher, Patrick Vinck, and Phuong N. Pham. 2010. "Stay the Hand of Justice: Whose Priorities Take Priority?" In Rosalind Shaw, Lars Waldorf, and Pierre Hazan (eds.). *Localizing Transitional Justice: Justice Interventions and Local Priorities After Mass Violence*. Stanford, CA: Stanford University Press.

World Bank. 2011. *World Development Report 2011: Conflict, Security, and Development*. Washington, DC: World Bank.

World Food Programme and the World Bank Group. 2011. "Violent Conflicts and Displacement in Central Mindanao: Challenges to Recovery and Development." Rome: World Food Programme and Washington, DC: The World Bank Group.

Peace and Conflict Editorial Advisory Board

Ted Robert Gurr, Chair
Distinguished University Professor Emeritus
University of Maryland

Victor Asal
Associate Professor
Department of Political Science
University at Albany

Mary Caprioli
Associate Professor
Department of Political Science
University of Minnesota at Duluth

Kristian Skrede Gleditsch
Professor
Department of Government
University of Essex
Colchester, United Kingdom

Birger Heldt
Associate Professor
Folke Bernadotte Academy
Sandöverken, Sweden

Will H. Moore
Professor
Department of Political Science
Florida State University

Monica Duffy Toft
Professor of Government and Public Policy
Blavatnik School of Government
University of Oxford

Acknowledgments

We are grateful to Jennifer Knerr at Paradigm Publishers, who has been tireless in her enthusiasm for this publication. In addition, we appreciate the generosity of the Center for International Development and Conflict Management at the University of Maryland, which provided the financial support necessary to permit the continued production of this publication in full color.

About the Authors

David A. Backer is a Research Associate Professor and Assistant Director of the Center for International Development and Conflict Management, as well as Director of the Minor in International Development and Conflict Management, at the University of Maryland. His research focuses on conflict dynamics and post-conflict processes. He is Co-Director of the West Africa Transitional Justice Project and the Constituency-Level Elections Archive.

Jonathan Wilkenfeld is a Professor of Government and Politics at the University of Maryland, where he serves as Director of the ICONS simulation project. His research and publications focus on conflict and crisis, with particular emphasis on negotiation and mediation at the interstate and intrastate levels. He is Co-Director of the International Crisis Behavior Project.

Paul K. Huth is a Professor of Government and Politics at the University of Maryland and Director of the Center for International Development and Conflict Management. He is also editor of the *Journal of Conflict Resolution*. He has published books and widely in journals on subjects related to the study of international conflict and war, including deterrence behavior, crisis decision making, territorial disputes, the democratic peace, international law and dispute resolution, and the civilian consequences of war.

About the Contributors

Ravi Bhavnani is an Associate Professor at the Graduate Institute of International and Development Studies (Switzerland). His research explores the microfoundations of patterns of violence, examining the endogenous relationships among the characteristics, beliefs, and interests of relevant actors, as well as social mechanisms and emergent structures that shape attitudes, decision making, and behavior. He uses agent-based modeling and disaggregated empirical data to link theoretical conjectures to concrete evidence, thereby identifying processes that tend to generate specific outcomes.

Joshua W. Busby is an Associate Professor at the LBJ School of Public Affairs at the University of Texas-Austin. He is the Crook Distinguished Scholar at the Strauss Center for International Security and Law and a lead researcher with the Climate Change and African Political Stability (CCAPS) program. He has written widely on climate and security in International Security and Security Studies, as well as for a number of think tanks.

Lars-Erik Cederman is Professor of International Conflict Research, ETH Zürich. His interests include nationalism, ethnic conflict, democratization, and state formation. He is the (co)author of *Emergent Actors in World Politics: How States Develop and Dissolve* (Princeton University Press, 1997), *Inequality, Grievances and Civil War* (Cambridge University Press, 2013), and recent articles in *American Political Science Review*, *International Organization*, *Journal of Conflict Resolution*, *Journal of Peace Research*, and *World Politics*.

Karsten Donnay is a PhD student in the Department of Humanities, Social and Political Science at ETH Zürich (Switzerland). His research uses detailed, disaggregated data on empirical violence and a range of statistical and computational modeling techniques to study micro-level conflict processes. Focusing mainly on asymmetric intrastate conflict, he has worked on the Israeli-Palestinian conflict—Jerusalem in particular—and the conflict in Iraq.

Laura Dugan is an Associate Professor in the Department of Criminology and Criminal Justice at the University of Maryland. Her research examines the consequences of violence and the efficacy of violence prevention/intervention policy and practice. She is a Co-Principal Investigator for the Global Terrorism Database (GTD) and the Government Actions in Terrorist Environments (GATE) dataset. She received an MS/PhD in Public Policy and Management and an MS in Statistics from Carnegie Mellon University.

Erica Frantz is an Assistant Professor in the Political Science Department at Bridgewater State University. Her research specialty is authoritarian politics, with interests that intersect comparative politics and international relations. She is the author of two books: *The Politics of Dictatorship* (Lynne Rienner Publishers) and *Dictators and Dictatorships* (Bloomsbury Publishing). She received her PhD in Political Science from UCLA.

Elena Gadjanova is a post-doctoral fellow at the Max Planck Institute for the Study of Religious and Ethnic Diversity. Her research explores the consequences of countries' ethnolinguistic diversity on governance and democratic processes. In particular, she studies how ethnic groups' interests are articulated and accommodated, with a focus on developing countries.

Luc Girardin began his journey at the Graduate Institute of International Studies in Geneva and later joined the UBS research laboratory (Ubilab), where he focused on novel approaches to support intuitive and interactive ways of thinking. Subsequently, he co-founded Macrofocus, a company that develops interactive visualization tools. He is currently CTO at Macrofocus and a researcher on complex adaptive systems at ETH Zürich (Switzerland). He holds a master's degree in computer science and telecommunication.

Amelia Hoover Green is an Assistant Professor of Political Science at Drexel University. She also serves as a consultant to the Human Rights Data Analysis Group, most recently performing analyses for prosecutions related to the civil war in El Salvador. Her current research explores how political education and indoctrination affect armed group violence against civilians. She has also written extensively on the politics of quantification in human rights. She received her PhD from Yale University.

Gary LaFree is Director of the National Consortium for the Study of Terrorism and Responses to Terrorism (START) and a Distinguished Scholar and Professor of Criminology and Criminal Justice at the University of Maryland. He is currently a Fellow of the American Society of Criminology (ASC) and a member of the National Academy of Science's Crime, Law and Justice Committee. He has served as President of the ASC and of the ASC's Division on International Criminology. Much of Dr. LaFree's ongoing research is on the Global Terrorism Database.

Patrick Meier is an internationally recognized thought leader on the application of new technologies for crisis early warning and humanitarian response. He presently spearheads the development of next-generation humanitarian technologies at the Qatar Foundation's Computing Research Institute. He holds an MA from Columbia University and a PhD from The Fletcher School and was a pre-doctoral scholar at Stanford University. His influential blog, iRevolution.net, has received well over one million hits. He tweets at @patrickmeier.

Phuong N. Pham, PhD, is a research scientist at Harvard School of Public Health and associate faculty with the Harvard Humanitarian Initiative. Her areas of expertise are applications of epidemiologic research methods and information technology in complex emergency settings with a focus on vulnerable populations. She designs and implements evidenced-based policy research in on-going and post-conflict countries, and co-founded KoBoToolbox, a digital data collection application to advance digital research methods.

Clionadh Raleigh is a Professor of Political Geography and Conflict at the University of Sussex. She is the creator and Director of the Armed Conflict Location and Event Dataset project, an affiliate of the International Peace Research Institute in Oslo (PRIO), and an associated researcher with the Minerva CCAPS project at the University of Texas. Her work focuses on African conflict patterns, the social and political consequences of climate change, and the political geography of developing states. She currently manages a European Research Council project on "Conflict Landscapes and Life Cycles," which tracks, models, and predicts local political violence patterns across Africa.

Idean Salehyan is an Associate Professor of Political Science at the University of North Texas and Co-Director of the Social Conflict in Africa Database. His research interests include civil and international conflict, refugee migration, and environmental security. He is the author of *Rebels without Borders: Transnational Insurgencies in World Politics* (Cornell University Press, 2009) and his articles appear in journals such as the *American Journal of Political Science*, *World Politics*, and *International Organization*. Dr. Salehyan received his PhD from the University of California, San Diego.

Patrick Vinck, PhD, is Associate Faculty with the Harvard Humanitarian Initiative and a Research Scientist at the Brigham and Women's Hospital and Harvard School of Public Health. His research at the nexus between social and public health sciences focuses on peacebuilding, conflict transition, vulnerability analysis, human rights, and food security.

Julian Wucherpfennig is a Lecturer (Assistant Professor) in International Security at University College London. His research addresses the role of interdependent decision making in conflict processes and has been published in *International Organization*, the *Journal of Politics*, and *World Politics*, among others. He holds an MA and a PhD in Political Science from ETH Zürich (Switzerland). His PhD dissertation, on ethnic conflict, was awarded the ECPR Jean Blondel Prize.

Center for International Development and Conflict Management

ABOUT THE CENTER FOR INTERNATIONAL DEVELOPMENT AND CONFLICT MANAGEMENT

The Center for International Development and Conflict Management (CIDCM) is an interdisciplinary research center at the University of Maryland. CIDCM seeks to prevent and transform conflict, to understand the interplay between conflict and development, and to help societies create sustainable futures for themselves. With research, policy, and training programs grounded in the insights of academic scholarship, CIDCM devises effective tools and pathways to constructive change.

The Center's programs are based on the belief that "peace building and development-with-justice are two sides of the same coin" (Edward Azar, CIDCM founding director). Our accomplished researchers, expertise in data collection and analysis, and direct involvement in regional conflict management efforts make the Center a unique resource for discovering enduring solutions to the world's most intractable conflicts.

Basic Research and Data Collections

CIDCM researchers examine a wide range of topics pertaining to domestic and international conflicts and their peaceful resolution. In so doing, researchers collect, analyze, and link data relevant to the study of the dynamics of societal conflicts. The aim is to produce cutting-edge basic research and to expand data capabilities to facilitate cross-disciplinary research among scholars and policy analysts concerned with aspects of societal conflict, state failure, and minority rights. The Center hosts several major international databases on societal conflict, including Minorities at Risk and International Crisis Behavior.

Policy Analysis

Strategically located at the nexus of policy and practice, CIDCM seeks to foster a conversation among scholars and policy makers and to use global analyses as a basis for concrete recommendations for the policy community. Extensive field experience, subject matter experts, and command of both quantitative and qualitative methods provide CIDCM researchers with a strong foundation for advancing cutting-edge policy analysis. In this regard, its biennial publication *Peace and Conflict* reports major global and regional trends in societal conflict, development, and governance issues. Other recent examples of analyses offered by the Center's researchers include assessments of the policies regarding the use of information technology in development, democratization, strategies for conflict mitigation and resolution, and approaches for sustainable development and peace.

Training and Education

The Center provides on-the-ground training for parties to specific conflicts, as well as programs that feature conflict resolution training for students and government officials. The Partners in Conflict program has provided training in citizens' diplomacy and conflict resolution in more than 15 countries, and the ICONS Project creates interactive tools for teaching and training in negotiation, leadership, and crisis management techniques. CIDCM also offers an undergraduate minor in International Development and Conflict Management and works closely with PhD students as they prepare to become accomplished scholars in their own right.

In addition, two CIDCM endowed chairs, the Anwar Sadat Chair for Peace and Development and the Baha'i Chair for World Peace, seek to bridge the gap between the academic and policy worlds and develop alternatives to violent conflict.

To learn more about CIDCM, please visit the website at: **http://www.cidcm.umd.edu**.

Paul K. Huth
Director